Truppenübungsplatz Grafenwöhr
Gestern - Heute

Grafenwoehr Training Area
Yesterday & Today

Gerald Morgenstern

Über den Autor

Gerald Morgenstern, geboren 1958 in Grafenwöhr, begann 1975 seinen Dienst bei der Bundeswehr. Nach verschiedenen Verwendungen an mehreren Standorten und Ausbildung zum Munitionsfachkundigen Übernahme als Berufssoldat. Seit 1990 eingesetzt beim DMV in Grafenwöhr als Feuerwerker im Innen- und Außendienst, Dienstgrad Stabsfeldwebel. In Zweitfunktion zuständig für Presse- und Öffentlichkeitsarbeit. Im Mai 2011 aus dem aktiven Dienst der Bundeswehr ausgeschieden.

Freier Berichterstatter für die Tageszeitung „Der Neue Tag". Mitglied in verschiedenen Vereinen seiner Heimatgemeinde. Politisch engagiert bei der CSU, Mitglied des Stadtrates von Grafenwöhr, von 2002 bis 2008 zweiter Bürgermeister, Kreisrat im Landkreis Neustadt an der Waldnaab.

About the Author

Gerald Morgenstern, born 1958 in Grafenwoehr, began his career in the German Army in 1975. After having served in various functions at several military installations, he began and completed his training as an explosive ordnance specialist and joined the German Army as a career NCO. He was stationed as an EOD NCO at the Office of the German Military Representative in Grafenwoehr from 1990 to May 2011 when he retired from active duty in the rank of Sergeant Major. He also served as the unit's public affairs officer and is a free-lance writer for „Der Neue Tag" daily newspaper. He is a member of several clubs in his hometown. A member of the Christian Social Union (CSU) party, he serves as a city councilman in Grafenwoehr, served as second mayor from 2002 to 2008, and is a member of the county parliament of Neustadt an der Waldnaab County.

Fotos/Bildnachweis / *Photo Credits:*

Fotostudio Spahn, Grafenwöhr; US-Armee Garnison Bavaria: Andreas Kreuzer, Franz Zeilmann, Ray Johnson; Umweltabteilung der Garnison / *Environmental Office of the U.S. Army Garrison Bavaria: Stefan Härtl;* 7th Army JMTC PAO, JMTC/TSAE: Markus Rauchenberger, Gertrud Zach; Bundeswehr, Karin Irmgard Bauer; Baudienststelle der Regierung der Oberpfalz, US-Bauverwaltung Grafenwöhr – Andrea Hösl; Köstler-Projektmanagement, Bayreuth; Bundesforst Grafenwöhr, Dr. Oliver Krone, Hubertus von Blum, Frank Gerstenmeier, Andreas Irle; Heimatverein; Stadt Grafenwöhr; Tourismus Neustadt/WN; Tourismus Amberg-Sulzbach; Stadtmarketing Amberg e.V. / Clemens Zahn; Feuerwehrmagazin, Alex Müller; Ingrid Popp, „Der neue Tag"; Joachim Gebhardt, „Sulzbach-Rosenberger Zeitung"; Fotostudio Gabi Müller, Vilseck; Sammler / Collector Hermann Dietl u. Hans Jürgen Kugler; Fotofreunde Eschenbach-Grafenwöhr, Kenny Vlasek; Eigene Bilder: Gerald Morgenstern

Karten / *Maps:*

© Bayerische Vermessungsverwaltung; Amt für Geoinformationswesen der Bundeswehr

Informationen und Quellen / *References:*

Eckehart Griesbach, Truppenübungsplatz Grafenwöhr, Geschichte einer Landschaft; Hans-Jürgen Kugler, Hopfenohe, Geschichte einer Pfarrgemeinde; Major Helmut Mädl, Die Geschichte des Truppenübungsplatzes Grafenwöhr; Paul Burckhardt, Die Truppenübungsplätze Grafenwöhr – Hohenfels – Wildflecken; History Line: Michael Beaton; Gerhard Müller, Ausstellungskatalog des Kultur- und Militärmuseums; Heimatverein Grafenwöhr; Historiker Olaf Meiler; Chronik des Bundesforstbetriebs Grafenwöhr / *Chronology of the Federal Forest Office Grafenwoehr;* Eigene Berichte und Recherchen Gerald Morgenstern / *Private stories and research by Gerald Morgenster*

Impressum / *Imprint:*

„Truppenübungsplatz Grafenwöhr gestern – heute" / *"Grafenwoehr Training Area yesterday – today"*
1. Auflage, 30. Juni 2010 / *1st Edition, June 30, 2010*
2. Auflage, 31. Oktober 2011 / *2nd Edition, October 31, 2011*
3. Auflage, 15. November 2015 / *3rd Edition, November 15, 2015*

Verfasser / *Author:* Gerald Morgenstern
Herausgeber / *Publisher:* G. und G. Morgenstern, Martin-Luther-Straße 20, 92655 Grafenwöhr
Übersetzung / *Translation:* Susanne Bartsch
Herstellung und Vertrieb / *Printing and Distribution:* Druckerei Hutzler GmbH, Im Gewerbepark 21, 92655 Grafenwöhr

Informationen und Versand / *Information and Sales*
www.grafenwoehr.trainingareabook.com

ISBN 978-3-00-036017-6

Vorwort - Preface

Als auf königlich-bayerischen Befehl der Truppenübungsplatz Grafenwöhr gegründet wurde, begann für die Stadt und die Region ein völlig neuer Abschnitt der Geschichte. Das 100-jährige Bestehen im Jahr 2010 war für mich Anlass, dieses Buch mit dem Titel „Truppenübungsplatz Grafenwöhr gestern – heute" zusammenzustellen.

Ein umfangreiches Archiv an eigenen Aufnahmen und viele Bilder, die mir von verschiedensten Seiten zur Verfügung gestellt wurden, motivierten mich, den Vergleich zwischen einst und jetzt zu dokumentieren. Geschichte und Geschichten aus dem Platz und der Militärgemeinde, herausragende Ereignisse, Begebenheiten und Aktionen, an denen ich selbst beteiligt sein durfte, lieferten den Inhalt für die einzelnen Kapitel. Der große Ausbau der Garnison Grafenwöhr, die Ausbildungsmöglichkeiten für die Soldaten, das 100. Jubiläum des Forstbetriebes, die einzigartige Pflanzen- und Tierwelt, auch die Unberührtheit und Schönheit von Natur und Landschaft sollen hier dargestellt werden.

Das Buch ist keineswegs eine wissenschaftliche, chronologische oder gar vollständige Abhandlung zur Geschichte des Übungsplatzes. Umfangreiche Literatur und die Darstellung im Kultur- und Militärmuseum sowie zahlreiche Einzelarbeiten sind dazu bereits vorhanden. Immer wieder wird in den Texten auf entsprechende Quellen hingewiesen. Die Verfasser dieser Werke haben sehr engagiert und umfassend gearbeitet und recherchiert. Mit den Bildern in diesem Buch sollen nicht das Militär und der Krieg verherrlicht werden. Aufnahmen und Namen aus der Zeit der Dritten Reichs dienen ausschließlich der geschichtlichen Darstellung.

Übungsplätze sind Ausbildungseinrichtungen, auf denen sich Soldaten auf ihre gefährlichen Einsätze vorbereiten können; Friedensmissionen, Einsätze und Kriege, zu denen sie entsandt und befohlen werden. Neben der militärischen Bedeutung stellt der Übungsplatz einen enormen Wirtschaftsfaktor für die Region dar. Die Menschen in und um den Übungsplatz leben von und mit ihm, mit all seinen Vor- und Nachteilen.

Dieses Werk soll einen Blick auf die andere Seite des Zauns, hinein in das militärische Sperrgebiet ermöglichen. Das Buch möge aber auch eine geistige Brücke zwischen Gestern und Heute sein. Es möge neue Verbindungen knüpfen und um Verständnis werben zwischen deutschen und amerikanischen Soldaten und den zivilen Anwohnern des Übungsplatzes. Den vielen hier stationierten amerikanischen Soldaten und ihren Familien möge es dazu dienen, ihre „bayerische Heimat auf Zeit" kennen zu lernen und in guter Erinnerung zu behalten.

A completely new chapter in history began for the city and the region when the Bavarian Royal family gave the order to establish Grafenwoehr Training Area. Its 100th anniversary in 2010 motivated me to put this book with the title "Grafenwoehr Training Area yesterday – today" together.

A huge archive of photos I took myself and many photos that had been provided to me for use by various sources, motivated me to make and document the comparison between then and now. The story of and stories from the training area and the military community, special events, occurrences and events which I had the chance to participate in myself, provided the content for the individual chapters. The large expansion of the Grafenwoehr garrison, the training possibilities for soldiers, the 100th anniversary of the forest office, the unique flora and fauna, the pristine and beautiful nature and landscape are to be documented here.

This book does not intend to provide a scientific, chronological or even complete history of the training area. Extensive literature and documentation in the Culture- and Military Museum as well as many single articles covering that have already been published. The respective sources have been mentioned in many publications. The authors of those publications were very committed, conducted excellent research and have provided extensive coverage. The photos in this book are not intended to glorify the military and war. Photos and names dating back to the Third Reich are merely published for historic documentation.

Training areas are training facilities which allow soldiers to prepare themselves for their dangerous missions; peace missions as well as other missions and war to which they are deployed. Apart from its military significance, the training area is also an important economic factor in the region. The people on and around the training area, with all its pros and cons, live with it and from it.

This publication intends to provide readers with a view across the fence and into the restricted military area. Additionally, the book shall be an intellectual bridge between yesterday and today. May it establish new relationships and promote the understanding between the German and American soldiers and the civilian neighbors of the training area For the many American soldiers who are stationed here and their families, it may be a tool to get to know and to fondly remember their "temporary Bavarian home away from home."

Gerald Morgenstern

Inhaltsverzeichnis / Index

Karte 1913 / Map 1913	
Über den Autor / About the Author / Impressum / Imprint	2
Vorwort / Preface	3
Grafenwöhr / Grafenwoehr	6
Landkreis Neustadt a. d. Waldnaab / County	12
Kultur- und Militärmuseum / Culture- and Military Museum	15
Bau des Lagers / Construction of the camp	18
Der erste Schuss / The first shot	25
Photostudio Spahn / The Spahn Photo Studio	30
Die Wachen / The Gates	32
Der Wasserturm / The Water Tower	36
Das Stalllager / The Stables	43
Pro Patria / Prisoner of war cemetery	48
Wolfsschützenkapelle / Wolf Hunter's Chapel	50
Bleidorn - Schwarzen Berg	52
Geologie / Geology / Ursprung	54
Ehemalige Ortschaften / Former villages	60
Pappenberg	65
Haag	71
Hopfenohe	76
Netzaberg – Vom Dorf zur Stadt Netzaberg / Netzaberg – from a village to a town	81
Netzaberg Chapel	90
Karte 1939 / Map 1939	92
Westwallbunker / West Wall Bunkers	94
Bombardierung / Air Raids	97
Einmarsch der Amerikaner / Arrival of the Americans	102
Jahrestag der Bombardierung / Anniversary of the Air Raids	103
Dora	104
Elvis	108
Vom Fesselballon zum Kampfjet / Aviation	111
D.U.S.T.O.F.F. / Amerikanische Rettungflieger / American MEDEVAC	118
Bundeswehr / German Army	121
Militär und Politik / Military and Politics	130
Gemeinsames Multinationales Ausbildungskommando der 7. US-Armee JMTC - 7th U.S. Army Joint Multinational Training Command	134
NCO-Akademie und Pattons Schreibtisch / NCO Academy and Patton´s Desk	138
JMSC Simulation Center	140
GTA Range Operations	142
Schießen und Üben / Training / EAS	144

Vilseck	154
Landkreis Amberg-Sulzbach / Amberg-Sulzbach County / DES / AFN	156
Südlager / South Camp / Rose Barracks	158
Gesundheitswesen / Health Care / BHC / BDENTAC	162
2CR / 2. Kavallerieregiment / 2nd Cavalry Regiment	164
Militär Polizei / 18th Military Police Brigade / Partnerschaftsbaum / Partnership Tree	169
15th Engineer Battallion / 15. Pionierbataillon	172
1-91 Cav / 1st-91st Cavalry Regiment (Airborne) / 1. Luftlande-Schwadron 91. Kavallerieregiment	173
4-319th AFAR / 4th Battalion 319th Airborne Field Artillery Regiment	174
18th CSSB / 18th Combat Sustainment Support Battalion / 18. Kampfunterstützungsbataillon	176
702nd EOD (Explosive Ordnance Disposal) / 702. Kampfmittelbeseitigungskompanie	178
44th ESB / 44th Expeditionary Signal Battalion / 44. Expediertes Fernmeldebataillon	179
US-Armee Garnison Grafenwöhr / U.S. Army Garrison Grafenwoehr	181
Wirtschaftliche Bedeutung / Economic Impact	184
Lagerfeuerwehr / Fire Department	186
Schulen / Schools	188
Tower Barracks Bücherei / Libary	189
Wild B.O.A.R.	190
Kontakt Club / Contact Club	190
Vom Empfang zum Volksfest / From the reception to the Volksfest / USO	192
EB-G Standortoptimierung Grafenwöhr / Efficient Basing - Grafenwoehr	202
Single Soldier Barracks	208
Community Service Center	209
Dining Facility	213
Physical Fitness Center	214
Shopping Center	216
Hotel	218
Umweltschutz / Environmental Protection	220
Forst / Forest	229
Himmel der Hirsche / Deer haven	232
Adler / Eagle	239
Impressionen	243
95 – 60 – 50	252
100 Jahre Truppenübungsplatz Grafenwöhr / 100 Years Grafenwoehr Training Area	254
Zitate / Remarks	262
Zeittafel 1900 – 2010 / Chronology 1900 – 2010	264
Zeittafel Forst / Chronology of the Forest Office	273
Frieden für die Welt / Peace for the world	278
Gedenkstein / Memorials	282
Zum Nachdenken / Something to think about	284
Dank / Thanks	286
Karte / Map 2010	

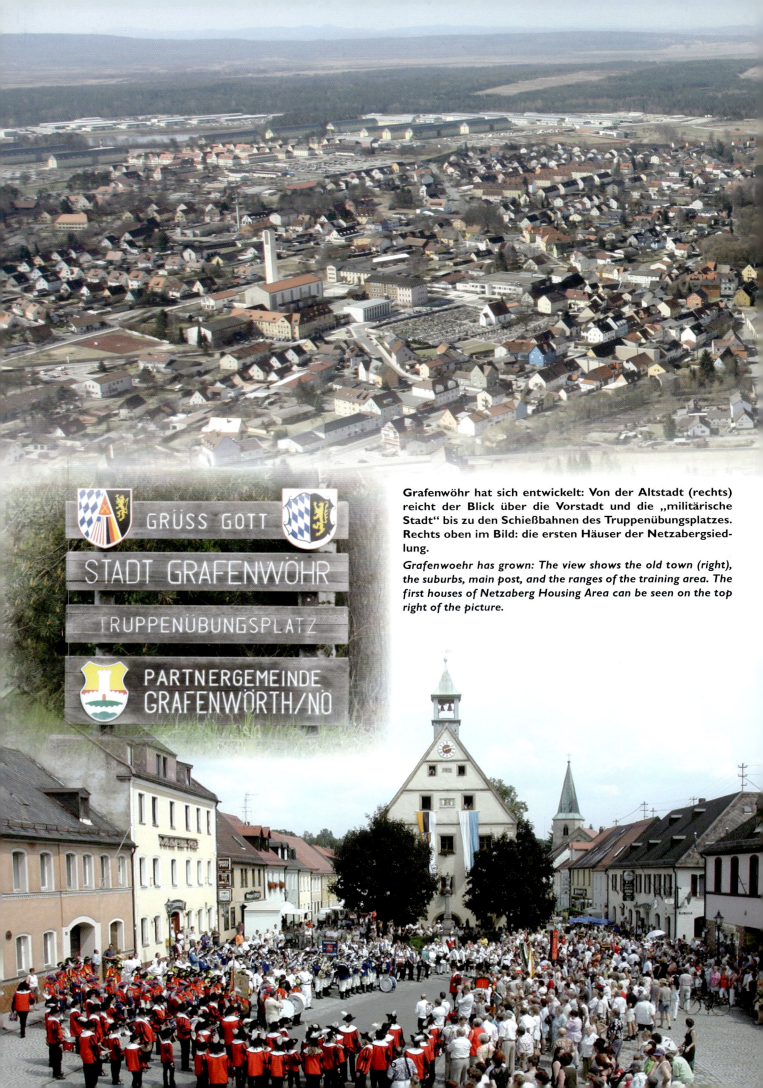

Grafenwöhr hat sich entwickelt: Von der Altstadt (rechts) reicht der Blick über die Vorstadt und die „militärische Stadt" bis zu den Schießbahnen des Truppenübungsplatzes. Rechts oben im Bild: die ersten Häuser der Netzabergsiedlung.

Grafenwoehr has grown: The view shows the old town (right), the suburbs, main post, and the ranges of the training area. The first houses of Netzaberg Housing Area can be seen on the top right of the picture.

Grafenwöhr

Grafenwöhr um 1950
Grafenwoehr around 1950

Liebe Leserinnen und Leser, mit dem Truppenübungsplatz – dem größten außerhalb der USA – kommt der Stadt Grafenwöhr in mehrfacher Hinsicht eine besondere Rolle zu:

1. Wir sind Heimat auf Zeit für die hier stationierten Amerikaner und ich darf behaupten, die amerikanischen Gäste sind hier herzlich willkommen. Wir wollen, dass die Soldaten und ihre Familien sich bei uns wohl fühlen. Dazu tragen auch die sehr guten Beziehungen zwischen der Stadt und den verantwortlichen der U.S. Army bei.

2. Der Übungsplatz ist ein beachtlicher Wirtschaftsfaktor. Er bietet als größter Arbeitgeber im Landkreis mehr als 2.000 Menschen einen Arbeitsplatz. Jährlich fließen ca. 650 Mio. € in die Region.

3. Der Truppenübungsplatz ist auch für uns Heimat. Das Amerikanische ist uns Grafenwöhrern seit jeher vertraut. Es ist wichtig, dass wir unsere eigenen, unsere bayerischen Traditionen pflegen und das machen wir auch gerne. Aber in Grafenwöhr gehört die amerikanische Mentalität mit zur Tradition und damit auch zur Heimat. Ich verstehe diesen engen Kontakt mit den Amerikanern als Alleinstellungsmerkmal und als Chance die es eben nur hier bei uns gibt.

Ich wünsche Ihnen viel Freude beim Durchblättern der vorliegenden Neuauflage, die durch das einzigartige Detailwissen des Autors über den Truppenübungsplatz höchste Qualität bietet.

Edgar Knobloch, 1. Bürgermeister der Stadt Grafenwöhr, Oktober 2015

Dear Readers, due to the training area, the largest outside of the USA, the city of Grafenwoehr assumes a particular role:

1. We are the temporary home for the Americans stationed here and I can say that the American guests a cordially welcome here. We want the soldiers and their families to feel comfortable during their stay here with us. The very good relations between the city and the commanders of the U.S. Army contribute to that.

2. The training area is a considerable economic factor. As the largest employer in the county, it provides a job for more than 2,000 people. Every year, about € 650 million flow into the region.

3. The training area is also our home. The residents of Grafenwoehr have always been very familiar with the American way of life. It is important that we uphold our own Bavarian traditions and we like to do that but the American mentality is part of Grafenwoehr's tradition and, therefore, also a part of our home. For me, this close contact with the Americans is a unique feature and a chance that is only available here.

Enjoy browsing through the pages of this new edition which offers the highest quality thanks to the author's detailed knowledge of the training area.

Edgar Knobloch, 1st Mayor, City of Grafenwoehr, October 2015

Postplatz um 1950
Post Square around 1950

Postplatz mit Kennedy-Stein heute
Post Square with Kennedy Memorial today

Aufschwung mit dem Truppenübungsplatz

Mit Gründung des Übungsplatzes verlor Grafenwöhr, einschließlich der Gemeindeteile Gmünd, Hütten und Gößenreuth, 2.820 ha und damit 2/3 seines Grundbesitzes sowie einen Teil seines Hinterlandes. Dennoch stellte sich mit den Militärs der große Aufschwung für die Stadt ein. Von 1909 bis 1910 verdoppelte sich die Einwohnerzahl innerhalb eines Jahres von 961 auf 1841 Bürger. 2010 zählt Grafenwöhr rund 6550 Einwohner.

Die Entwicklung von Grafenwöhr mit Höhen und Tiefen geht seit 1910 mit der Entwicklung des Truppenübungsplatzes einher. Zum eigentlichen Wahrzeichen der Stadt, dem gotischen Rathaus auf dem Jahr 1462, gesellte sich der Wasserturm.

Training area caused economic boom

With the establishment of the training area, Grafenwoehr and its subdivisions Gmünd, Hütten and Gößenreuth lost 2.820 hectare, or two-thirds of its real estate as well as a portion of its back country. Nevertheless, the military caused an immense economic boom in Grafenwoehr. The number of inhabitants doubled between 1909 and 1910 from 961 to 1.841. In 2010, Grafenwoehr had 6.550 inhabitants.

Since 1910, the development of Grafenwoehr with all its highs and lows has been closely connected to the development of the training area. The Water Tower joined the city's original landmark, the gothic town hall built in 1462.

www.grafenwoehr.de

Waldbad mit Sportpark
Grafenwoehr Outdoor Pool and Sport Park

Friedenskirche
"Church of Peace" in Grafenwoehr

Blick vom Süden auf Lager und Stadt
View of main post and city from the south

Der Schirmherr der 650-Jahr-Feier, Weihbischof Reinhard Pappenberger, Bürgermeister und Stadtrat in historischen Gewändern zusammen mit deutschen und amerikanischen Gästen beim Jubiläumsabend. Hier wurde auch offiziell die Partnerschaft mit der US-Armee Garnison Grafenwöhr besiegelt.

Auxiliary bishop Reinhard Pappenberger, the chairman of the city's 650th anniversary festivities, mayor and city council in historic clothes together with German and American guests at the fest evening. The official partnership with the U.S. Army Garrison Grafenwoehr was also sealed here.

Sphärische Nacht und Party im Kulturellen Zentrum

Spherical night and party at the Cultural Center

Kleinstadt mit internationalem Flair

Da weite Teile des Übungsplatzes seit der Gebietsreform zum Stadtgebiet gehören, ist Grafenwöhr heute mit 21621 Hektar die viertgrößte Flächengemeinde in Bayern. Grafenwöhr hat sich zu einer modernen Kleinstadt mit einer guten Infrastruktur, Einkaufsmöglichkeiten sowie einer vielfältigen Gastronomie und Hotelerie entwickelt. Ein Waldfreibad, ein modernes Sportzentrum, eine Stadthalle und weitere Einrichtungen sowie ein reges Vereinsleben bieten gute Freizeitmöglichkeiten. Eine Partnerschaft unterhält die Stadt mit der Marktgemeinde Grafenwörth in Niederösterreich. Beim Stadtjubiläum wurde auch die offizielle Partnerschaft mit der US-Armee Garnison Grafenwöhr besiegelt. Den amerikanischen Soldaten und ihren Familien will Grafenwöhr eine „Heimat auf Zeit" geben.

Small town with an international flair

As a result of the district rezoning, large parts of the training area belong to the city of Grafenwoehr. Therefore, Grafenwoehr is the fourth largest city in Bavaria with a land area of 21,621 hectare.

Grafenwoehr has developed into a small modern city with a good infrastructure, shopping opportunities and a variety of restaurants and hotels. An outdoor pool, a modern sports center, a community hall and other facilities as well as lots of active clubs offer excellent leisure opportunities. The city has a partnership with the city of Grafenwörth in Lower Austria. An official partnership with the US Army Garrison Grafenwoehr was established during the festivities of the city anniversary. It is one of Grafenwoehr's goals to provide the American soldiers and their families with a home away from home.

Vom Volkstanz über Rock and Roll und Elvis-Show reichten die Vorführungen.
The show events ranged from traditional dances to rock and roll.

Festbetrieb und „Grafenwöhr International" auf dem Markt- und Marienplatz.
Fest activities and „Grafenwoehr International" on the Market Square and on St. Mary's Square.

Zoigl-Bier und Stimmung im Kommunbrauhaus
Zoigl beer and fun at the community brewery

650 Jahre Stadt Grafenwöhr

Im Jahr 1361, 131 Jahre bevor Columbus Amerika entdeckte, wird Grafenwöhr durch Kaiser Karl IV zur Stadt erhoben. Der 650. Geburtstag der Stadt wurde 2011 mit verschiedenen Veranstaltungen groß gefeiert.

Die Geschichte des kleinen Ackerbürger-Städtchens ist wechselvoll.

Während des 30-jährigen Krieges (1618-1648) wurde der Ort durch die Schweden belagert, mehrmals geplündert und gebrandschatzt. 1636 wird die Stadt von der Pest heimgesucht. Die Bürger flehten damals um Hilfe und legten ein Gelübde beim Ortsheiligen St. Sebastian ab. Der Sebastianstag, der 20. Januar, wird auch heute noch als örtlicher Feiertag begangen.

650th Anniversary of the City of Grafenwoehr

In 1361, 131 years before Columbus discovered America, the city received its town charter from Emperor Charles IV. Grafenwoehr celebrated its 650th anniversary with several events in 2011.

The small farm town had a changeful history.

During the Thirty Years' War (1618-1648) the city was besieged by the Swedish, marauded and burned. In 1636, the city was infested with the plague. The citizens prayed for help and made a vow to the city saint Saint Sebastian. Sebastian's Day, the town holiday, is still celebrated every year on January 20.

„Grafenwöhr feiert anders! Feiern Sie mit!"
war 2011 das Motto der 650-Jahr-Feier
"Grafenwoehr celebrates differently! Celebrate with us!"
was the motto of the city's 650th anniversary in 2011

Die Theatergruppe orakelt über die Zukunft der Stadt.
The theater group performed a sketch about the future of the city.

Sturm auf die Stadtmauern im Schwedenkrieg
Attack on the city wall during the Swedish War

Ein Leuchtturm im Landkreis – der schönste Basaltkegel Europas - der Parkstein im bayerisch-böhmischen Geopark
Parkstein, Europe's most beautiful basalt cone, is a county landmark and part of the Bavarian-Bohemian Geopark

Landkreis Neustadt a. d. Waldnaab
Neustadt a. d. Waldnaab County

Die Stadt Grafenwöhr liegt in der nördlichen Oberpfalz im Landkreis Neustadt an der Waldnaab und somit im geographischen Zentrum Europas. Die aufstrebende Wirtschaftskraft der Region steht in Symbiose mit Landschaft und Natur. Als Teil eines grünen Bandes entlang der bayerisch-tschechischen Grenze dehnt sich der Naturpark Nördlicher Oberpfälzer Wald über den gesamten Landkreis Neustadt an der Waldnaab aus. Ein gut ausgeschildertes Radwegenetz und Fernwanderwege verbinden die Sehenswürdigkeiten des Naturparklandes, die vom Rußweihergebiet in Eschenbach, dem Kloster Speinshart, dem Rauhen Kulm, dem Parkstein als schönstem Basaltkegel Europas, über die wasserumspülten Granitfelsen des Waldnaabtals, zahlreiche Burgen, die Glasmacher- und Kreisstadt Neustadt bis zur kontinentalen Tiefbohrung in Windischeschenbach reichen.

The city of Grafenwoehr is located in the northern Oberpfalz region in Neustadt an der Waldnaab County and thus in the geographical center of Europe. The increasing economic power of the region forms a symbiosis with the landscape and nature. The Northern Upper Palatinate Nature Park is part of a green belt along the Bavarian-Czech border, spread across the entire Neustadt an der Waldnaab County. A well-developed network of bike and hiking trails connects the sights of the nature park which spreads from the Rußweiher Lake in Eschenbach, the Speinshart Monastery, the Rauhe Kulm mountain, Parkstein – Europe's most beautiful basalt cone – to the granite rocks of the Waldnaab valley that are surrounded by wild waters, the many castles, the glass maker town and county seat Neustadt to the continental deep-drilling hole at Windischeschenbach.

www.neustadt.de
www.oberpfaelzerwald.de

Der Rußweiher mit seinen Bootshäusern in Eschenbach
Rußweiher Lake with its boathouses in Eschenbach

Glasmacher- und Kreisstadt Neustadt an der Waldnaab
glass maker town and county seat Neustadt an der Waldnaab

Kloster Speinshart
the Speinshart Monastery

Doost zwischen Neustadt und Floß
Doost between Neustadt and Floß

Burgruine Weißenstein im Steinwald
The ruins of Weißenstein Castle in the Steinwald Mountains

Der „Steinreichtum" der Region wird im grenzüberschreitenden bayrisch-böhmischen Geopark präsentiert. Die Menschen in der Oberpfalz sind bodenständig und fleißig und pflegen Gastlichkeit und Tradition beim „Zoigl-Bier". Ausflüge bieten sich zu den Nachbarn im böhmischen Bäderdreieck sowie nach Regensburg, Nürnberg oder Bayreuth an. In der Mitte des Landkreises liegt die Stadt Weiden, die auch eine Partnerschaft mit der US-Armee Garnison Grafenwöhr unterhält.

The geologically versatile region is part of the border-crossing Bavarian-Bohemian Geopark. The people in the Oberpfalz region are down to earth, industrious and keep the tradition of hospitality with the "Zoigl" beer. Trips may be taken to the neighbors in the Bohemian spa triangle and to Regensburg, Nuremberg, or Bayreuth. The city of Weiden, which also has an official partnership with the U.S. Army Garrison Grafenwoehr, is located in the center of the county.

www.weiden-oberpfalz.de

Am 21. April 1945 wurde das Untere Tor von den Amerikanern gesprengt. Die Durchfahrt war für die Panzer zu eng.

The lower gate was blown up by the Americans on April 21, 1945. It was too small for tanks.

Grafenwöhr, Stadtweiher, Stadttor und Kastenhaus (links), in dem heute das Museum i

Grafenwoehr, city pond, city gate and granary (left), where the museum is located today

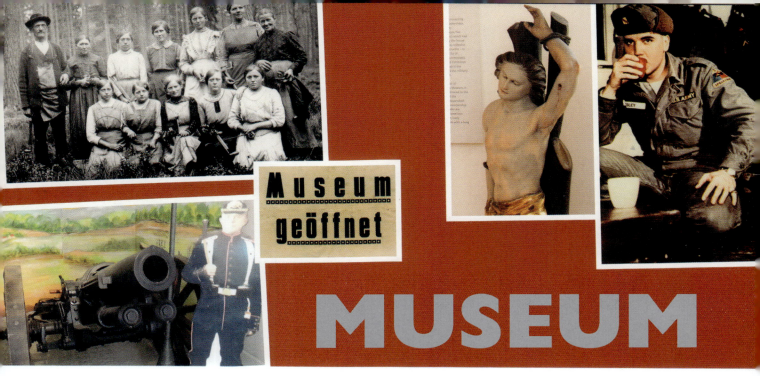

Kultur und Militär

Im Kultur- und Militärmuseum wird in einer deutschlandweit einmaligen Ausstellung die Entwicklung des Truppenübungsplatzes und das Zusammenleben von Deutschen und Amerikanern dargestellt. Bilder, Filme und Exponate berichten von der Ablösung der ehemaligen Ortschaften, über den Bau des Lagers, die Zeit des Ersten Weltkrieges mit dem Kriegsgefangenenlager, die Wehrmachtszeit, die Bombardierung und den Einzug der Amerikaner. Auch Hitlers Wunderwaffe „Dora" ist mit einem Originalstück des Rohres im Militärteil zu sehen. Im Obergeschoss der Militärabteilung stehen das Soldatenleben, dessen Faszination und Schicksal im Mittelpunkt. Es wird die Entwicklung vom „Bunten Rock zum Kampfanzug" dokumentiert.

Culture and Military

The history of the training and the social interaction between Germans and Americans is shown in a nationwide unique exhibition in the Culture- and Military Museum. Many photos, films and exhibits tell about the disbandment of the former villages, the construction of the training area, the World War I era with the prisoners of war camp, the Wehrmacht era, the bombardment and the arrival of the Americans. Even an original piece of the muzzle of Hitler's silver bullet "Dora" is on display in the military section. The first floor of the military section focuses on the fascination and fate of the life of a soldier. It documents the uniform development from the so-called "colored jacket" to the camouflage battle dress uniform.

Kultur- und Militärmuseum, Ausstellungshalle, Kastenhaus und Torschusterhaus am Stadtweiher
Culture and Military Museum, exhibition hall, granary and gate house at the city pond

Hitlers-Wunderwaffe „Dora" im Modell mit einem Originalstück des Rohres
A model of Hitler's silver bullet "Dora" with an original piece of the muzzle

Die Militärabteilung des Museums
The military section of the museum

Museum im historischen Kastenhaus

Mit Hilfe von professionellen Museumsgestaltern und mit großem ehrenamtlichen Engagement, haben die Mitglieder des Heimatvereins die Ausstellung 2015 umfassend modernisiert und erneuert. Von der Gründung der Stadt im Jahr 1361, über das religiöse Leben, Handwerk und Landwirtschaft, die Aufrüstung in der NS-Zeit bis zum deutsch-amerikanischen Zusammenleben heutzutage reicht der gespannte Bogen. Als prominentester amerikanischer Soldat war Elvis Presley in Grafenwöhr. Der Flügel, an dem Elvis ein Konzert in der legendären Micky Bar gab, ist ebenfalls Teil der neuen Ausstellung. Texte und Medienstationen im Museum sind zweisprachig in Deutsch und in Englisch

Der Museumskomplex ist direkt am Stadtweiher in einer neuen Ausstellungshalle sowie im historischen Kastenhaus, einem Speicher aus dem Jahre 1532 und im Torschusterhaus untergebracht. Neben dem Torschusterhaus stand einst das Untere Tor. Es gehörte zur Stadtbefestigung. Am 21. April 1945 wurde es von den Amerikanern gesprengt, um die Durchfahrt mit Panzern und Großgerät zu ermöglichen.

Das Kultur- und Militärmuseum ist am Sonntag, Dienstag, Mittwoch und Donnerstag jeweils von 14 bis 16 Uhr geöffnet. Gruppenführungen sind jederzeit möglich. Von April bis Oktober bietet der Heimatverein einmal monatlich eine Fahrt durch den Truppenübungsplatz an. Informationen gibt es auch auf der Internetseite www.museum-grafenwoehr.de.

Museum in the historic granary

In 2015, the members of the historic society volunteered many hours to modernize and renew the exhibition with the help of professional museum designers. It covers local history from the founding of the city in 1361, religious life, craftsmanship and agriculture, armament during the Third Reich to Germans and Americans living together today. The most famous American soldier ever stationed in Grafenwoehr was Elvis Presley. The piano Elvis played when he gave a concert at the Micky Bar is also part of the new exhibition. Texts and media stations in the museum are bilingual (German and English).

The museum is located directly next to the city pond in a new exhibition hall, the historic granary – a storage building built in 1532 - and the gate house. The lower gate was once located next to the gate house and was part of the city's fortification. On April 21, 1945 it was blown up by the Americans so they could pass through with their tanks and other large equipment.

The Culture and Military Museum is open on Sunday, Tuesday, Wednesday and Thursday from 2-4 p.m. Guided tours for groups are possible anytime. From April to October, the historic society offers a tour through the training area once a month. For more information, go to www.museum-grafenwoehr.de.

www.museum-grafenwoehr.de

Gäste bei der Museumseinweihung im Oktober 2015
Guests at the museum opening in October 2015

Vitrine Drittes Reich
The Third Reich display

Der Flügel an dem Elvis Presley ein Konzert in der Micky Bar gab
The piano Elvis played when he gave a concert at the Micky Bar

Bau des Lagers
Construction of the military camp

Architektonische Leistung

Als beachtliche architektonische Leistung kann der Bau des Truppenlagers, das im Volksmund nur kurz „Lager" heißt, bezeichnet werden. Erste Entwurfsplanungen fertigte die Intendantur und Baurat Ernst Feder. Vorstand der Bauleitung des Truppenübungsplatzes war der königliche Baurat Wilhelm Kemmler, als bauleitender Architekt wurde Jürgen Sievers zugeteilt. Nach der Versetzung Kemmlers wurde Sievers 1913 Vorstand der Bauleitung (bis 1933).
Von 1907 bis 1915 wurde geplant, vorbereitet und gebaut. Der Platz südlich von Grafenwöhr bot das ideale Gelände, wo, vorausschauend bis in die heutige Zeit, auch Erweiterungsmaßnahmen möglich waren.

Ein Heer von Bauarbeitern

Nach einer Straßenverlegung, der Entwässerung und den Rodungsarbeiten folgten dann die Erschließung mit großzügigen Straßen, der Bau der Wasserversorgung, der Kanalisation und die Errichtung der elektrischen Versorgung. Das Lager wurde an die Bahnlinie Weiden-Kirchenthumbach angeschlossen. Ein Heer von Bauarbeitern, darunter auch viele ausländische Arbeiter, zog es in das kleine Städtchen Grafenwöhr. Mit 1692 Mann wurde im April 1910 der Höchststand angegeben. Die Unterbringung und Versorgung der Arbeiter und das Zusammenleben untereinander gestaltete sich als schwierig. Ausführlich beschäftigen sich die Militärabteilung des Museums und der Museumskatalog mit der Thematik des Lagerbaus.

Architectural achievement

The construction of the military camp, commonly called "the camp," must be considered an architectural achievement. The first architectural designs were done by the intendant's office and government engineer Ernst Feder. Royal Engineer Wilhelm Kemmler headed the construction team and Jürgen Sievers was the head architect. In 1913, after Kemmler's permanent change of station, Sievers was named head of the construction team. He remained in that position until 1933. Planning, preparation and construction began in 1907 and ended in 1915. The area south of Grafenwoehr was ideal for the purpose and offered and still offers until today a lot of room for expansion.

An army of construction workers

First, a road was relocated, the area was drained and trees were cut. The construction of wide streets, the water supply and sewage systems and the electrical power supply followed. The camp was connected to the Weiden-Kirchenthumbach railroad line. An army of construction workers, among them many foreign workers, moved into the small town of Grafenwoehr. The number of workers reached its peak with 1692 men in April 1910. The lodging, the supply and the living conditions of the workers were difficult. The military section of the museum and the museum catalogue describe the construction of the camp in great detail.

Bau eines Hauses im Offizierslager. Zum Materialtransport wurden Loren auf einem Schienensystem benutzt.

Construction of a house in the officers' camp. Lorries on a railroad track were used to transport material.

Schmucke Fachwerkbauten

250 Gebäude für insgesamt 8,9 Millionen Mark wurden beiderseits der Alten Amberger Straße gebaut. Die Straßen teilen das Lager in einen Verwaltungs-, Offiziers- und Mannschaftsbereich und das Stalllager. Die schmucken Fachwerkbauten, die an einen fränkischen Stil erinnern, entstanden an den Straßen in symetrischer Weise. Die Gebäude waren für damalige Verhältnisse mit modernsten sanitären Anlagen ausgestattet und hatten elektrischen Strom. Zusammen mit den vielen Parkanlagen und Grünflächen wirkte die Anlage wie aus einem Guss.

Pretty half-timbered buildings

250 buildings for a total of 8.9 million mark were built on both sides of Alte Amberger Straße. The streets divide the camp into an administrative, officers' and enlisted section, and the stable complex. The pretty half-timbered buildings, which resemble a Franconian style of architecture, were symmetrically built along the streets. The buildings were equipped with the most modern sanitary facilities of the time and were connected to electrical power. With its many parks and green areas the camp had a very harmonious appeal.

Die Fachwerkbauten im Offizierslager. Die Gebäude, die 1945 bei der Bombardierung unversehrt blieben, werden auch heute noch genutzt.

The half-timbered buildings of the officers' camp. The buildings that were not damaged during the air raids in 1945 are still being used today.

Ein Wirtschaftsgebäude mit Truppenküche, dahinter eine Mannschaftskaserne, das heutige Gebäude 500, Hauptquartier der US-Armee-Garnison.

A supply building with dining facility, behind it a barracks building (today Bldg. 500, the U.S. Army garrison headquarters' building).

Die Warmbadeanstalt südlich der Pumpstation hatte mehrere Wannenbäder und Brauseräume. Offiziere, Feldwebel und Mannschaften hatten unterschiedlich lange Badezeiten. Heute ist in der Warmbadeanstalt der „Military Clothing Sales Store" beheimatet.

The warm baths, south of the water pumping station, had several baths and showers. The bathing times of officers, NCOs and soldiers differed. Today, the warm baths are the home of the military clothing sales store.

Das Lazarett, unterhalb des Wasserturms, dahinter sind der Höhenzug des Annabergs und der Rosenhof zu sehen. Das alte Lazarettgebäude ist heute ein Teil des Hauptquartier-Komplexes für das JMTC.

The military hospital below the Water Tower, behind it Annaberg mountain and the Rosenhof subdivision. Today, the old military hospital is a part of the JMTC headquarters' building.

Der königliche Baurat Wilhelm Kemmler wirkte von 1907 bis 1913 in Grafenwöhr. 1910 erhielt er von Prinzregent Luitpold den Königlichen-Militärverdienst-Orden für Errichtung und Ausbau des Truppenübungsplatzes Grafenwöhr.

Royal Engineer Wilhelm Kemmler was assigned to Grafenwoehr from 1907 to 1913. In 1910, Prince Regent Luitpold awarded him the Royal Military Achievement Medal for the construction and the expansion of Grafenwoehr Training Area.

Johnson Street während des Baus 1910 und heute (rechts)

Johnson Street during construction in 1910 and today (right)

Blick vom Wasserturm auf das Militärgasthaus um 1912. Im Hintergrund ist die Stadt zu sehen, die damals aus der Altstadt und wenigen Häusern der Vorstadt bestand.

View from the Water Tower on the military restaurant circa 1912. The city can be seen in the background. It only consisted of the old town and a few houses in the Vorstadt subdivision.

Die Schmalspur-Feldbahn führte zunächst bis nach Langenbruck und wurde dann als Ringbahn um den alten Teil des Platzes gebaut. Hier die Lokomotive am Schaumbach beim Wassertanken.
Initially, the railway system ended in Langenbruck, then it was expanded into a circular railroad track that ran around the entire original section of the training area. The photo shows the engine being refilled with water at the Schaumbach river.

MUNA und Feldbahn

Es entstand auch ein Lazarett und in östlicher Richtung die Munitionsanstalt (MUNA), wo Munition gelagert und schießfertig gemacht wurde.

Als Einrichtungen im Gelände wurden die Schießbahnen, die Artilleriefliegerschule und die Feldbahn gebaut. Mit der Schmalspurbahn konnten kleine Truppenabteilungen, deren Gepäck, Geschütze, Munition, Zielbaukommandos und Material innerhalb des Platzes befördert werden. Die Schmalspur-Feldbahn führte zunächst von Grafenwöhr nach Langenbruck und wurde später als Ringbahn um den gesamten alten Platz gebaut. Das Gleisbett der Feldbahn ist noch heute an vielen Geländeabschnitten zu erkennen.

MUNA and light railway system

A military hospital and an ammunition facility, known as MUNA, where ammunition was stored and prepared for firing were also built.

Facilities built on the training area included the ranges, the artillery pilots' school and the light railway system. Small groups of soldiers, their equipment, weapon systems, ammunition, as well as range workers and other material were transported with the narrow-gauge track system. At first, the railway system connected Grafenwoehr and Langenbruck, then it was expanded into a circular railroad track that ran around the entire original section of the training area. The tracks can still be seen at many parts of the training area.

Blick auf das ehemalige Militärgasthaus und die angrenzende Stadt
View of the former military guest house and the adjacent city today

Blick vom Birka auf das östliche Lager um 1910 - *View from Birka mountain to the eastern part of main post circa 1910*

Werkstätten der Kommandantur heute Wache 3 | Bäckerei Neuberger | Fam. Bauer | Kaserne 14 Arbeitskommando | Kommandantur

Auto Witt | Weizenbierbrauerei heute Restaurant „Luigi" | Fam. Mark Schneiderei Fellner | Zement Deyerling heute Steinmetz Reiter | Bayerischer Hof | Magazin und Kohlenhof

Mannschaftskaserne 1910 und heute - *Soldiers' Barracks 1910 and today*

Der erste Schuss
The first shot

Am 30. Juni 1910 wurde offiziell der erste Artillerie-Schuss abgefeuert

Der Kanonier Michael Kugler aus Nitzlbuch gab am 30. Juni 1910 den ersten Schuss auf dem Truppenübungsplatz ab. Es war fast hundert Jahre ein Geheimnis, welche Einheit, welches Geschütz oder gar welcher Soldat den ersten Schuss auf dem Übungsplatz abgefeuert hat. Nur ein Marterl, dessen Nachbau im Zielgebiet des Übungsplatzes bei der Flurbezeichnung „Am Dreieck" zu finden ist, weist auf das Ereignis hin.

The first artillery shot was officially fired on June 30, 1910

The first shot on Grafenwoehr Training Area was fired on June 30, 1910 by cannoneer Michael Kugler from Nitzlbuch. Which soldier, which unit and which weapon fired the first shot on the training area remained a secret for almost a hundred years. Only a small monument, whose replica is located in the impact area of the training area near the lot "By the Triangle" serves as a reminder of the event.

Nach 99 Jahren lüftet sich das Geheimnis

Erst im Jahr 2009 knüpfte durch Zufall der Geschäftleiter der Stadt Grafenwöhr, Willi Keck, Kontakt zu Herbert Kugler, der in Kehrham bei Ampfing in Oberbayern wohnte. Zusammen mit Historiker Olaf Meiler vom Grafenwöhrer Museum und den Stabsfeldwebeln Michael Hiller und Gerald Morgenstern, die sich von der Seite der Bundeswehr mit der Truppenübungsplatzgeschichte befassen, besuchte Willi Keck im Mai 2009 die Familie Kugler.
Herbert Kugler gab an, dass sein Vater Michael Kugler als junger Kanonier und Angehöriger der 3. Batterie des 2. königlich-bayerischen Fußartillerie-Regiments diente. Im Juni 1910 gab er den ersten offiziellen Artillerieschuss auf dem Truppenübungsplatz ab. Die Bilder aus dem Familienerbe und die Erzählungen des 77-Jährigen waren sehr aufschlussreich.

Secret is disclosed after 99 years

It wasn't until 2009 that Grafenwoehr's city manager Willi Keck made contact with Herbert Kugler, who lived in Kehrham near Ampfing in Upper Bavaria, with the help of relatives of the Kugler family. Willi Keck visited the Kugler Family in May 2009 together with Olaf Meiler, historian of the Grafenwöhr Museum and Sergeants Major Michael Hiller and Gerald Morgenstern, who document the history of the training area for the German Army. Herbert Kugler said that his father Michael Kugler served as a young cannoneer with the 3rd Battery of the 2nd Royal-Bavarian Foot Artillery Regiment and fired the first official artillery shot at the training area in June 1910. The family photos and the stories told by the 77 year-old were a lot of help.

Der Kanonier Michael Kugler gab den ersten offiziellen Artillerie-Schuss auf dem Truppenübungsplatz ab. Der Ausschnitt aus seinem Reservistenbild zeigt ihn mit der „15 cm schweren Feldhaubitze" von Krupp.
The cannoneer Michael Kugler fired the first official artillery shot at the training area. This cutout of his reservist's photo shows him with the heavy 15 cm Krupp field howitzer.

Michael Kuglers großes Regiments-Erinnerungsbild zeigt die Soldaten der „3. Batterie des königlich-bayerischen 2. Fußartillerie-Regiments Metz". Abgebildet sind auch ihre Geschütze und die Luftschiffe der Luftbeobachter. Das Original-Bild ist im Kultur- und Militärmuseum ausgestellt.

Michael Kugler's large reservist's photo shows the soldiers of the 3rd Battery, 2nd Royal-Bavarian Foot Artillery Regiment Metz. Shown also are the cannons and the blimps of the aerial observers. The original photo is on display at the 1st Upper Palatinate Culture and Military Museum.

Die Fotografie von Michael Kugler wurde im Atelier Spahn aufgenommen und trägt dessen Firmenstempel.

This photo of Michael Kugler was taken at the Spahn Photo Studio and carries the company stamp.

Erst 2009 wurde bekannt, wer den ersten Schuss abgegeben hat. Historiker Olaf Meiler (von rechts), Willi Keck und die Stabsfeldwebel Gerald Morgenstern und Michael Hiller im Gespräch mit Herbert Kugler (†) (Mitte), dessen Vater Michael der Kanonier des ersten Schusses war.

It was not known until 2009 who fired the first shot. Historian Olaf Meiler (from right to left), Willi Keck and Sergeants Major Gerald Morgenstern and Michael Hiller talk to Herbert Kugler (†) (center), whose father Michael was the cannoneer of the first shot.

Eine Gedenktafel an der Einschlagstelle erinnerte an den ersten Schuss. Das Original-Marterl wurde später umgesetzt und schließlich von einem Souvenierjäger entwendet.

Die Inschrift auf der Tafel lautete wörtlich: „O Wanderer stehe still und hör´ was ich dir sagen will! 25 Meter südlich dieser Stelle hat am 30. Juni 1910 früh 8 Uhr eine 15 cm Granate 80Z, aus s. Feldhaubitzen v. der Grünhundhöhe kommend, als erstes Artillerie-Geschoss auf dem Truppenübungsplatze, 800 Meter vor dem Ziele ihren Geist aufgegeben".

A plaque at the point of impact commemorates the first shot. The original plaque was later moved and then stolen.

The inscription on the plaque reads: Dear hiker, rest and listen to what I want to tell you! On June 30, 1910 at 8 a.m., the first artillery round fired at the training area, a 15 cm grenade 80Z coming from a howitzer located at Grünhund Hill, impacted here 800 meter short of its destination."

Der erste Schuss war ein Fehlschuss

„Weil s so guad woar n", sei die Geschützbesatzung von Michael Kugler für den historischen Moment ausgesucht worden, erinnert sich der Sohn an die Schilderungen des Vaters. Das Geschütz hatte sechs Mann Besatzung und ist von vier Pferden gezogen worden. Geschossen wurde von der Grünhundhöhe, die oberhalb des Grünhundweihers bei der Schießbahn 114 liegt. Allerdings ging die Vorführung gehörig daneben, denn die Granate schlug schon 800 Meter vor dem eigentlichen Ziel im Boden ein. Deshalb wurden die Artilleristen des ersten Schusses „mächtig aufgezwickt". „Wir haben halt daneben g´schossen", habe der Vater immer erzählt. Nach dem Ereignis ist in der Kaserne trotzdem gefeiert worden. Mit verschiedenen Bildern belegte Herbert Kugler eindeutig, dass sein Vater der Kanonier des ersten Schusses war.

The first shot was a miss

"Because they were so good," that's why the howitzer crew of Michael Kugler was selected for that historic moment, remembers the son of his father's stories. The howitzer had a six-men crew and was drawn by four horses. The shots were fired from Grünhund Hill, above Grünhund Lake near Range 114. Unfortunately, the demonstration was a failure because the grenade impacted 800 meters short of its destination. That's why the artillery men who fired the first shot caught a lot of flak. "We simply missed," is what the father used to say. Nevertheless, there was a party at the barracks afterwards. Herbert Kugler shows a lot of photos that prove without a doubt that his father was the cannoneer of the first shot.

Am Fuße des Schwarzen Berges bei der Flurbezeichnung „Am Dreieck" steht heute ein Nachbau des Marterl, wo am 30. Juni 1910 der 1. offizielle Artillerieschuss einschlug. Lange Jahre kennzeichnete nur ein Steinhaufen mit einer aufgesetzten Geschosshülle den Platz, der im gesperrten Gefahrenbereich der Schießbahnen liegt.

Today, a replica of the commemorative plaque is located at the bottom of the Schwarzen Berg mountain near the lot "By the Triangle." For many years a pile of stone with a grenade shell on top marked that spot which is located in the danger zone of the ranges.

So könnte die Szene während der Schussabgabe 1910 ausgesehen haben. Das Bild zeigt Soldaten der königlich- bayerischen Artillerie mit der Feldhaubitze 02. Dahinter steht der Protzenwagen, der zum Transport der Munition und zum Vorspannen der Pferde diente.

This photo demonstrates what the firing scene of the first shot in 1910 may have looked like. The photo shows soldiers of the Royal-Bavarian Artillery with a howitzer 02. Behind them is the wagon that was used to transport the ammunition. It was drawn by horses.

Eine „VH 99" (Versuchs-Haubitze vor der Serienfertigung der sFH 02) wurde im Jubiläumsjahr von der Bundeswehr an das Museum übergeben.

The German Army donated a „VH 99" (trial howitzer before the sFH 02 howitzer went into series production) to the museum during the 2010 anniversary year.

Die schwere Feldhaubitze 02

Durch das vorliegende Reservistenbild, eine Farbkollage mit eingesetztem Gesicht des Kanoniers Michael Kugler, steht nun auch endgültig der Geschütztyp fest. Es war die „15 cm schwere Feldhaubitze 02" (sFH 02) von Krupp. Die alten Gruppenfotos und Einzelbilder aus dem Nachlass von Michael Kugler tragen den Firmenstempel des Ateliers Spahn. Viele der Fotos wurden vor den Fachwerkbauten des Grafenwöhrer Lagers aufgenommen. Ein großes Regiments-Erinnerungsbild zeigt neben den damaligen Soldaten in verschiedenen Zeichnungen die Waffen und die Ausstattung der „3. Batterie des königlich-bayerischen 2. Fußartillerie-Regiments Metz". Auf einer Artillerie-Granate sind alle Namen der Soldaten aufgeführt, die von 1909 – 1911 in der Batterie ihren Wehrdienst ableisteten. Vermutlich stammten etliche der Soldaten auch aus der Region um Grafenwöhr.

Im Ersten Weltkrieg wurde Michael Kugler mit seinem Regiment an der Somme und vor Verdun eingesetzt. Er wurde mit dem EK II (Eisernen Kreuz 2. Klasse) ausgezeichnet. Zeitweise diente er unter dem Generalfeldmarschall Albert Kesselring, der auch den Beinamen „Blutsäufer" trug.

The heavy field howitzer 02

The existing reservists' photo, a colored collage with the face of cannoneer Michael Kugler pasted into it, now also shows for sure which cannon was used. It was the heavy 15 cm field howitzer 02 (sFH 02) made by Krupp. The old group and individual photos from Michael Kugler's estate carry the company stamp of Spahn Photo Studio. Many of the photos were taken in front of the half-timbered buildings of the old Grafenwoehr camp. The large reservist's photo shows paintings of the soldiers and the weapons and equipment of the 3rd Battery, 2nd Royal-Bavarian Foot Artillery Regiment Metz. The names of all soldiers who served in the battery from 1090 to 1911 are listed on an artillery grenade. It can be assumed that many of the soldiers came from the region around Grafenwoehr.

During World War I, Michael Kugler served with his regiment at the Somme river and near Verdun, France, and was awarded the Iron Cross, Class II. He temporarily served under the command of General Field Marshal Albert Kesselring who was also known as the "Blood Drinker."

Artillerie-Schießen heute: Die amerikanische Feldhaubitze M 777 im Einsatz.
Artillery fire today: A deployed American howitzer.

Die Haubitzen des deutschen Heeres mussten gemäß dem Versailler-Vertrag vernichtet werden. Ein sehr seltener Fund der Feldhaubitze 02 tauchte in Frankreich in einer Scheune auf.
In accordance with the Treaty of Versailles, the German Army had to demolish its howitzers. In France, a howitzer 02 was found in a barn – an extremely rare find.

Artillerie-Schießen damals: Die Postkarte um 1910 zeigt die Haubitzenbatterie mit der sFH 02 in Stellung.
Artillery fire then: The post card from around 1910 shows the emplacement of a howitzer battery sFH 02.

Kuglers Heimat lag im heutigen Übungsplatz

Nach dem Ersten Weltkrieg heiratete Michael Kugler Katharina Pirkl aus Welluck und übernahm einen Hof in Sommerhau, das zur Pfarrei Hopfenohe gehörte. Die Orte liegen auf dem Gelände des Übungsplatzes und existieren heute nicht mehr. 1938 folgte die Umsiedelung, die Herbert Kugler als Kind miterlebte und von der er noch einiges zu berichten wusste. Die Familie erhielt von der Reichsumsiedlungsgesellschaft einen Hof in Kerham im Landkreis Mühldorf am Inn in Oberbayern.

Michael Kugler, der Kanonier des ersten Schusses, verstarb 1974 im Alter von 86 Jahren.

Kugler's home was located where the training area is today

After World War I, Michael Kugler married Katharina Pirkl from Welluck and took over a farm in Sommerhau which belonged to the Hopfenohe parish. Both towns were located on the training area and do not exist anymore today. Herbert Kugler was a child when the resettlement, of which he could still remember, took place in 1938. The so-called Reich Resettlement Company gave the family a farm in Kerham, Mühldorf am Inn County in Upper Bavaria. Michael Kugler, the cannoneer of the first shot, died in 1974 at the age of 86.

Tausende von Soldaten hielt die Familie Spahn im Bild fest. Hier eine Aufnahme königlich- bayerischer Artilleristen vor dem Atelier Spahn.

Thousands of soldiers were photographed by the Spahn family. This photo shows Royal-Bavarian Artillery soldiers in front of Spahn Photo Studio.

Photostudio Spahn

Ein Militärfotograf aus Hammelburg

Mit der Gründung des Truppenübungsplatzes wurde vom königlich-bayerischen Armeekorps 1910 Hans Spahn nach Grafenwöhr gerufen.

Hans Spahn, geboren 1881, entstammte einer Fotografenfamilie aus der Nähe von Hammelburg, dort existierte bereits damals ein Übungsplatz. Auf Glasplatte hielt er Szenen vom Bau des Lagers sowie Soldaten in Gruppen oder im Einzelportrait fest.

Ein modernes Atelier

An der Grenze zum Übungsplatz ließ Fotografenmeister Spahn sein eigenes Atelier bauen.

Kernstücke waren die rundum verglasten Studios, da nur Naturlichtaufnahmen gemacht werden konnten.

In den Sommermonaten musste Hans Spahn Fotografen aus Polen beschäftigten, um alle vom Militär geforderten Aufnahmen liefern zu können Vermutlich alle bekannten Bilder aus der Gründerzeit und aus der Geschichte des Truppenübungsplatzes stammen von Fotomeister Spahn. Im Besitz einer Kamera war in der damaligen Zeit auch der königliche Baurat Wilhelm Kemmler, er hielt weitere Szenen vom Bau des Lagers fest und machte Aufnahmen von Ausflügen in die Gegend.

A military photographer from Hammelburg

When the training area was established by the Royal-Bavarian Army Corps in 1910, Hans Spahn was called to Grafenwoehr. Spahn, born in 1881, was the descendant of a family of photographers from the Hammelburg area, where another training area was already located. He photographed the construction of the camp as well as group and single portraits of soldiers on glass plates.

A modern photo studio

Spahn built his own photo studio at the border of the training area. Its core were the glass studios because photos could be taken only in natural light. During the summer months, he had to hire photographers from Poland to take all the photos required by the military. It can be assumed that all photos dating back to the founding years of the training area were taken by Spahn. Another camera was owned in those days by royal government building officer Wilhelm Kemmler, who also photographed the construction of the camp and trips into the surrounding areas.

Das Fotostudio Spahn an der Wache 1, der Zuschnitt des ursprünglichen Gebäudes von 1910 ist noch zu erkennen. 2014 wurde das Fotoatelier endgültig geschlossen.

The Spahn Photo Studio at Gate 1. The floor plan of the old building from 1910 can still be recognized. The photo studio was closed for good in 2014.

1910 wurde das Fotoatelier Spahn errichtet. Damals ein hochmoderner Bau mit zwei verglasten Studios. In der hinteren Reihe (vierter von links) ist der Bauherr Hans Spahn selbst mit auf dem Bild.

The Spahn Photo Studio was built in 1910. At the time, it was a state-of-the-art building with two glass studios.

Ein Schnappschuss Hitlers

Soldaten aller Dienstgrade, Größen des Kaiserreichs, der Reichswehrzeit, der Wehrmacht und auch den italienischen Duce hielt Hans Spahn im Bild fest. Ein seltener Schnappschuss gelang ihm beim Besuch Adolf Hitlers in Grafenwöhr am 24. Juni 1938. Während der Vorbeifahrt der Führerlimousine überreichte Spahns Sohn Josef einen Blumenstrauß um die Fahrt des Wagens für die Aufnahme zu verlangsamen. Der Führer durfte damals eigentlich nur von seinem Leibfotografen abgelichtet werden.

Fotografentradition endet 2014

In die Fußstapfen von Fotografenmeister Hans Spahn stieg Sohn Erich, geboren 1914., Nach seiner Rückkehr aus der Gefangenschaft 1945 fand er das Fotoatelier in Schutt und Asche vor. Trotz des Fotografierverbots hielt er gleich die Ausmaße der Zerstörungen durch die Bombardierung Grafenwöhrs für die Nachwelt fest. Der unvergessene Erich Spahn verstarb 2002 im gesegneten Alter von 88 Jahren. Das Fotostudio Spahn wurde von Alexander Kneidl weitergeführt, er erlernte bei Erich Spahn das Fotografenhandwerk und übernahm das Geschäft 1996. Mit dem weiteren Fortschritt der digitalen Fotografie gab er das Geschäft 2014 auf.–

A snapshot of Hitler

Soldiers of all ranks, the important people of the Emperor's times, the Reichswehrzeit, the Wehrmacht and the Italian Duce were photographed by Hans Spahn. He successfully took a rare snapshot during Adolf Hitler's visit to Grafenwoehr on June 24, 1938. When Hitler's sedan drove by, Spahn's son Josef presented Hitler with a bouquet of flowers to slow the vehicle for the photograph. In those days, only Hitler's personal photographer had the right to take pictures of the "Führer."

A photographer's tradition ends in 2014

Son Erich, born in 1914, followed in his father's footsteps. After his return from captivity as a prisoner of war, he found the photo studio destroyed. Despite the ban on photography, he immediately documented damages caused by air raids on Grafenwoehr. The unforgotten Erich Spahn passed away 2002 at the age of 88. In 1996, Alexander Kneidl, Spahn's former apprentice, took over the photo studio. He closed the studio in 2014 due to the continuing progress of digital photography.

Selten stehen Fotografen selbst vor der Kamera. Dieses Bild vereint drei Generationen der Familie Spahn: Hans Spahn, sein Sohn Erich und Erich Spahn junior. Die Aufnahme entstand um 1960.

Photographers rarely take pictures of themselves. This photo shows three generations of the Spahn family: Hans Spahn, his son Erich and Erich Spahn junior. The photo was taken around 1960.

Hans Spahn fotografierte 1938 den Führer bei seinem Besuch in Grafenwöhr

In 1938, Hans Spahn took a photo of the "Führer" during his visit to Grafenwoehr.

Bilder in aller Welt bekannt

Viele offizielle Empfänge, Feierlichkeiten, Paraden und das Leben im Lager wurden auf Zelluloid gebannt. Die markanten Bauten des Lagers und natürlich der Wasserturm waren Motive für unzählige Postkarten. Die Aufnahmen und Ansichtskarten des Fotostudios Spahn vom Lager, das mit seinen Fachwerkbauten für die Amerikaner das „Rothenburg der Übungsplätze" ist, machten Grafenwöhr in aller Welt bekannt. Noch immer gibt es die „Schatzkammer" der Spahns, ein Archiv mit Glasplatten, weiteres Material wurde an den Heimatverein übergeben.

Photos known around the world

Many official receptions, celebrations, parades and life in the camp were put on celluloid. The camp's landmarks and naturally the Water Tower became motifs for countless postcards. The photos and postcards taken by Spahn's photo studio of the training area and its half-timbered buildings, which Americans consider the "Rothenburg of the training areas," established Grafenwoehr's world-wide fame. However, the Spahn's "treasury," an archive of glass plates, is still in the family's possession. Other material was given to the local historic society.

Die Wachen
The Gates

Wache 1 – das Tor zum Lager

Niemand hat sie je gezählt, die Soldaten und Zivilisten die das „Gate 1" im Laufe der letzten 100 Jahre passiert haben. Das Bild der Wache 1 aus den 1960er Jahren mit dem markanten Eingangsbogen und der Aufschrift „U.S. Army Training Area Grafenwöhr" sowie dem alten Wachhäuschen aus Holz hat sich eingeprägt. Auf Bildern und Postkarten ging es um die Welt.

Die Hauptwache

In der Geschichte des Übungsplatzes haben sich die Tore und Einfahrten zum Lager wiederholt verändert. Das Wachgebäude an der Lagereinfahrt in der Alten Amberger Straße stand nicht immer an der heutigen Stelle. Die große Hauptwache mit Schreibstube, Wachlokal und sechs Arrestzellen wurde bei der Gründung des Übungsplatzes als eingeschossiges Gebäude gegenüber dem Wasserturm gebaut. Zwischen dem Forsthaus und dem Militärgasthof (MG), dem heutigen „Tower View Restaurant and Conference Center" war das Eingangstor mit den Wachposten. Der Militärgasthof hatte zur Stadt hin einen Nebeneingang, der auch zivilen Gästen den Besuch ermöglichen sollte. Dieses Schlupfloch wurde oft genutzt, um durch das Gasthaus auch ohne Ausweiskontrolle in die Kaserne zu gelangen. Später wurde die alte Hauptwache aufgestockt; das Fachwerk und der Uhrenturm waren nach dem Umbau prägend. Bei den Luftangriffen im April 1945 fiel die Hauptwache den Bomben zum Opfer. Heute erinnert dort ein Stein mit einer Gedenktafel an die Errichtung des Übungsplatzes. Eine Historientafel erzählt die Geschichte der Wache.

Gate 1 – the gate to the camp

Nobody ever counted them – the soldiers and civilians that have passed through Gate 1 during the past 100 years. This picture of Gate 1, taken in the 1960s, shows the distinctive entrance arc. The inscription "U.S. Army Training Area Grafenwoehr" and the old wooden guard house are well-known. On photos and post cards it was sent around the world.

The Main Gate

The gates and access routes into the training area have changed over the years. The guard house at Gate 1 on Alte Amberger Straße has not always been located where it is today. When the training area was established, the main gate and one-story guard house with an office and six prison cells was built across from the Water Tower. The gate and the guards were located between the Forest House and the military restaurant, known today as the Tower View Restaurant and Conference Center. The military restaurant had a side door to the city that allowed civilian guests to frequent the club. This loophole was often used to access post via the guest house and without having to go through the pass control at the gate. Later, a second floor was added to the old guard house. Its half-timbered architecture and the clock tower became its most significant features. The guard house was destroyed during the air raids in April 1945. Today, a stone marker is located there to commemorate the establishment of the training area and to tell the story of the main gate.

Bis Juli 1990 stand das alte Holzhäuschen am Lagereingang der berühmten Wache 1. Das Motiv mit der jungen Frau, zwei Soldaten der Wachkompanie und dem markanten Torbogen wurde in den 1950er und 60er Jahren auf tausenden von Postkarten und Bildern in der ganzen Welt verbreitet.

The old wooden guard house stood at the entrance of the training area, the famous Gate 1, until July 1990. The picture of the young woman, two guard soldiers and the distinctive arc was sent around the world on thousands of photos and post cards in the 1950s and 60s. Hermann Dietl.

Als Gartenlaube und Lagerraum hat das alte Wachhäuschen nur 100 Meter vom ehemaligen Standort entfernt eine neue Verwendung gefunden.

The old guard house has found a new use as a gazebo and storage room only 100 meters away from its former location.

Fotomeister Spahn schoss von seinem Fenster aus Anfang der 1950er Jahre dieses Bild der Wache 1. Über den Grund, weshalb die Menschenmenge dort Schlange stand, gibt es nur Vermutungen. Sie könnten sich um Arbeit oder um einen Ausweis beworben haben.

At the beginning of the 1950s, master photographer Spahn took this photo of Gate 1 from his window. There are only assumptions why so many people stood in line there. They could have been applying for work or for an installation pass.

So sieht das Gate 1 heute aus. Das 2009 gebaute Wachhaus gewährt den Guards mehr Platz, Schutz und Sicherheit.

Gate 1 today. The guard house built in 2009 offers the guards more room, protection and security.

Die Wache 1 als Postkartenmotiv

Gate 1 -- a motif for post cards

Die Häuser, die im Lager bis zur Wache 1 stehen, wurden schon vor 1938 für die Bauverwaltung und als Wohnungen errichtet. Beim Fotohaus Spahn wurde ein Holzhäuschen für die Wachposten aufgestellt. Kurz vor dem Militärgasthaus war das Passbüro. In den 1960er Jahren ließ die US-Armee den markanten Torbogen aufstellen.

Erst im Juli 1990 wurde das alte hölzerne Wachhäuschen durch ein Fertiggebäude im „Bavarian Style" ersetzt. Nur wenige wissen, dass das Relikt aus früheren Zeiten, gar nicht weit vom alten Standort entfernt, heute noch existiert. Erich Spahn, der bereits verstorbene Chef des gleichnamigen Fotogeschäfts, ließ das ihm vertraute Schildhaus vor seinem Schaufenster durch die Baufirma, die es entsorgen sollte, einfach in seinen Garten am Lagerzaun hieven. „Für ein paar Mark Trinkgeld", so erzählte seine Frau Edith im Jahr 2010 „hat der Erich die viel fotografierte Wache für die Nachwelt gesichert." Im Garten der Spahns wird die Holzhütte idyllisch zwischen Büschen und Sträuchern nun als Gartenlaube und Lagerraum genutzt.

The houses on the training area located next to Gate 1 were built prior to 1938 to house the construction office and apartments. A wooden guard house for the guards was built next to Spahn Photo Studio. The installation pass office was located shortly before reaching the military restaurant. During the 1960s, the U.S. Army built the distinctive entrance arc. The old wooden guard house was not replaced by a modern "Bavarian-style" prefab building until July 1990. Only a few people know that the old guard house still exists not far from its old location. Erich Spahn, the late owner of the photo studio of the same name, asked the construction company, which had been tasked to destroy the familiar guard building in front of his store window, to simply lift it over his fence and put it in his garden adjacent to the camp's fence. "For a tip of a few marks," says his wife Edith in 2010, "Erich saved the often photographed guard house for future generations." Today, the wooden shed between the bushes in the Spahn's garden is used as a gazebo and for storage.

Wache 1 heute

Im November 2009 erhielt die Wache 1 ihr heutiges Aussehen. Das Staatliche Bauamt ließ im Auftrag der US-Armee ein neues Funktionsgebäude errichten.

Wände, Fenster und Türen sind schusssicher. Mit der Holzschalung soll sich das Gebäude harmonisch in die Umgebung einfügen. Mit der Postkartenromantik der 1950er und 60er Jahre hat der neue Bau zwischen dem Fotohaus Spahn und der evangelischen Michaelskirche allerdings nicht mehr viel zu tun.

Gate 1 today

In November 2009, Gate 1 received its current look. The U.S. Army asked the State Construction Office to build a new functional building. Walls, windows and doors are bullet-proof. With its wooden side panels, the building was designed to adapt to its surroundings. The new building, however, has nothing in common with the romantic post card atmosphere of the 1950s and 60s between the Spahn Photo Studio and the protestant St. Michael's Church.

Die ursprüngliche Hauptwache mit Diensträumen für die Wachmannschaft und dem Arrestbereich
The former main gate with offices for the guards, and holding area

Noch vor dem Zweiten Weltkrieg wurde die alte Hauptwache aufgestockt. Fachwerk und der Uhrenturm prägten das Gebäude. Die Wache stand direkt gegenüber dem Wasserturm und fiel der Bombardierung im April 1945 zum Opfer.

A second floor was added to the old main gate before World War II. Its half-timbered architecture and the clock tower became its most significant features. The guard house was located directly across from the Water Tower and destroyed during the air raids in April 1945.

Die Wachposten standen einst zwischen dem Forsthaus und dem Militärgasthof (MG).
The guards were formerly located between the Forest House and the military restaurant.

Die Hauptwache und der Militärgasthof, das heutige „Tower View Restaurant and Conference Center"

The main gate and the military restaurant, now the Tower View Restaurant and Conference Center

Truppenübungsplatz Grafenwöhr
Kaserne des Arbeitskommando

Ein stattlicher Komplex war die Kaserne 14, das Arbeitskommando. In den Gründerjahren war dort die heutige Wache 3. Die Kaserne wurde bei der Bombardierung 1945 völlig zerstört.

Barracks building 14 was a huge complex and home of the labor command. Gate 3 was located there during the founding years. The barracks building was completely destroyed during the air raids in 1945.

Wache 3 am Lagerbahnhof

Auch die Wache 3 am Lagerbahnhof war bei der ursprünglichen Gründung des Platzes an einer anderen Stelle. Die Wachposten standen damals auf Höhe der Kaserne 14, dem Sitz des Arbeitskommandos, das ebenfalls 1945 bei der Bombardierung vollends zerstört wurde. Die Wache 3 konnte auch über den Alten Weg und die Gartenstraße erreicht werden. Erst 1937/38 wurden dann die Heeresbäckerei und die Silos errichtet und die Zufahrt endgültig zum Lagerbahnhof verlegt.

Im Zuge der großen Erweiterungsmaßnahmen und des Baus des Community Service Centers wurde im Jahr 2005 die Wache 3 als funktionelle Hauptzufahrt umgestaltet. Kontrollhalle, Wachhaus, Schranken, Einfahrtssperren und Lärmschutzwand prägen heute das Bild. Im alten Lagerbahnhof haben die Guards der privaten Wachfirma ihr Büro. Gleich hinter den Bahngleisen und dem Rolltor steht ein alter M-24-Chaffee Panzer. Die Wache 3 hat auch repräsentativen Charakter.

Weitere Einfahrten zum Lager Grafenwöhr sind die neu gebaute Lkw-Zufahrt 6 am Flugplatz sowie die Wache 20 an der Netzaberg Straße. Im Süden bei Tanzfleck ist das Tor 4 Zufahrt zum Übungsplatz.

Gate 3 at the camp's train station

When the training area was founded, Gate 3 at the camp's train station was also located elsewhere. In those days, the guards were standing next to barracks building 14 which was also completely destroyed during the air raids in 1945. Gate 3 could also be accessed via the Alte Weg and Gartenstraße. In 1937/38 the Army bakery and the silos were built and the gate ultimately relocated to the train station.

In 2005, as part of the vast construction measures and the construction of the Community Service Center, Gate 3 was remodeled to become a functional main gate with a roofed-over control point, a guard house, barriers road blocks and a noise abatement wall. The old train station now houses the offices of the guards of a private security firm. An old M-24 Chaffee tank is located behind the rails and the rolling gate. Other gates to the training area include the newly built truck gate, Gate 6 near the airfield and Gate 20 on Netzaberg Road. Gate 4, near Tanzfleck, is the southern access gate to the training area.

Der Wasserturm
The Water Tower

**Der „große alte Herr des Übungsplatzes"
ist 100 Jahre alt**
*The "great old gentlemen of the training area"
celebrated its 100th birthday*

Wahrzeichen des Übungsplatzes und der Stadt

Seit Gründung ist der Turm das Wahrzeichen des Übungsplatzes und der Stadt Grafenwöhr. Auf Tausenden von Postkarten, Bierkrügen, Bildern und anderen Souvenirs trug er den Namen Grafenwöhr in alle Welt hinaus und wurde zusammen mit dem Forsthaus zum unverwechselbaren Erkennungszeichen für das Militärareal. Durch seinen Baustil mit dem Fachwerk, Erkern, dem Treppenturm mit Spitze und aufgesetzter Kanonensilhouette unterscheidet sich der Grafenwöhrer Wasserturm deutlich von Turmgebäuden, die anderenorts für den nötigen Wasserdruck im Leitungsnetz sorgen.

Landmark of the training area and the town

The tower has been the landmark of the city and the training area since its establishment. On thousands of post cards, beer mugs, photos and other souvenirs it carried Grafenwoehr's name into the world and together with the Forest House became the distinctive landmark of the military training area. The Water Tower with its half-timbered architecture, its bay windows, the tower for the staircase with its top and a silhouette of a cannon attached to it is distinctly different from other towers in the region. Its purpose is to ensure there is enough pressure in the water system.

Der Wasserturm um 1911, kurz nach der Fertigstellung. Ein stattliches Gebäude, das sich in seinem Baustil deutlich von Türmen unterscheidet, die anderenorts für den Wasserdruck in den Leitungen sorgen.
The Water Tower around 1911, shortly after its completion. The huge building's architectural style differs vastly from other water towers in the region.

Die Firma Weiß aus Weiden erbaute in den Jahren 1909 bis 1911 den Wasserturm. Vorne das Forsthaus, das im Rohbau schon fertig ist.
The Weiß Construction Co. from Weiden built the Water Tower from 1909 to 1911. The Forest House, its building shell already finished, is seen in the foreground.

Aus der Vogelperspektive eine Aufnahme aus dem Jahr 2011: Rechts neben dem Forsthaus sind die Stallungen und die Scheune des ehemaligen Militärforstamtes zu sehen.

A bird's eye view taken in 2011: The stables and the barn of the former military forest office are seen to the right of the Forest House.

Planung und Bau

„Entworfen von Intendantur und Baurat Feder. Ausgeführt von Militärbauinspektor Kemmler. In der Zeit vom 26. August 1909 bis zum 30. Juni 1911". Die Übereinstimmung von Plan und Ausführung des Bauwerks wird auf dem noch vorhandenen Originalplan durch den inzwischen zum Baurat beförderten Wilhelm Kemmler am 24. Februar 1912 bestätigt.

Errichtet wurde der 43,5 Meter hohe Turm von der Firma Peter Weiß aus Weiden. Gemauert wurde mit sogenannten Reichsformat-Ziegelsteinen. Der Sockel sowie die Treppen und der Eingangsbogen sind mit heimischem Sandstein gestaltet. Zwei riesige Wasserbehälter im zweiten und achten Stockwerk stellten den Leitungsdruck im Wassernetz des Lagers sicher. Auch heute noch ist der rund 450 Kubikmeter fassende Behälter in der oberen Etage in Betrieb.

Planning and construction

"Designed by the intendant's office and government engineer Feder. Executed by Military Construction Officer Kemmler from August 26, 1909 to June 30, 1911." That the tower was constructed as designed was confirmed by Wilhelm Kemmler, who had since been promoted to government engineer, on February 24, 1912 with a note on the original building plan.

The 43.5 meter-high tower was constructed by the Peter Weiß Construction Co. in Weiden with so-called Reich's-formatted bricks. Its base, the entrance arc and the stairs were built with local sandstone. Two large water basins on the second and the eighth floor ensure there is enough pressure in the camp's water system.

Die handgezeichneten Originale sind noch in der Plankammer vorhanden.
The original hand-drawn plans can still be seen in the plans' archive.

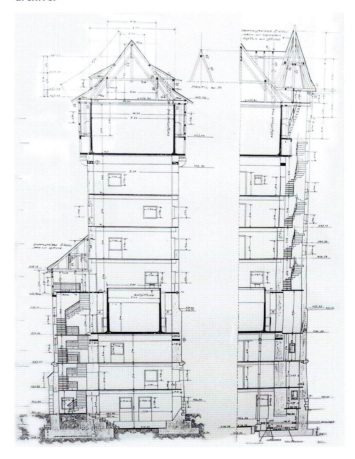

Der „große alte Herr des Übungsplatzes" wurde 100 Jahre alt. Die Zeichnung zeigt den Wasserturm als Jäger mit umgehängter Büchse. Ein weiteres Geburtstagskind ist das Rathaus (rechts), die Stadt feierte 2011 ihr 650-jähriges Bestehen. Die Figuren von Rathaus und Wasserturm sollen die gute Zusammenarbeit von Stadt und Lager symbolisieren. Die Karikatur stammt von Oskar Schieder (†) und wurde für eine Jugendorganisation gezeichnet.

The Grafenwoehr Water Tower celebrated its 100th birthday The „great old gentlemen of the training area," as the locals often refer to the Water Tower, is portrayed on this cartoon as a hunter with a rifle. Another birthday child is the town hall (right) because the city celebrated its 650th anniversary in 2011. The town hall and Water Tower characters symbolize the great cooperation between the city and the training area. The cartoon was sketched by the late Oskar Schieder for use by a youth organization.

Der Wasserturm und das Forsthaus heute, eine Ansicht wie sie auf tausenden von Bildern zu sehen ist.
The Water Tower and the Forest House today – a motif seen on thousands of photos.

Wasserturm und Forsthaus wurden auf unzähligen Postkarten, Bildern und Souvenirs abgebildet – man behauptet sogar, dass der Wasserturm öfter als der Eiffelturm fotografiert wurde.
Water Tower and Forest House were pictured on countless post cards, photos and souvenirs. Some people even say that more pictures have been taken of the Water Tower than the Eiffel Tower.

Die Bombardierung überstanden

Im April 1945 entgingen der Wasserturm und das in seinem Schatten stehende Forsthaus bei den verheerenden Bombenangriffen nur um Haaresbreite der Zerstörung. Der Turm war damals in einer Tarnfarbe gestrichen. Es war reiner Zufall und großes Glück, dass die Spreng- und Brandbomben das Ensemble Forsthaus/Wasserturm nicht trafen. Rundum waren die Gebäude zerstört und überall gab es Bombentrichter. Mit dem Bombenhagel erlebte der „große alte Herr des Übungsplatzes" wohl das traurigste Kapitel in seiner Geschichte. Das Lager wurde zu 80 Prozent zerstört, mehrere Hundert Menschen fanden den Tod.

Surviving the air raids

In April 1945, the Water Tower and the adjacent Forest House barely survived the devastating air raids and their resulting destruction. In those days, the tower was painted with camouflage color. It was a mere coincidence and a lot of luck that the demolition and fire bombs did not hit the architectural ensemble of Forest House and Water Tower. All surrounding buildings were destroyed and there were bomb craters everywhere. The air raids were the darkest chapter of the training area. Eighty percent of the camp was destroyed and several hundred people were killed.

Der Wasserturm auf einer gezeichneten Postkarte; hier wurden die Spätheimkehrer auf die Schippe genommen.
The Water Tower shown on a painted post card that makes fun of late returnees from prisoner-of-war-camps.

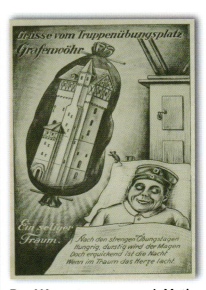

Der Wasserturm war auch Motiv auf sogenannten Witzpostkarten. Träumen vom Wasserturm.
The Water Tower also became a motif on funny post cards. Dreaming of the Water Tower.

Im Lichterschein: Das Forsthaus ist heute Wohnung für den ranghöchsten US-Offizier und seine Familie.
In the lights' glow: Today, the Forest House is the home of the highest-ranking U.S. officer and his family.

Der Wasserturm im Gerüst 1946
The scaffolded Water Tower in 1946

1910 drückte Baurat Wilhelm Kemmler auf dem Dachboden des Wasserturms auf den Auslöser seiner Kamera. Die Aufnahme ermöglicht einen Blick auf das östliche Lager, die Dachziegel liegen zum Eindecken bereit. Auch 2010 ließ sich wieder durch das Gebälk des Wasserturms nach außen blicken.

In 1910, engineer Wilhelm Kemmler took this photo from the attic of the Water Tower. The photo shows the eastern section of the cantonment area with piles of roof tiles waiting to be put up. In 2010, one could look through the framework of the Water Tower's roof again.

Mehrmals gründlich renoviert

1946 wurde der Wasserturm eingerüstet und neu getüncht. Es folgte der Wiederaufbau des Lagers. Die neuen Hausherrn, die Amerikaner, fanden Gefallen an den Fachwerkbauten, dem Wasserturm und den historischen Gebäuden und sorgten für eine dementsprechende Pflege. 1974 und 1994 wurde der „alte Herr" gründlich renoviert. Eine halbe Million D-Mark investierte die US-Armee allein im Jahr 1994. Nach den ursprünglichen Mustern wurden im Juli 2008 die Fensterläden am Wasserturm wieder vervollständigt.

Im Herbst 2010 ist der Wasserturm erneut eingerüstet, einzelne Balken des Fachwerks müssen ausgetauscht werden, der Turm erhält einen neuen Anstrich. Auf dem Dach sind in Nachbarschaft zur alten Kanonensilhouette das Dreh-Anflugfeuer für den Flugplatz und verschiedene Antennen installiert.

In der zweiten Etage des Bauwerks richtete die US-Armee einen Konferenzraum mit modernster, technischer Ausstattung ein. In weiteren Stockwerken ist seit dem Übungsplatzjubiläum eine Ausstellung zur Geschichte des Platzes zu sehen.

Seit dem Bau des neuen Hauptquartiers für das Joint Multinational Training Command (JMTC), der Neuplatzierung der Flaggenmasten und der Abholzung von Bäumen ist das Übungsplatz-Wahrzeichen auch vom Paradeplatz her gut und vollständig zu sehen.

Im Jahr 2010 wurde der Wasserturm auch in die Denkmalliste aufgenommen, er ist somit ein staatlich anerkanntes, schützenswertes Bauwerk.

Various in-depth renovations

In 1946, the Water Tower was scaffolded and newly painted. The reconstruction of the camp followed. The Americans, the new landlords, liked the half-timbered buildings, the Water Tower and the historic buildings and took care of them accordingly. The Water Tower was fully refurbished in 1974 and 1994. The U.S. Army invested a half a million D-Marks in 1994 alone. Based on the original pattern, several missing window shutters of the Water Tower were added in July 2008. In the fall of 2010, the Water Tower was scaffolded again. Several beams of the half-timbered frame had to be replaced and the tower received a fresh coat of paint.

The revolving approach lights of the airfield and various antennas are installed on the roof next to the canon silhouette. The U.S. Army installed a conference room with state-of-the-art technical equipment on the second floor. Since the 100th anniversary, the other floors feature an exhibition about the history of the training area.

After the construction of the new headquarters building of the Joint Multinational Training Command (JMTC), the relocation of the flag poles and cutting of some trees, the training area's landmark can now also be fully and very well seen from the parade field.

In 2010, the Water Tower was also put on the list of protected historic monuments which makes it a state-recognized building that must be protected.

Neue Kanonen-Silhouette

Exakt 100 Jahre thronte die alte Windfahne in Form einer Kanonen-Silhouette auf dem Wasserturm. 2012 wurde sie von einem Windstoß umgedrückt und fiel zu Boden. 1912 war in eingeschlagenen Zahlen im Drehlager der Windfahne zu lesen. Eine Spezialfirma fertigte die originalgetreue Kopie und setzte im April 2013 die „neue Kanone" wieder auf die Spitze des Grafenwöhrer Wahrzeichens. Die Gesamtmaßnahme kostete über 32.000 Euro, da ein Spezialgerüst mit eigener Statik notwendig war. Die „alte Kanone" fand im Museum neben dem Modell des Wasserturms einen angemessenen Platz.

New canon silhouette

The old vane, shaped like a canon silhouette, sat on top of the Water Tower for exactly 100 years. In 2012, a wind gust knocked it over and it fell to the ground. "1912" was engraved into the pivot bearing of the vane. A specialized company produced a true to original replica. In April 2013, it put the "new canon" on top of Grafenwoehr's landmark. Replacing and installing the new vane cost more than 32,000 Euro because a special scaffold with its own statics had to be installed. In the museum, the „old canon" was appropriately put next to the model of the Water Tower.

Historische Ausstellung im Wasserturm.
Historic exhibition in the Water Tower.

Erneuerung der Windfahne im Jahr 2013
Replacement of the vane in 2013

Wasserturm und Forsthaus als Motiv. Die Radierung von Otto Dünne ziert das Etikett einer Weinflasche. Der „Grafenwöhrer Zapfenstreich" ist ein Rheinriesling aus der niederösterreichischen Partnergemeinde Grafenwörth.

Water Tower and Forest House. This etching by Otto Dünne decorated the label of a wine bottle. The "Tattoo of Grafenwoehr," is Riesling wine from the Lower-Austrian partner community of Grafenwörth.

Ein Platz mit Atmosphäre. 2005 wurden 95 Jahre Übungsplatz, 60 Jahre US-Armee in Grafenwöhr und 50-jähriges Bestehen der Bundeswehr im Schatten des Turms gefeiert.

A square with a lot of atmosphere: The 95th anniversary of the training area, the 60th anniversary of the U.S. Army in Grafenwoehr and the 50th anniversary of the German Armed Forces were celebrated in 2005 in the shade of the tower.

Zwischen 1909 und 1911 wurde das Stalllager gebaut. Es bot über 3700 Pferden Platz.
The stable complex was built from 1909 to 1911. It provided room for more than 3,700 horses.

Das Stalllager — The Stables

Tankstelle statt Pferdetränke

Kein Platz mehr für die Kavallerie. Die letzten noch erhaltenen Stallungen des einst riesigen Stalllagers fielen während der Neubaumaßnahmen der letzten Jahre der Spitzhacke zum Opfer. Wo in den Gründerjahren des Übungsplatzes einst Pferde in ihren Boxen standen, parken nun Fahrzeuge; wo die Pferde zur Tränke kamen, stillen Motoren an den Zapfsäulen ihren Durst. Über 3700 Gäule hatten einst im großen Stalllager Platz.

Pferde und Kriegsgefangene

Bereits 1909 begannen die Arbeiter unter dem königlichen Baurat Wilhelm Kemmler mit der Errichtung des großen Stalllagers. Auch Reithallen, Pferdekrankenställe, eine Bespannabteilung und Hufbeschlagschmieden gehörten dazu. Nach zwei Jahren war das Projekt noch in der Regierungszeit des Prinzregenten Luitpold abgeschlossen. Doch nicht nur die Rösser des königlich-bayerischen Armee-Korps waren hier eingestellt. Unter damals mit Sicherheit unzureichenden Umständen wurde das Stalllager während des Ersten Weltkriegs zum Quartier für Kriegsgefangene umfunktioniert. Ein Großteil der 24 000 Häftlinge hatte in den Pferdebaracken ein Dach über dem Kopf.

Gas station instead of horses' drinking trough

No room anymore for the cavalry. The last remaining stables of the former stable complex were demolished as a result of the new construction measures. Vehicles now park where horses once stood in their stables during the founding years of the training area. Vehicle engines now quench their thirst where horses used to come to the trough. There was once room for more than 3,700 horses in the stable complex.

Horses and prisoners of war

Construction of the stable complex started in 1909 under the direction of royal engineer Wilhelm Kemmler. It also included an indoor riding hall, stables for sick horses, an area to bridle the horses and blacksmiths' shops. After two years, still during the reign of Prince Regent Luitpold, construction was completed. But not only the horses of the Royal-Bavarian Army Corps were put up here. During World War I, the stables were transformed into quarters for prisoners of war who were housed there under less than comfortable conditions. A majority of the 24,000 prisoners lived under the roof of the horse stables.

Im Stalllager vor dem Wasserturm
The stable complex in front of the Water Tower

Kriegsgefangene
Prisoners of war

Hoch zu Ross war auch die Regimentskapelle unterwegs.

The regimental band also moved on horseback.

Von den Bomben zerstört

In der Reichswehrzeit und im Zweiten Weltkrieg wurde das Stalllager wieder für seine ursprüngliche Bestimmung genutzt. Der Reichsarbeitsdienst war für die Beaufsichtigung der Baracken und für die Betreuung und Pflege der Gäule zuständig.

Im April 1945 flogen Bomber der Alliierten ihren zweiten Angriff auf die Stadt und den Truppenübungsplatz. Das Stalllager wurde bis auf drei Baracken völlig zerstört. Die Bevölkerung durfte nach den Bombenangriffen mit amtlicher Genehmigung die Ruinen als Baumaterialdepot nutzen und die Reichsformat-Ziegel zum Wiederaufbau der eigenen Wohnhäuser verwenden.

Destroyed by bombs

The stable complex was used again for its original purpose during the so-called Reichswehrzeit from 1921-1935 and during World War II. The so-called Reich's Work Force was in charge of the stables and took care of the horses. In April 1945, allied bombers flew their second attack on the city and the training area. The stable complex was destroyed except for three stables. After the air raids, the town's population was allowed by the authorities to use the debris as construction material with the so-called Reichsformat bricks to rebuild their destroyed houses.

Soldaten des III. Königlich-Bayerischen Fußartillerieregiments mit den Pferden der Offiziere vor einem Stall

Soldiers of the Third Royal-Bavarian Foot Artillery Regiment with the officers' horses in front of a stable

Im Ersten Weltkrieg waren Kriegsgefangene in den Pferdeställen einquartiert.

Prisoners of war were put up in the stables during World War I.

Der Ausschnitt der Fliegeraufnahme lässt die riesige Dimension des Stalllagers (linke obere Bildhälfte) gut erkennen. Die Aufnahme entstand vermutlich 1927. Rechts der Wasserturm mit Forsthaus, darüber der Gefangenenfriedhof.

The huge dimensions of the stable complex (upper left corner) can easily be seen in this detail of an aerial photo. The photo was probably taken in 1927. The Water Tower and the Forest House can be seen on the right with the prisoners-of-war cemetery above it.

Blick vom Wasserturm: die Artilleriekasernen und das Stalllager

A view from the Water Tower: The artillery barracks and the stable complex

Nach der Bombardierung 1945: Die Artilleriekasernen und fast alle Ställe wurden von den Bomben weggefegt. Nur drei steinerne Stallungen (in der oberen Bildhälfte) blieben stehen.

After the 1945 air raids: The artillery barracks and almost all stables had been destroyed by the bombs. Only three stables (in the upper half of the photo) were left.

Lagerraum, Bowlingbahn und Mal- und Bastelladen

Die drei unbeschädigten Ställe wurden nach 1945 als Lagerräume genutzt. Auch ein Kleinkaliber-Schießstand, eine Kegel- und Bowlingbahn sowie das Outdoor Recreation-Center waren zeitweise dort eingerichtet. Nur der dritte Stall hat in seinen Grundmauern heute noch Bestand. Der Mal- und Bastelladen mit Kunststudio direkt hinter dem neuen Hotel ist eine umgebaute und umgestaltete längliche Stallbaracke.

Storage area, bowling alley and arts and crafts shop

After 1945, the three undamaged stables were used as storage areas. A small-caliber weapons' range, a bowling alley and the outdoor recreation center were temporarily located there. Only the third stable remained unchanged. The arts and crafts shop with the attached art studio behind the new hotel is a remodeled and redesigned oblong stable.

Blick vom Wasserturm im Jahr 2000

A view from the Water Tower in 2000

April 2010: Neue Straßen sind angelegt, das Shopping Center mit Parkplätzen steht, der Rohbau des Hotels ist fertig.
April 2010: New roads, the shopping center and parking lot, and the structural work of the new hotel have been completed.

Der Spitzhacke zum Opfer gefallen

2006 und 2008 rückten die Abbruchbagger an und machten die letzten Ställe dem Erdboden gleich. Vorher wurden die Gebäude entkernt, noch gutes Material wiederverwendet. Im Innenraum war die ursprüngliche Struktur an vielen Stellen noch gut erkennbar. Zwischen der Balkenkonstruktion standen die Pferde an Halteringen und den betonierten Futtertrögen. An den Außenmauern waren die Ösen zu sehen, an denen die Pferde zum Appell angebunden waren.

Fast ausnahmslos sind die Planer im Hauptlager bemüht, die historische Bausubstanz zu erhalten. Die Stallbaracken passten leider nicht ins Konzept. Mit dem Abriss der letzten noch erkennbaren Pferdeställe verschwand somit ein Stück der Übungsplatz-Geschichte endgültig von der Bildfläche.

Demolished

In 2006 and 2008 the last remaining stables were demolished. Before they were demolished, the buildings were stripped and good material was recycled. On the inside, the building's original purpose could still be seen in many areas. The horses stood between the beams, attached to holding rings and in front of concrete feeding troughs. On the outside walls, one could see the holding rings to which the horses were attached during roll call. With hardly any exceptions, planners attempted to preserve the historic buildings on main post. Unfortunately, the stables did not fit into the new construction concept. So when the last stables were demolished, a piece of the training area's history disappeared from the face of the earth as well.

In den entkernten Gebäuden war der Zuschnitt der Ställe noch eindeutig erkennbar. Zwischen den Pfeilern links und rechts der Stallgasse standen die Pferde. Unter widrigen Umständen waren während des Ersten Weltkriegs auch Kriegsgefangene in den Baracken untergebracht.
The floor plan of the stables could easily be seen after the buildings had been stripped to the core. The horses stood in-between the beams to the left and the right of the stable aisle. During World War I, prisoners of war who were housed in the stables under less than comfortable conditions.

Für Tankstelle, Parkplatz, Straße und Kreisverkehr mussten die letzten noch im Original vorhandenen Ställe weichen. 2008 wurde das Gebäude 600 (Bildmitte), früher Bowlingbahn und Outdoor Recreation-Center, abgebrochen.

The last original stables had to be demolished to make room for the gas station, the parking lot, access road and traffic circle. In 2008, building 600 (center), the former bowling alley and outdoor recreation center, was demolished.

Abrissbagger leisten ganze Arbeit.

Demolition of the stables.

Tankstelle, Parkplatz und Kreisverkehr

2,9 Millionen Euro ließ sich der Auftraggeber AAFES (Army and Air Force Exchange Service), der für die Versorgung der amerikanischen Soldaten und Familien zuständig ist, den Bau der neuen Tankstelle kosten. Zur großzügigen Anlage gehört auch ein kleiner Einkaufsmarkt.
Die Stallabbrüche machten Platz für die Zufahrt zu den Zapfsäulen sowie für einen neuen Parkplatz am Burger King. Wo einst der Eingang zur Stallbaracke war, bewältigt heute ein Kreisverkehr den rasant gestiegenen Autostrom.

Gas station, parking lot and traffic circle

AAFES (Army and Air Force Exchange Service), which is responsible for the provisioning of the American soldiers and their families, invested 2.9 million Euro into the construction of the new gas station. The large complex also includes a shoppette. Demolishing the stables provided room for the access road to the gas pumps and for a new parking lot next to Burger King. A traffic circle, managing the increased traffic flow, is now located were the entrance to a stable used to be.

2007 wurde die neue Tankstelle eröffnet. Für ihre Zufahrt und die Straße musste das historische Stallgebäude abgebrochen werden.

The new gas station was opened in 2007. The historic stable had to be demolished to make room for the street and the access road to the gas station.

Auf dem Gefangenenfriedhof vor dem Denkmal „Pro Patria". Die bislang unbekannte Fotografie lässt im Hintergrund den Annaberg mit der Turmspitze der Kirche erkennen.

At the prisoner of war cemetery in front of the monument "Pro Patria." This newly discovered photo shows the Annaberg mountain and the top of the church tower in the background.

Pro Patria

Fern der Heimat

Ein fast in Vergessenheit geratener Gefangenenfriedhof erinnert auf dem Gelände des Truppenlagers an das Schicksal ausländischer Soldaten zur Zeit des Ersten Weltkrieges. Durch das Kriegsministerium wurden in Bayern sechs Unterbringungsorte für Kriegsgefangene bestimmt. Grafenwöhr war mit einer „Belegungsfähigkeit" von nahezu 24000 Häftlingen das größte Gefangenenlager in Bayern. Ausführlich stellt das Militärmuseum das Leben und das Schicksal der damals inhaftierten Franzosen, Russen, Rumänen, Engländer, Belgier und Italiener dar.

Friedhof für Kriegsgefangene

Bereits kurz nach Kriegsausbruch im August 1914 trafen in Grafenwöhr von der französischen Front Kriegsgefangene ein. Viele waren schwer verletzt und starben bald nach der Ankunft. Für sie wurde am Rande des Truppenlagers an der Vilsecker Straße ein eigener Gefangenenfriedhof eingerichtet. Er wurde am 3. November 1914 eingeweiht. An Verwundungen, Krankheiten oder auch an mangelnden hygienischen Umständen starben 482 Franzosen, etwa 210 Russen, 51 Rumänen, sechs Engländer und sechs Italiener, die auf dem Militärfriedhof beigesetzt wurden.

Far away from home

An almost forgotten prisoner of war cemetery on Grafenwoehr main post reminds us of the fate of foreign soldiers during World War I. The war ministry established six prisoner of war camps in Bavaria. Grafenwoehr was the largest prisoner of war camp in Bavaria with room for 24,000 prisoners. The military museum shows in a very detailed manner the life and fate of the incarcerated French, Russian, Romanian, English, Belgian and Italian soldiers.

Prisoner of war cemetery

Shortly after the beginning of the war in August 1914, the first French prisoners of war arrived in Grafenwoehr. Many of them were severely injured and died shortly after their arrival. A separate prisoner of war cemetery was established for them near Vilsecker Strasse and dedicated on November 3, 1914. 482 Frenchmen, about 210 Russians, 51 Romanians, six Englishmen and six Italians died from their wounds, illnesses and bad hygiene and were buried in the military cemetery.

Das übriggebliebene Areal des Grafenwöhrer Gefangenenfriedhofs heute

The remaining area of the Grafenwoehr prisoner of war cemetery today

Auf dem französischen Gefangenenfriedhof in Sarrebourg/Lothringen
At the French prisoner of war cemetery in Sarrebourg/Alsace-Lorraine

Pro Patria

Der französische Kriegsgefangene und Bildhauer, Professor Freddy Stoll, schuf für diesen Friedhof ein Denkmal. Aus einem 500 Zentner schweren Granitblock, der aus dem Fichtelgebirge geholt wurde, meißelte er mit einigen Helfern eine kniende Männergestalt. Sie stellt einen sterbenden Soldaten dar. Die Inschrift des massiven Sockels lautete: „Pro Patria" – „Für das Vaterland". Im Juni 1928 wurde dieses Denkmal aus Grafenwöhr abtransportiert und nach Frankreich gebracht, wo es auf dem Soldatenfriedhof von Sarrebourg einen Platz erhielt.
Die Gebeine von 579 in Grafenwöhr bestatteten Franzosen, Engländern und Italienern wurden in den Wintermonaten der Nachkriegsjahre exhumiert und in ihre Heimatländer überführt.
Im April 1945 wurden nach der verheerenden Bombardierung die Opfer der Angriffe in einem Massengrab auf dem Militärfriedhof beigesetzt. Später überführte die deutsche Regierung deren sterbliche Überreste zu einem Zentralfriedhof in Bayern.

16 Kreuze und zwei Grabsteine

Heute ist nur noch ein kleiner Teil des Gefangenenfriedhofs vorhanden. Hinter der alten Holzturnhalle, östlich der Dining Facility (Truppenküche), liegt umfriedet von einer niedrigen Kalksteinmauer und einer Hecke das übriggebliebene Areal. 16 Betonkreuze und zwei Grabsteine unter den Laubbäumen weisen auf die verbliebenen Gräber hin. An der Westseite des Friedhofs steht als Denkmal ein steinernes Kreuz mit den Jahreszahlen 1914 – 1918. Am Eingangsportal ist auf einer Gedenktafel unter dem Symbol der Kriegsgräberfürsorge in deutscher und englischer Sprache zu lesen: „Hier ruhen fern der Heimat als Opfer des Ersten Weltkrieges 261 Russen und Rumänen".

Pro Patria

The French prisoner of war and sculptor Professor Freddy Stoll built a memorial for that cemetery. He and some helpers sculpted the figure of a kneeling man from a 500 centner (25,000 kilograms) granite block that was brought down the Fichtelgebirge mountains. It depicts a dying soldier. The inscription on the massive base reads: "Pro Patria" – For the Fatherland." In June 1928, the monument was transported from Grafenwoehr to France were it was placed at the soldiers' cemetery at Sarrebourg. The remains of 579 French, English and Italian soldiers were disinterred and taken to their home countries during the winter months of the first years after the war.
In April 1945, the victims of the devastating bombardments were buried in a mass grave on the military cemetery. Later, the German government transferred their remains to a central war cemetery in Bavaria.

16 crosses and two headstones

Today, only a small portion of the prisoner of war cemetery is left. It is located behind the old wooden gymnasium, east of the main dining facility, and fenced off with a low wall made out of limestone and a hedge. Sixteen concrete crosses and two headstones under the decidious trees mark the graves. A stone cross monument with the dates 1914 – 1918 is located on the western side of the cemetery. There is an information board with the symbol of the German War Graves Commission at the entrance which states in German and English: "261 Russians and Romanians, victims of World War I, were laid to rest here far away from home."

Abbau des Denkmals am 14. Juni 1928
Dismantling of the monument on June 14, 1928

Wolfsschützenkapelle
The Wolf Hunter's Chapel

Die Sage vom Wolfsschützen

„Im 17. Jahrhundert ereignete sich auf diesem Platz die Darstellung, wo der alte Förster einen Wolf anschoss, welcher auf ihn losging und über diesen herfiel; aber in dem Augenblick der größten Gefahr durch Anrufung der hl. Dreifaltigkeit des Försters Sohn hinzukam, mit einem wohlgezielten Schuss den Wolf tötete und dadurch seinen Vater aus der Lebensgefahr errettete." Dies war die Inschrift am alten Bild in der Wolfsschützenkapelle. Die Kapelle mitten in den dunklen, ausgedehnten Wäldern nahe dem Erzhäusl ist als letztes noch intaktes Kirchlein auf dem gesamten Übungsgelände ein Kleinod. 1967 rettete der Bundesforst die schlichte Kapelle vor dem Verfall. Die Waldarbeiter restaurierten sie nach alten Unterlagen. Das Gnadenbild mit der schaurigen Szene aus der Wolfsschützensage wurde neu gemalt und ziert den Innenraum. Alljährlich am Dreifaltigkeitssonntag findet eine kleine Wallfahrt der Pfarrei Vilseck zu dem Kirchlein im Übungsgelände statt. Der Weg vom ehemaligen Erzhäusl wurde erst in diesem Jahr durch den Revierförster mit einer Lindenallee bepflanzt. Der Bundesforst hat sich auch der Pflege der Wolfsschützenkapelle angenommen.

In Gottes Hand

Eckehart Griesbach geht in seinem Buch detailliert auf die Geschichte dieses Kleinods ein. In seinen abschließenden Bemerkungen schreibt er: „Die Wolfsschützenkapelle erinnert daran, dass hier seit Jahrzehnten Soldaten ausgebildet werden zum Schutz des Vaterlandes und zur Erhaltung des Friedens. Die Kapelle soll die Soldaten, woher sie auch kommen mögen, daran erinnern, dass über der weltlichen Macht eine göttliche waltet, und den Jäger mahnt sie, dass das Glück der Jagd auch in Gottes Hand liegt."

The legend of the wolf hunter

"The following events took place here in the 17th century: The old hunter shot at and wounded a wolf which then attacked him. During that moment of clear and present danger he prayed to the Holy Trinity and the hunter's son arrived and killed the wolf with a perfect shot, saving his father's life." That was the inscription on the old painting in the Wolf Hunter's Chapel. The chapel, located in the midst of the dark forest near the former Erzhäusl forest house is the last, completely undamaged chapel on the entire training area and a treasure. The Federal Forest Office preserved the simple chapel from dilapidation in 1967 and renovated it based on old documents. The miraculous image depicting the horrible scene from the old legend was replaced with a new painting. It decorates the interior. Every Trinity Sunday, the Vilseck parish organizes a small pilgrimage to the chapel on the training area. This year, the responsible forest ranger planted an alley of linden trees along the road from the former Erzhäusl forest house to the chapel. The Federal Forest Office is also responsible for the maintenance of the chapel.

In God's hands

In his book, Eckehart Griesbach describes the history of this treasure in a very detailed manner. In his final remarks he says that "The Wolf Hunter's Chapel is a reminder that soldiers have been trained here for years to protect their home country and to preserve peace. The chapel is to remind the soldiers, regardless of where they might come from, that a divine power reigns above all secular power. In the same way it reminds the hunter that the luck of hunting lies in God's hands as well.

Alljährlich am Dreifaltigkeitssonntag pilgern Gläubige aus der Pfarrei Vilseck zur Wolfsschützenkapelle.

Every year on Trinity Sunday, parishioners from Vilseck make a pilgrimage to the Wolf Hunter's Chapel.

1967 restaurierten die Arbeiter des Bundesforstes die Wolfsschützenkapelle. Das kleine Kirchlein liegt idyllisch in den Wäldern beim Erzhäusl und ist ein Kleinod auf dem Übungsplatz.

The workers of the Federal Forest Office renovated the Wolf Hunter's Chapel in 1967. The little chapel is idyllically located in the forest near the Erzhäusl forest house and is one of the treasures of the training area.

Das Gnadenbild zeigt die schaurige Szene der Wolfsschützensage.

The miraculous image depicts the horrible scene from the wolf hunter's legend.

Bleidorn

Blick vom Schwarzen Berg über die nebelverhangene Impact Area nach Norden
View from Schwarzen Berg mountain across the foggy impact area to the north

1926 wurde der Bleidorn-Turm auf dem Schwarzen Berg für die Artilleriebeobachter gebaut.
The Bleidorn Tower on Schwarzen Berg mountain was built in 1926 for the artillery observers.

Der alte Bleidorn-Turm steht heute im Schatten des neuen Stahlriesen.
Today, the old Bleidorn tower stands in the shadow of the new steel tower.

Blick gen Osten in die aufgehende Morgensonne. Rechts der neue Antennenmast auf dem Schwarzen Berg
View to the east during sunrise: The new antenna on Schwarzen Berg mountain (right)

Schwarzen Berg

Beobachtungsturm auf dem Schwarzen Berg

Zur Beobachtung des Artillerieschießens wurde 1926 auf dem Schwarzen Berg ein 21 Meter hoher Turm aus Reichsformatziegeln und einer betonierten Beobachtungskanzel gebaut – der Bleidorn-Turm. Benannt ist er nach General Rudolf Bleidorn, dem Inspekteur der Artillerie in der Reichswehrzeit, der November 1927 aus dem Dienst ausschied. Der 563 Meter über dem Meeresspiegel liegende Schwarzen Berg – die zweithöchste Erhebung im Übungsplatz – bietet den Artillerie- und Feuerbeobachtern einen hervorragenden Blick in das Zielgebiet. Dieser „Feldherrnhügel" bot nicht nur den verschiedenen Armeen und Soldaten aller Nationen einen hervorragenden Überblick. Als das am Fuße des Berges liegende Erzhäusl noch Forsthaus und Ausflugslokal war, kamen auch Gäste auf den Berg, um dem Scharfschießen der Artillerie zuzusehen. Heute beherbergt der alte Bleidorn-Turm nur mehr Relaisstationen der Bundeswehr-Funkanlagen und steht quasi als „Denkmal" im Schatten eines neuen Stahlriesen.

Stahlriese als großer Bruder

Im Jahr 2001 ließ die US-Armee mit einem Kostenaufwand von zirka 450 000 Mark den derzeitigen Beobachtungsturm neben dem Bleidorn-Turm bauen. Der Stahlriese ist 27 Meter hoch und ersetzte einen kleineren Vorgänger aus Stahl und Holz. Kernstück des Turms ist auf der obersten Etage eine gläserne Beobachtungskanzel. Sie dient in erster Linie für die Beobachtung des Luftraums und zur Leitung der Luftwaffeneinsätze. Dementsprechend ist der Raum mit Instrumenten, Funkgeräten und Antennen ausgestattet. Ein weiterer freistehender Antennenmast wurde 2009 auf dem Schwarzen Berg östlich der beiden Türme aufgestellt.

Blick bis ins Nürnberger Land

Nicht nur dem Militär bietet der Berg mit dem Turm einen hervorragenden Ausblick. Von der obersten Etage des neuen Turms ist bei günstiger Witterung die Sicht einzigartig. Hinter dem Rauhen Kulm im Norden ist das Fichtelgebirge mit dem Ochsenkopf und dem Schneeberg zu sehen. Über dem Parkstein im Osten schweift der Blick bis zum Grenzturm auf tschechischem Gebiet bei Eslarn. Im Süden ist die Maria-Himmelfahrtskirche bei Amberg sichtbar, und im Westen erkennt man den Fernsehturm bei Betzenstein im Nürnberger Land.

Observation tower on the Schwarzen Berg mountain

The Bleidorn Tower, a 21 meter-high tower made of so-called Reichsformat bricks with a concrete observation pulpit, was built on Schwarzenberg mountain in 1926 to observe the shooting of the artillery. It was named after General Rudolf Bleidorn, the Inspector of the Artillery during the so-called Reichswehrzeit period, who retired in November 1927. The Schwarzenberg mountain is located 563 meters above sea level and the second highest elevation in the training area. It offers artillery and fire observers an excellent view across the impact area. But this Commander's hill did not only offer the armies and soldiers from various nations a good overview. When the Erzhäusl, located on the foot of the hill, was still a forest house and restaurant, guests also came up the mountain to observe the live shooting of the artillery. Today, the old Bleidorn Tower houses only the relay stations of the German Army's radio system and, like a monument, stands in the shadow of a new steel tower.

Steel tower a big brother

In 2001, the U.S. Army built the current observation tower next to the Bleidorn Tower at a cost of nearly 450,000 D-Marks. The steel tower is 27 meters high and replaced a smaller predecessor made of steel and wood. The center of the tower is the observation pulpit made of glass on the top level. It is mainly used to observe the air space and guide the missions of the Air Force. Therefore, the room is filled with electronic instruments, radios, and antennas. A second, stand-alone antenna was erected east of the two towers in 2009 on Schwarzen Berg mountain.

View of the Nürnberger Land region

The tower not only offers the military an excellent view. The view from the upper level of the new tower is excellent when the weather is good. Located to the north, behind the Rauhe Kulm mountain, are the Fichtelgebirge mountains with the Ochsenkopf and the Schneeberg mountain. Across the Parkstein mountain to the east, the Czech border near Eslarn comes into view. To the south, you can see Maria-Himmelfahrts-Church in Amberg and to the west you can see the television tower near Betzenstein in the Nürnberger Land region.

Geologie
Geology

Faszinierend und fesselnd

„Man kann sich nur schwer dem Zwang entziehen, das Innere dieser Gegend zu erforschen", heißt es in einer Ausarbeitung von 1934, die der damalige Platzkommandant, Oberst Max Renz, über den geologischen Aufbau des Truppenübungsplatzes und seiner Umgebung schrieb. Zu den Bodenschätzen der Gegend zählten Torf, Eisen und Bleierze sowie Sand, Steine und Erden. Aufgelassene Steinbrüche, Juraformationen, Tümpelquellen im Keuper, Abraumhalden des Erzabbaus, alte Sand- und Farberdegruben mit faszinierenden Farbspielen, aber auch noch aktuelle Steinbrüche sind Zeugen der beeindruckenden Geologie.

Freihunger Störungszone

Das Gelände des Übungsplatzes wird zwei verschiedenen geologischen Räumen zugerechnet. Beide sind durch die von Nordwesten nach Südosten verlaufende so genannte Freihunger Störungszone getrennt. Im westlichen Teil stoßen Ausläufer des fränkischen Jura in den Platz, der Ostteil gehört zum Weidener Becken. Die besondere geologische Situation mit der Verwerfungszone machte das Gebiet seit alters her interessant für die Ausbeutung von Bodenschätzen. Dieter Freitag vom Geo-Archiv Nordostbayern war Initiator und versierter Führer bei verschiedenen Exkursionen ins Sperrgebiet. Er brachte auch alte Unterlagen mit, die den Abbau von Bodenschätzen belegen.

Fascinating and captivating

"It is hard to withstand the urge to explore the earth's interior of this region," writes Col. Max Renz in a study about the geologic makeup of the training area from 1934. The natural resources of the region include peat, iron, lead ore, sand, stones and earth. Abandoned quarries, Jurassic formations, limnocrenes in the saliferous marl, mining dumps from ore mining, old sand and colored earth caverns with fascinating plays of colors, along with active quarries bear witness to a fascinating geology.

The Freihung fault line

The training area belongs to two different geological areas. They are separated by the so-called Freihung fault line which runs from the northwest to the southeast. In the west, branches of the Franconian Jura mountains reach into the training area while the eastern part belongs to the Weiden Basin. This special geologic formation, including the fault line, has always made it a much sought-after area for the mining of natural resources. Dieter Freitag of the Geo-Archive North-Eastern Bavaria was the initiator and an expert guide for various field trips to the training area. He also brought old documents with him that verified the mining of natural resources.

Faszination im Untergrund: Die Silbersandgruben von Pappenberg. „Farben aller Art von reinstem Weiß, bis zum tiefsten Braunrot und Violett begleiten den Weg", heißt es in der geologischen Betrachtung von 1934.
Underground fascination: The silver sand mines of Pappenberg. "All kinds of colors from pure white to deep brownish red and violet accompany the way," states the geologic report from 1934.

Einfache Holzaufbauten schützen die Eingangsschächte der Ockergruben gegen den Regen. Mit einer alten Fotografie legt Hauptfeldwebel Christian Schmidt anhand der abgelichteten Höhenzüge den möglichen Standort der Grube fest.

Simple wooden covers protect the entrances to the ocher mines against rain. Master Sergeant Christian Schmidt determines the possible location of the mine with the help of mountain ranges shown on an old photo.

Im Ockerbergwerk bei Pappenberg: Arbeiter füllen ihre Transportgefäße mit der Farberde.

In the ocher mine near Pappenberg. Workers fill their transport bins with colored earth.

Silbersand und Ocker

Im Bereich des Höhenzugs der aufgelassenen Ortschaft Pappenberg verläuft ein Band aus hellweißem Sand, der in der Bevölkerung den Namen Silbersand erhielt. Dieser wurde im vorigen Jahrhundert in den Glashütten des alten Platzes, insbesondere in der Annahütte, verarbeitet. Die Sandgasse westlich der Wüstung Pappenberg zeigt noch heute viele offene Felsenkeller, in denen das feine Quarzmaterial gewonnen wurde. Die Wände und Decken der Keller glänzen in hellem, marmoriertem Gelb. „Farben aller Art von reinstem Weiß, bis zum tiefsten Braunrot und Violett begleiten den Weg", heißt es in der geologischen Betrachtung von Oberst Renz.

Noch bekannter als der Silbersand war jedoch der Pappenberger Ocker. In Jahrmillionen wurde der gelbbraune bis rote, stark eisenhaltige Lehm zum Farbstoff Ocker gebildet. 30 Meter gruben sich die Bergleute in die Tiefe, bevor Stollen auf der Sohle in die Farbschächte getrieben wurden. Die Vorkommen gehörten zu den bedeutendsten im süddeutschen Raum, hält die Ausarbeitung von 1934 fest.

Silver sand and ocher

A strip of bright white sand, called silver sand by the inhabitants, runs through the mountain range of the abandoned village of Pappenberg. In the last century, it was processed in the glass factories of the old training area, especially in the Anna Hut. There are still many open rock caverns in the strip of sand west of Pappenberg in which fine quartz was mined. The walls and ceilings of the caverns shine brightly in light, marbled yellow. "All kinds of colors from pure white to deep brownish red and violet accompany the way," writes Col. Renz in his geologic report. Even more famous than the silver sand, however, was the ocher of Pappenberg. The yellow-brownish to red clay contained a lot of iron and over millions of years turned into ocher. Miners dug holes 30 meters into the ground before galleries were driven into the color shafts on the base. The report from 1934 states that the deposits were the most significant ones in southern Germany.

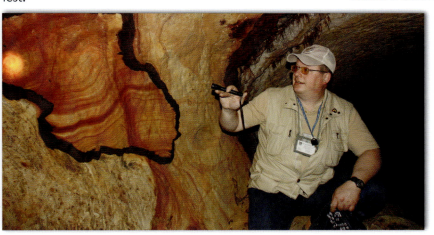

Ein besonderes Farbenspiel: Eine tiefbraune bis violette Erzlinse aus Jura, dem Dogger. Auf zirka 160 Millionen Jahre bezifferte der Geologe Dieter Freitag das Alter des Erzeinschlusses.

A special play of colors: A dark brown to violet ore inclusion made of Jura, the so-called "dogger." Geologist Dieter Freitag estimates that the ore inclusion is about 160 million years old.

Gestern und Heute - ein Naturdenkmal im Jura von besonderer Schönheit: Felsentor und Felsnadel bei Beilenstein.
Yesterday and today - a natural monument in the Jura mountains forms a special beauty: The mountain gate and mountain needle near Beilenstein.

Beilnsteiner Felsenpartie bei Auerbach, Oberpfalz

Pingen am Erzhäusl, Bergbau im Westen

Weitere Zeugen der geologischen Vielfalt des Übungsplatzes und der verschiedenen Vorkommen an Bodenschätzen sind die Erzsteine rund um den Schwarzen Berg sowie die Pingen, die Abraumhalden des früheren Erzabbaus, beim ehemaligen Forsthaus Erzhäusl.

Als „Grabenfeld der Eisensteinzeche St. Phillip bei Langenbruck" wird das 40 Hektar große Areal direkt beim Erzhäusl in der Verleihungsurkunde des königlichen Bezirksbergamtes aus dem Jahr 1872 bezeichnet. Erzsteine und Werkkalke wurden an der Südflanke des Schwarzen Berges gebrochen.

Bis 1978 wurden am Platzrand bei Auerbach mächtige Doggererzvorkommen unter Tage abgebaut. Die Stollenanlagen der Zeche Maffei in Nitzlbuch reichten tief in das Gebiet des Übungsplatzes hinein. Zurückgeblieben sind bei Bernreuth ausgedehnte Bergsenkungsfelder. Viele Ortsnamen im Platz weisen auch auf das Verarbeiten der Erze hin, wie beispielsweise Hellziechen (Helle Zeche) oder Hammergänlas (ein früherer Eisenhammer).

Glory holes at the Erzhäusl, mining in the west

The ore inclusions around the Schwarzenberg mountain, the glory holes and the mining dumps from ore mining at the old Erzhäusl forest house bear further witness to the geological diversity of the training area and its multiple natural resources. The 40 hectare-wide area directly near Erzhäusl is called "the mining area of the iron mine St. Phillip near Langenbruck" in the award certificate from 1872 of the Royal District Mining Office. Ore inclusions and working lime were mined on the southern slope of the Schwarzenberg mountain.

Until 1978, huge "dogger" iron deposits were mined underground on the border of the training area in Auerbach. The galleries of the Maffei mine in Nitzlbuch extended far into the training area. Left behind were extended cuttings near Bernreuth. Many villages' names in the training area point to the mining of ores such as Hellziechen (bright mine), or Hammergänlas (a former iron hammer)

Die Pingen am alten Forsthaus Erzhäusl sind Abraumhalden des Eisenerzabbaus.
The glory holes at the old Erzhäusl forest house are mining dumps from ore mining.

Naturdenkmäler aus Jura

Die Gugelplatte, eine Erhebung an der nordwestlichen Übungsplatzgrenze, markiert den Übergang zum fränkischen Jura. Landschaftlich einzigartig sind das Felsentor und die Felsennadel oberhalb der alten Ortschaft Beilenstein. Die imposante und weithin sichtbare Jurafelsformation war schon damals als Naturdenkmal Wahrzeichen der Ortschaft. Der Beilenstein liegt zwischen dem Gottvaterberg bei Auerbach und dem Glatzenberg, der mit 590 Metern auch die höchste Erhebung im Übungsplatz ist. Weitere Felsengruppen sowie kleinere Jurahöhlen sind in der Südwestecke des Platzes zu finden.

Jurassic natural monuments

The so-called Gugelplatte, a mountain on the northwestern border of the training area marks the changeover to the Franconian Jura. The mountain gate and the mountain needle above the former town of Beilenstein are unique landmarks. This impressive and monumental Jura rock formation and natural monument is visible from far away and has always been the landmark of the village. The Beilenstein is located between the Gottvaterberg mountain near Auerbach and the Glatzenberg mountain. At 590 meters, it is the highest mountain in the training area. Other rock formations as well as smaller Jura caverns can be found in the southwestern corner of the training area.

Der Abbau von Quarzsand am südlichen Platzrand um 1910 und 2010
The mining of quartz sand on the southern border of the training area around 1910 and 2010

Ursprung aus dem Quarzsand

Am südlichen Platzrand wurde im großen Umfang bereits im 19. Jahrhundert Quarzsand abgebaut. Die Quarzsandgrube der Firma Strobel aus Freihungsand wurde 1909 mit einer damals hochmodernen Drahtseilbahn ausgestattet, die den Quarzsand zum Werk transportierte. Die bis zu 100 Meter tiefen Geländeeinschnitte gleichen einem Canyon. Auch heute baut die Firma dort noch Quarzsand ab. Das Band mit dem weißen Sand zieht sich über die gesamte Südflanke des Platzes, was am Quellbereich des Altenweiher Urspung in einem faszinierenden Naturschauspiel deutlich wird. In unberührter Natur sprudelt als artesische Quelle glasklares Wasser aus dem hellen Quarzsand. Professor Reinhold Rosner (†) von der Uni Erlangen bezeichnete dies bei einem Besuch als hydro-geologische Besonderheit, nur selten kommen derartige Tümpelquellen im Keuper vor.

Spring from the quartz sand

A large amount of quartz sand were mined on the southern border of the training area as early as the 19th century. In 1909, the quartz sand mine of the Strobel Company from Freihungsand was equipped with a state-of-the-art cable railway which transported the quartz sand to the factory. The road cuts, which are up to 100 meters deep, resemble a canyon. The company still mines quartz sand there today.

The strip of white sand runs through the entire southern part of the training area which leads to a fantastic display of nature at the Altenweiher Ursprung spring. Crystal clear water flows from the bright quartz sand in this pristine natural environment. During a visit, Professor Reinhold Rosner (†) of the University of Erlangen called this a hydro-geological peculiarity. Such limnocrenes are seldom found in the saliferous marl.

Glasklares Wasser sprudelt aus dem hellen Quarzsand: Die artesische Quelle des Altenweiher Ursprung ist eine hydro-geologische Besonderheit.
Crystal clear water springs from the bright quartz sand: The Altenweiher Ursprung spring is a hydro-geological peculiarity.

Am Ursprung „atmet die Erde"
"The Earth breathes" at the Ursprung spring

Am Ursprung „atmet die Erde"

„Der Altenweiher Ursprung ist ein Diamant im Kronjuwel Grafenwöhr", sagte Professor Dr. Holger Weiß. Der Umweltwissenschaftler offenbarte neue geologische Erkenntnisse: Aus der artesischen Quelle im Sperrgebiet des Übungsplatzes steigen Gase auf, die teilweise aus einem Magma-Reservat in zirka 30 Kilometer Tiefe stammen. Dies ist der erste wissenschaftliche Nachweis einer Querverbindung zum Egergraben, der 75 Kilometer weiter östlich liegt.

Professor Weiß ist Mitarbeiter des Helmholtz-Zentrums für Umweltforschung in Leipzig. Sein Cousin Heiko Weiß, der als Förster auf dem Truppenübungsplatz arbeitet, machte ihn auf den Ursprung aufmerksam. Das wissenschaftliche Interesse veranlasste Weiß und seine Kollegen, die aufsteigenden Gase mittels einer Isotopen-Massenspektrometrie zu untersuchen. Holger Weiß gab bekannt, dass dieser „Atem der Erde" vulkanischen oder subvulkanischen Ursprungs in der Region bislang nur an den Mineralquellen und Mofetten (Gasaustrittslöchern) der böhmischen Bäder Karlsbad, Marienbad und Franzensbad festgestellt wurde. Für Professor Weiß und die Wissenschaftler steht damit fest: Der Altenweiher Ursprung ist mit dem Egergraben verbunden und es steigt Gas aus dem Mantel der Erde auf.

Der Ursprung liegt idyllisch im dichten Wald des Übungsplatzes. Kristallklar sprudelt das Wasser und bewegt den weißen Quarzsand des Weihergrundes, der teilweise durch Laub und Nadeln tiefgrün gefärbt ist. Das Wasser ist gering mineralisiert und hat Trinkwasserqualität. Eine Fassung als Mineralquelle, großen Besucherandrang oder auch nur einzelne Wanderer gibt es hier nicht: Die Lage im militärischen Areal und im Gefahrbereich der Schießbahnen lassen dies nicht zu.

„The Earth breathes" at the Ursprung spring

"The Altenweiher Ursprung spring is a diamond in the crown jewel Grafenwoehr," says Professor Dr. Holger Weiß. The environmental scientist presented new geological research results: Gases welling up from the artesian spring in the impact area of the training area partially come from a magma chamber located approx. 30 kilometers below ground. This is the first scientific proof of a link to the Eger Rill which runs 75 kilometers further east.

Weiß works for the Helmholtz-Center of Environmental Science in Leipzig. His cousin Heiko Weiß, a forest ranger at Grafenwoehr Training Area, told him about the hydrological peculiarity at the Ursprung spring. Following their scientific interest, Weiß and his colleagues determined the isotopic composition of the ascending gases with the help of isotopic mass spectrometry. Weiß announced that this "breath of the earth" is of volcanic or sub-volcanic origin in the region and had previously only been detected at the mineral springs and mofettes of the Bohemian spas in Karlovy Vary, Mariánské Lázně and Františkovy Lázně. Weiß and the other scientists are certain that the Altenweiher Ursprung is linked to the Eger Rill and that gas is welling up from the inner mantle of the Earth.

The Ursprung spring is idyllically located in the deep forests of the training area. Its crystal-clear water forms bubbles and moves the white quartz sand on the bottom of the lake which is partially dyed green by leaves and fir needles. The water is slightly mineralized and of drinking water quality. The spring is neither tapped nor crowded, and not even a single hiker can be found there because of its location on the training area and in the danger zone of the firing ranges.

Naturidyll und hydro-geologische Besonderheit erster Güte: Der Altenweiher Ursprung im Sperrgebiet des Übungsplatzes. Professor Dr. Holger Weiß (links) erbrachte zusammen mit Doktorand Pablo Borges De Amorim (rechts) den Beweis: Die Gasblasen steigen aus großer Tiefe auf. Die Forstleute Jochen Scharrer und Heiko Weiß (von rechts) begleiteten die Wissenschaftler bei ihrer Exkursion.
The Altenweiher Ursprung spring in the impact area of the training area is an idyllic place and a rare hydro-geological peculiarity. Professor Dr. Holger Weiß (left) and postgraduate student Pablo Borges De Amorim (right) found proof that the gas welling up at the Ursprung comes from the inner mantle of the Earth. Forest rangers Jochen Scharrer and Heiko Weiß (from right to left) accompanied the scientists on their excursion.

Ehemalige Ortschaften
Former Villages

Schmerzhafter Verlust der Heimat

Rund 250 Einwohner aus zehn Ortschaften, Gehöften und Weilern mussten in den Jahren 1907 bis 1910 für die Errichtung des Übungsplatzes ihre Heimat verlassen. Bei der großen Erweiterung des Übungsgeländes auf die heutige Größe waren es 3500 Menschen, die aus 57 Dörfern, Weilern und Einzelgehöften abgesiedelt wurden. Die eigens gegründete Reichsumsiedlungsgesellschaft (RUGES) nahm mit mehr oder weniger Druck des Dritten Reichs in den Jahren 1937/38 die Absiedelung vor. Den Familien wurden in anderen Gemeinden wieder Häuser und Grund zugewiesen oder sie wurden finanziell entschädigt. Auch wenn für die Kommission der Grundsatz gelten sollte: „Niemand darf wirtschaftlich geschädigt werden", war der Verlust der eigenen Scholle und der angestammten Heimat für die Betroffenen doch überaus schmerzlich. Besonders den alten Menschen fiel es schwer sich von den über Jahrhunderte erarbeiteten und weiter vererbten Höfen sowie von der Heimaterde zu trennen. Die Dorfgemeinschaft mit dem gesellschaftlichen und kirchlichen Leben, der Verwandten- und Bekanntenkreis, die Erinnerung vor Ort und die Bindung an die Toten auf den Friedhöfen mussten aufgegeben werden.

Painful loss of home

Approximately 250 residents of ten villages, farms and hamlets had to leave their homes between 1907 and 1910 as a result of the establishment of the training area. During the large expansion of the training area to its current size, 3,500 residents of 57 villages, farms and hamlets were resettled. The Reich's Resettlement Corporation (RUGES) organized the resettlement with more or less pressure from the Third Reich in 1937/38. The families either received new houses and land in other communities or were financially compensated for their loss. While the commission's intent was that "nobody would suffer any financial loss," the loss of their property and homeland was very painful for the affected residents. It was especially painful for the older people to bid farewell to their homeland and to property for which they had worked for several hundred years and that had been passed on from generation to generation. Everything had to be given up: The local community with its social and church life, relatives and friends, all the memories connected to home and the ties to the deceased at the cemeteries.

Kaundorf

Am Grünhundweiher, von den Amerikanern „L-Lake" genannt

At Grünhundweiher Lake, called "L-Lake" by the Americans

Karte mit Dörfern und Weilern des Übungsplatzes

Map with the villages and hamlets of the training area

Hebersreuth

Vor den Ruinen des Elternhauses in Leutzenhof
Former residents in front of the ruins of their home in Leutzenhof

Ebersberg

Kopfsteinpflasterstraße bei Ebersberg
Cobblestone street near Ebersberg

Erinnerung an einst blühende Ortschaften

In der Militärabteilung des Grafenwöhrer Museums wird auf die Absiedelung eingegangen. Gezeigt werden auch Ausschnitte eines Schwarz-Weiß-Films, den der Lehrer Paul Huber 1938 über das Leben in Haag und die Absiedelung gedreht hat. Sehr detailliert geht Eckehart Griesbach in seinem Buch „Truppenübungsplatz Grafenwöhr – Geschichte einer Landschaft" auf die ehemaligen Ortschaften des Platzes ein. Hans Jürgen Kugler stellt in seiner Publikation „Hopfenohe – Geschichte der Pfarrgemeinde" die Dörfer und das Leben in diesem Bereich vor.

Nur noch wenige Mauerreste, Kellergewölbe, Grundmauern, Brunnenlöcher, die Reste von Kirchen und Kapellen sowie die alten Obstbaumkulturen zeugen heute noch von den einst blühenden Ortschaften. Nach dem Krieg wurden die Dörfer freigegeben zur Entnahme von Baumaterial. Wind und Wetter trugen des weiteren zum Verfall der Gebäude bei, oft wurden die Ruinen dann auch geschliffen.

Eine Maßnahme zum Erhalt der Kirchenruine Hopfenohe wurde im Jahr 2005 durchgeführt. Hopfenohe, Pappenberg und Haag waren die drei größten Orte bei der Erweiterung des Platzes. Auf Maßahmen in diesen Ortschaften, auf Besuche und Erinnerungen der ehemaligen Bewohner und ihrer Nachkommen soll in den folgenden Kapiteln dieses Buches eingegangen werden.

Memories of once blossoming landscapes

The military section of the Grafenwoehr museum covers the resettlement. The museum also shows scenes from a movie that was shot in 1938 by teacher Paul Huber about the life and the resettlement of the village of Haag. In his book "Grafenwoehr Training Area – History of a Landscape" Eckehart Griesbach covers the former training area villages in great detail. In his publication "Hopfenohe – History of a Parish" Hans Jürgen Kugler portrays the villages and the life in the villages.

Today, only a few walls, cellars, foundation walls, well holes, the ruins of churches and chapels as well as old fruit trees bear witness of the once blossoming landscapes. After the war, the villages were opened so that construction material could be taken out. Wind and weather contributed to the dilapidation of the buildings and often, the structures were demolished into ruins. The ruins of Hopfenohe Church were preserved in 2005. Hopfenohe, Pappenberg and Haag were the three largest villages when the training area was expanded. The following chapters of this book cover what has since been done in those villages and tell about visits and memories of former residents and their relatives.

Ruinen von Schloss Frankenohe
Ruins of Frankenohe Castle

Die Natur holt sich zurück, was ihr einst mühsam abgerungen wurde.
Nature takes back what men once tediously gained.

Pappenberg mit der Wallfahrtskirche Maria Himmelfahrt. Im Hintergrund der Ortsteil Hermannshof

Pappenberg and Maria Himmelfahrt Church. The subdivision of Hermannshof can be seen in the background

Pappenberg

Weinend sind sie abgezogen

„Die Pfarrei Pappenberg wurde aus militärischen Gründen aufgelöst (Propter res militares). Die Pfarrangehörigen sind in alle Teile Bayerns zerstreut, weinend sind sie abgezogen (Flentes abierunt)," so schließt der damalige Pfarrer von Pappenberg, Wolfgang Ederer, nach der Spende des letzten Taufsakramentes am 13. Februar 1938 die Taufmatrikel ab. Pappenberg war einer der zentralen Orte bei der Erweiterung des Übungsplatzes während des Dritten Reichs. Der Ort besaß eine vielbesuchte Marienwallfahrtskirche, deren Ruine heute die alte Wüstung am Rande der Impact Area dominiert. Ein Großteil der Pappenberger wurde nach Wolfskofen bei Regensburg umgesiedelt.

They left crying

"Pappenberg parish was disbanded for military reasons (Propter res militares). The parishioners are scattered around Bavaria. They left crying (Flentes abierunt)." Those are the last words that the former chaplain of Pappenberg, Wolfgang Ederer, put in the baptism register after baptizing the last child on February 13, 1938. Pappenberg was one of the major villages during the expansion of the training area during the Third Reich. The village had a well-visited pilgrimage church dedicated to the Virgin Mary whose ruins dominate the deserted village on the border of the impact area today. A majority of the former Pappenberg residents were resettled in Wolfskofen near Regensburg.

Die Ruine der Wallfahrtskirche Maria Himmelfahrt in Pappenberg im Jahr 2008

The ruins of the pilgrimage church Maria Himmelfahrt in Pappenberg in 2008

Morgenstimmung in Pappenberg
Morning in Pappenberg

Ein mahnender Zeigefinger

Wenig steht heute noch von der einst blühenden Gemeinde Pappenberg. Die Grundmauern der Sandsteinhäuser verschwinden immer mehr. Was noch steht, ist die Kirchenruine. Die Reste des einst fünfgeschossigen Turms deuten wie ein mahnender Zeigefinger gen Himmel. Mannshohe Trümmer des eingefallenen Deckengewölbes, Schutt, Steine, Bäume und Strauchwerk füllen das Kirchenschiff. Trotz des Verfalls fällt heute noch die reiche Architektur mit teilweise erhaltenen Spitzbogenfenstern und anderen Verzierungen auf. Die Witterung nagt an den Mauerresten – die Natur holt sich zurück, was ihr einst die Pappenberger mühsam abgerungen haben.

Die Grundmauern der Kirche gehen auf das 12. Jahrhundert zurück. Die Maria-Himmelfahrts-Kirche Pappenberg war ein einschiffiges, gotisches Bauwerk aus drei Perioden. Sie war eine viel besuchte Wallfahrtskirche und stand bis zur Auflösung unter Denkmalschutz. „Das ganze ist ein für die Gegend ungewöhnlich schöner Bau", vermerkte der Oberpfälzer Kirchenführer bereits im vorherigen Jahrhundert.

A warning symbol

Today, little is left of the once prospering Pappenberg. The foundations of the sandstone houses continue to disappear. All that is still left are the church ruins. The remnants of the once five-story high church tower points into the sky like a warning symbol. Head high debris of the collapsed ceiling, rubble, stones, trees and bushes fill the nave. Despite the decay, the formerly rich architecture with remaining parts of pointed arch windows and other trimmings are still visible. The weather is taking its toll on the walls and nature is taking back what the residents of Pappenberg once tediously built. The church's foundation walls date back to the 12th century. Pappenberg's Maria Himmelfahrt Church was a gothic building with one nave dating back to three time-periods. It was a well-visited pilgrimage church that was a protected historic monument until the village was disbanded. "It is an extraordinarily beautiful building in this region," as stated in an Upper Palatine church guide dating back to the last century.

Postkarte von Pappenberg. Ein Dorf mit einer reichen Geschichte und regem gesellschaftlichen Leben
A post card showing Pappenberg – a village with a rich history and a vivid social life

Die Reste des „Roten Ochsen"
Relics of the "Red Ox"

Der Sebastians-Altar in Wolfskofen. Die Pappenberger Altäre mit reichen Verzierungen stehen nun seit über 70 Jahren in der Kirche des kleinen Ortes bei Regensburg.
The St. Sebastian altar in Wolfskofen. The altars from Pappenberg with their rich ornamentation have been located for more than 70 years in the church of the small village near Regensburg.

Das Gnadenbild aus der alten Wallfahrtskirche. Im Volksmund wurde es die „Schwarze Margreth von Pappenberg" genannt.
The miraculous painting from the old pilgrimage church which was vernacularly called the "Black Margreth of Pappenberg."

Die „Schwarze Madonna von Pappenberg"

1938 wurden bei der Erweiterung des Truppenübungsplatzes die Pappenberger wie die weiteren Bewohner der ehemaligen Dörfer durch die RUGES (Reichsumsiedlungsgesellschaft) aus ihrer Heimat verwiesen. Im Thurn- und Taxis-Gut Wolfskofen fanden viele Familien aus Pappenberg, Erlhof, Leuzenhof und weitere Angehörige der Pfarrei eine neue Heimat.

Fünf herrliche Altäre, die Kanzel, Beichtstühle, die Orgel und der Taufstein sowie weitere Teile der Inneneinrichtung wurden aus der alten Kirche nach Wolfskofen gebracht. Sie stehen nun in dem 1939 dort erbauten, schlichten, kleinen Gotteshaus. Die kunstvollen Altäre sind Werke des Auerbacher Bildhauers Michael Doser und des Malers Johann Wild. Besonders stechen in Wolfskofen die zwei Akanthus-Seitenaltäre ins Auge, die dem heiligen Sebastian und dem heiligen Florian geweiht sind. Reiches Muschelwerk ziert den Herz-Jesu-Altar und den Frauenaltar. Letzterer zeigt die malerische Nachbildung des alten Gnadenbildes der „Schwarzen Madonna von Pappenberg", die im Volksmund „Schwarze Margreth von Pappenberg" genannt wurde. Das Originalbild der Gottesmutter von Pappenberg, zu der einst viele Pilger kamen, wurde im Dreißigjährigen Krieg nach Prag in die Stiftskirche Strahhof in Sicherheit gebracht.

The "Black Madonna of Pappenberg"

In 1938, the residents of Pappenberg and the other former villages were resettled by the Reich's Resettlement Company (Reichsumsiedlungsgesellschaft, short: RUGES). Many families from Pappenberg, Erlhof, Leuzenhof and other parishioners found a new home at the Thurn- and Taxis Manor at Wolfskofen.

Five beautiful altars, the pulpit, confessionals, the organ, the baptismal font and other interior fittings were taken from the old church to Wolfskofen. They are now located in the small, plain church that was built in 1939. The ornate altars were made by Michael Doser, a sculptor from Auerbach and the painter Johann Wild. The Akanthus side altars, dedicated to St. Sebastian and St. Florian are especially eye-catching. The Herz-Jesu altar and the women's altar are richly decorated with rocaille ornaments. The latter shows a painted replica of the old miraculous painting of the "Black Madonna of Pappenberg," which was vernacularly called the ""Black Margreth of Pappenberg." The original painting of Pappenberg's Virgin Mary, which was once visited by many pilgrims, was taken to safety at Strahhof Church in Prague during the Thirty Years' War.

Ein gotischer Bau mit prachtvoller Innenausstattung
A Gothic building with a beautiful interior

Kreuzgewölbe in der Seitenkapelle der Kirche
Cross vault in the church's chapel

Wiedersehen am Gedenkkreuz der Eschenbacher. Sie wurden noch in Pappenberg getauft und empfingen zum Teil auch noch die Erstkommunion in der alten Kirche.
Reunion at the commemorative cross of the Eschenbach residents. They were baptized in Pappenberg and often also received their first Holy Communion in the old church.

Gottesdienste vor der Ruine

Nur selten ist wegen des Schießbetriebs und der Lage der Wüstung am Rande der Impact Area ein Besuch in Pappenberg möglich. 1988 fand anlässlich der 50 Jahre zurückliegenden Absiedlung ein Gottesdienst in Pappenberg statt. Ein Kreuz mit einer Gedenktafel wurde vor der Kirchenruine zur Erinnerung aufgestellt. Auf Initiative des Katholischen Männervereins St. Michael Eschenbach mit seinem Vorsitzenden Manfred Neumann wurde das Kreuz 2008 durch Arnold Mirwald aus Eschenbach erneuert. Der Eschenbacher Stadtpfarrer Thomas Jeschner und der Grafenwöhrer Ruhestandsgeistliche Karl Wohlgut hielten im Juni 2008 zum 70. Jahrestag wiederum vor den Kirchenmauern eine Gedenkmesse. Viele ehemalige Pappenberger, die zum Teil noch in der Kirche die Taufe erhalten und ihre Erstkommunion gefeiert hatten, waren dabei.

Church services in front of the ruins

A visit to Pappenberg is rarely possible due to the military training and the location of the deserted village on the border of the impact area. In 1988, a church service was held in Pappenberg to commemorate the 50th anniversary of the resettlement. A cross with a commemorative plaque was erected in front of the church ruins. In 2008, the cross was renewed by Arnold Mirwald from Eschenbach upon the initiative of the Catholic Men's Club St. Michael Eschenbach and its chairman Manfred Neumann. In June 2008, Eschenbach's city chaplain Thomas Jeschner and Grafenwoehr's retired chaplain Karl Wohlgut held another church service in front of the ruins to commemorate the anniversary. It was attended by many former Pappenberg residents, some of who had still been baptized and received their first Holy Communion in the church.

Gedenkgottesdienst im Jahr 2008 vor den Mauerresten der Kirche
Memorial service in 2008 in front of the church ruins

Weihbischof Reinhard Pappenberger und Frater Lukas vom Kloster Speinshart gestalteten im September 2010 die Feier. Gesegnet wurde eine Tafel mit dem Gnadenbild der Madonna von Pappenberg.
Auxiliary bishop Reinhard Pappenberger and Brother Lukas from the Speinshart Monastery co-celebrated the prayer in September 2010. A monument with a devotional image of the Pappenberg Madonna was blessed.

Namensverwandt mit Pappenberg: Weihbischof Reinhard Pappenberger vor dem Hochaltar Maria Himmelfahrt in Wolfskofen
A namesake of Pappenberg: Auxiliary bishop Reinhard Pappenberger in front of the high altar Maria Himmelfahrt in Wolfskofen

„Nachfolge-Kirche" von Pappenberg in Wolfskofen bei Regensburg
The "successor church" of Pappenberg in Wolfskofen near Regensburg

„Wir sind alle Pappenberger"

In Wolfskofen wurde im August 2008 das Patrozinium der dortigen Nachfolgekirche von Pappenberg gefeiert. Am 15. August, dem Maria Himmelfahrtstag, zelebrierte der Weihbischof der Diözese, der gebürtige Grafenwöhrer Reinhard Pappenberger, das feierliche Pontifikalamt. Seine Namensverwandtschaft lässt die Abstammung seiner Ahnen aus dem Übungsplatzdorf vermuten. „Wir sind alle Pappenberger und stehen unter dem besonderen Schutz der Gottesmutter", bekannte er bei der Messe in Wolfskofen. Gesegnet wurde in dem kleinen Dorf bei Regensburg auch ein Marterl, das an die Umsiedlung erinnern soll. Chronist Karl Matok präsentierte eine Ausstellung mit Dokumenten aus der Geschichte der Pfarrgemeinde.

Abendandacht mit 400 Gläubigen

„Gnadenorte haben ihre Anziehungskraft in der Bleibe und im Niedergang" stellte Weihbischof Reinhard Pappenberger im September 2010 fest. Mit 400 Gläubigen zelebrierte er eine Abendandacht vor der Kirchenruine in Pappenberg. Bundeswehr, Bundesforst und US-Armee hatten im Rahmen des 100jährigen Truppenübungsplatz-Jubiläums den Besuch ermöglicht.

"All of us are residents of Pappenberg"

In August 2008, the anniversary of the Wolfskofen church was celebrated. On Ascension Day, August 15, Reinhard Pappenberger, the auxiliary bishop of the diocese who was born in Grafenwoehr, celebrated the ceremonial Pontifical Mass. Based on his last name, it can be assumed that his ancestors were from the village in the training area. "All of us are residents of Pappenberg and enjoy the special protection of the Virgin Mary," he said during the mass in Wolfskofen. A small religious monument that commemorates the resettlement was also blessed in the small village near Regensburg. Historian Karl Matok presented an exhibition of official documents about the history of the parish.

Evening prayer with 400 believers

"Places of grace have an attraction in good times and in bad times," said auxiliary bishop Reinhard Pappenberger in September 2010 as he celebrated an evening prayer with more than 400 believers in front of the ruins of Pappenberg church. The German Army, the Federal Forest Office and the U.S. Army had made that visit possible as part of the festivities celebrating the 100th anniversary of the training area.

Abendliche Andacht vor der Kirchenruine. Vereinsfahnen, die ehemals in Pappenberg geweiht wurden, standen Spalier.
Evening prayer in front of the ruins of Pappenberg church. The flags that once were consecrated in Pappenberg formed an honor guard.

Bei einer Feier wurde durch Pater Benedikt Schuster und Frater Lukas vom Kloster das neue Kreuz auf dem Kumpfberg gesegnet. D Kumpfberg ist die einzige Stelle von der aus eine Blickverbindung zu Kloster Speinshart besteht.

Father Benedikt Schuster and Brother Lukas from the monastery bless the new cross on Kumpfberg hill during a celebration. Kumpfberg hill is t only location from where Speinshart Monastery can be seen.

Kreuz auf dem Kumpfberg

Ein neues Kreuz auf dem Kumpfberg, in der Schießbahn 305, erinnert an eine alte Verbindung vom Kloster Speinshart zum ehemaligen Übungsplatzdorf Zissenhof/Heilig Geist. Dem Kloster gehörte damals die Kapelle „Zum Heiligen Geist". In der Nähe stand einst auch ein wuchtiges Steinkreuz und ein Holzkreuz mit einer aus Blech geschnittenen Christusfigur. Mitarbeiter des Bundesforstes errichteten das neue Kreuz im Juli 2011, am Fuß des Kreuzes liegen Sandsteine von der Kirchenruine Pappenberg. Der Prior des Klosters, Pater Benedikt Schuster, und Frater Lukas segneten das neue Flurdenkmal.

Cross on Kumpfberg Hill

A new cross on Kumpfberg hill, inside of range 305, serves as a reminder of the old connection between Speinshart Monastery and the former village of Zissenhof/Heilig Geist (Holy Ghost). The monastery once owned the "Holy Ghost" chapel. A huge stone cross and a wooden cross with a figure of Jesus Christ cut from tin was once located nearby. Workers from the Federal Forest Office put up the new cross in July 2011. Sandstone blocks from the ruins of Pappenberg church lie at the foundation of the cross. Father Benedikt Schuster, the prior of the monastery, and Brother Lukas blessed the new wayside cross.

Vor dem Holzkreuz mit der Christusfigur liegen Sandsteine von der Kirchenruine Pappenberg, eine Tafel weist auf die Bedeutung der Stelle hin.

Sandstone blocks from the ruins of Pappenberg church lie at the foundation of the wooden cross. A plaque explains the religious significance of the location.

Das alte Kreuz auf dem Kumpfberg in den 30er Jahren

The old cross on Kumpfberg hill in the 1930s

„Kapelle zum Heiligen Geist" im ehemaligen Übungsplatzdorf Zissenhof

"Holy Ghost" chapel in the former village of Zissenhof

Das verschneite Haag von der Friedhofshöhe aus. Das Dorf hatte kleinstädtischen Charakter.
Snow-covered Haag seen from the top of the cemetery hill. The village had the character of a small town.

Haag

Friedhof Haag

„Haag war ein sehr schön gebautes Dorf, das beinahe kleinstädtischen Charakter hatte", schreibt Eckehart Griesbach in seinem Buch „Truppenübungsplatz Grafenwöhr – Geschichte einer Landschaft". Die alte Haupt-, Heer- und Handelsstraße (spätere Reichsstraße 85) von Regensburg über Amberg nach Bayreuth führte mitten durch den Ort und war die Lebensader für Handel und Verkehr. Die Panzerstraße durch die ehemalige Dorfstelle zeigt heute noch den Verlauf der R-85 an. Haag war der zentrale Ort des Erweiterungsgebietes für den Übungsplatz. Die politische Gemeinde hatte damals bereits über 500 Einwohner. 1938 wurde der Ort aufgelöst. Nur Mauerreste, Kellergewölbe, ein Granitstein mit Kreuz, Geschichtstafeln und der alte Dorfweiher weisen noch auf die Ortschaft hin. Ehemalige Bewohner, deren Nachkommen und andere Gruppen besuchen jedes Jahr den Haager Friedhof. Der historische Gottesacker wurde 1992 wieder hergerichtet.

Haag Cemetery

"Haag was a beautifully built village that had the character of a small town," writes Eckehart Griesbach in his book "Grafenwoehr Training Area – History of a Landscape." Reich's Road 85 (R-85), the old main Army and trade thoroughfare from Regensburg via Amberg to Bayreuth, ran through the center of town and was a lifeline for trade and traffic. The tank trail though the former village follows the route of R-85. Haag was centrally located in the expansion area of the training area. It had more than 500 inhabitants. In 1938, the village was disbanded. Only walls, cellars, a granite stone with a cross, history boards and the old village pond bear witness of the village. Former residents, their family and other groups visit Haag Cemetery every year. The historic cemetery was restored in 1992.

Der Haager Friedhof heute: Das Friedhofskreuz, errichtete Georg Stümpfl (†).
Haag Cemetery today. The cross that was erected by Georg Stümpfl (†).

Haag lag an einer alten Handelsstraße, der späteren Reichsstraße 85. Die Straße wurde bei der Platzerweiterung nach Westen verlegt und trägt heute die Bezeichnung Bundesstraße 85.

Haag was located on an old trade thoroughfare, later known as Reich's Road 85. The road was moved to the west after the expansion of the training area and is known today as Bundesstraße 85 (B-85).

Generalsanierung des Friedhofs

Auf der östlichen Anhöhe über dem Dorf, auf dem Weg zum Ortsteil Bergfried, liegt der Haager Friedhof. Wie die Gebäudereste der einst blühenden Ortschaft verfiel auch der Friedhof. Die Holzkreuze und Grabsteine stürzten um und wurden im Laufe der Jahrzehnte von der Natur überwuchert. Nicht selten trugen auch menschliche Unvernunft und Pietätlosigkeit zur Zerstörung bei.

Erst im Jahre 1992 wurde dem weiteren und endgültigen Verfall des Friedhofs Einhalt geboten. Ehemalige Haager und der Heimatverein Grafenwöhr waren Initiatoren für die „Generalsanierung". Der Bundesforst nahm die Ausholzung vor und die US-Armee ließ den Weg zum Friedhof aufschottern. Über 600 Arbeitsstunden investierte der Straßenbautrupp des damaligen Bundeswehr-Verbindungskommandos, des heutigen DMV. In mühevoller Kleinarbeit wurden von Hand die in der Erde liegenden Grabsteine wieder aufgerichtet. Ein altes Bild vom Friedhof zeigte den Standort der Grabsteine an. Meist standen über den Gräbern auch nur Holzkreuze. Auf historischen Bildern ist die Gruft der Familie von Grafenstein zu sehen; ihr gehörte die Brauerei in Hammergänlas. Der untere Teil der Gruft ist heute noch erhalten. Das Gruft-Gebäude wurde abgebrochen.

Complete restoration of the cemetery

Haag Cemetery is located on the eastern hill above the village on the way to the subdivision Bergfried. The cemetery has decayed like the rest of the once booming village. The wooden crosses and the headstones overturned and were overgrown by nature during the course of the decades. Often, human stupidity and impiety contributed to the destruction.

Further and final decay was not stopped until 1992. Former Haag residents and the Historic Society of Grafenwoehr initiated the complete restoration. The Federal Forest Office cut the trees and the U.S. Army put gravel on the road to the cemetery. The road construction team of the former German Army Liaison Command, known today as DMV, invested more than 600 work hours. The headstones which were buried in the earth had to be re-erected by hand. An old photo of the cemetery shows the location of the old headstones. A lot of graves were only marked by wooden crosses. Historic photos show the tomb of the Grafenstein Family. They owned the brewery at Hammergänlas. The lower part of the tomb still exists today.

1992 stellten Arbeiter der Bundeswehr die Grabsteine auf dem verwüsteten Friedhof von Haag wieder auf.

In 1992, employees of the German Army re-erected the headstones on the destroyed Haag Cemetery.

Der Friedhof von Haag, rechts auf der sehr unscharfen Schwarz-Weiß-Fotografie ist die Gruft der Familie von Grafenstein zu erkennen.
Haag Cemetery, the tomb of the Grafenstein Family can be seen on the right of this very blurred photo.

Kunstvolle Grabsteine

Die oft kunstvollen Grabsteine stammen zum größten Teil aus der Zeit vor 1900 und sind überwiegend aus Sandstein. Der sonst witterungsanfällige Sandstein hat sich durch das Liegen in der Erde selbst patiniert und konserviert. Die Inschriften sind vielfach noch gut lesbar und geben neben den Namen der Verstorbenen auch Geburts- und Sterbedatum sowie den Beruf oder Familienstand an. Die reich verzierten Grabstellen finden immer wieder große Beachtung. Auch die Steinmetz-Innung aus Weiden bestätigte bei einem Besuch die Seltenheit solcher Grabmäler.

Der in Bergfried bei Haag geborene Georg Stümpfl zimmerte für den Gottesacker ein neues Friedhofskreuz. Kurz vor seinem Tod im Oktober 1997 – der „Stümpfl Girch" wurde 90 Jahre alt – brachte er mit seinen Söhnen am Kreuz noch eine farblich gefasste Christus–Figur an. Gepflegt wird der Friedhof von Mitarbeitern der Bundeswehr. 2003 wurde nach einem Wildschaden ein neuer Zaun um den Friedhof gebaut.

Ornate headstones

Most of the many ornate headstones date back to the time before 1900 and are mainly made from sandstone. While buried in the earth, the sandstone, which usually weathers easily, patinated and conserved itself. Many of the inscriptions are still well legible and state the name, date of birth and death and the profession and marital status of the dead. The richly ornated headstones are often met with a lot of admiration. During a visit, the Weiden Masons' association confirmed the rarity of such headstones.

Georg Stümpfl, born in Bergfried near Haag, built a new cross for the cemetery. Together with his sons, he mounted a colored figure of Christ on the cross shortly before his death in October 1997. The "Stümpfl Girch" turned 90. The cemetery is maintained by the employees of the German Army. In 2003, a new fence was built around the cemetery.

Die Grabsteine der Familie Kohl
The headstones of the Kohl Family

Nur selten sind heute auf Friedhöfen Sandstein-Grabmäler mit derart prachtvoller Verzierung zu finden.
Today, ornate headstones made of sandstone can rarely be found on cemeteries.

Friedhofbesuche der alten „Hoocher"

„Wenn wir ferne sind und weit, wer wird dann am Grabe beten, zu der Allerseelenzeit?" Diese Frage aus dem Gedicht „Abschied vom Friedhof" des Haager Heimatdichters Erhard Trummer - dem „Alten Dohler" - beantworten seit 1992 die ehemaligen „Hoocher" und weitere Besucher. Alle Jahre um den Allerseelentag im November brechen sie zum Gräberbesuch nach Haag und Langenbruck auf.

Toni Englhardt, ein gebürtiger Haager und ehemaliger Bürgermeister der Übungsplatzgemeinden Langenbruck und Sorghof, gab 1992 mit den Anstoß zur Sanierung des Friedhofs in Haag. Seither ist er auch Initiator der Friedhofsbesuche. Mit Liedern und Gebeten gedenken Geistliche aus Vilseck, Schlicht, Sorghof und Grafenwöhr jedes Jahr zusammen mit den Besuchern der Verstorbenen auf den Friedhöfen im Truppenübungsplatz. Begleitet werden die Fahrten von Mitarbeitern des Büros für Presse- und Öffentlichkeitsarbeit der US-Armee Garnison, meist vom Vilsecker Franz Zeilmann sowie von den Feuerwerkern der Bundeswehr.

Der Langenbrucker Friedhof

Eine Andacht wird bei den Fahrten auch auf dem alten Friedhof von Langenbruck gehalten, der am Rande der Rose Barracks in Vilseck liegt.

Toni Englhardt erinnerte beim Besuch 2005 an US-Sergeant Abraham, der vor 40 Jahren hier stationiert war und sich freiwillig der Pflege und des Erhalts des alten Friedhofs in Langenbruck annahm. Die Tochter des Sergeants übermittelte Toni Englhardt Grüße des Vaters. Die junge Frau ist ebenfalls Soldatin und war 2005 in Heidelberg stationiert.

Seit 1992 werden alljährlich um die Allerseelenzeit Andachten auf den Friedhöfen im Truppenübungsplatz gefeiert. Wehmut begleitet die Besucher beim Gang zu den Gräbern ihrer Vorfahren.

Since 1992, prayer services are held every year around All Souls' Day on the cemeteries. Sadness accompanies the visitors during their trip to the graves of their ancestors.

Cemetery visits by former Haag residents

"If we are far away and gone, who will pray at the graves on All Souls' Day?" This question is asked in the poem "Bidding the Cemetery Farewell" by Haag poet Erhard Trummer and answered every year since 1992 by former Haag residents and other visitors. Every year on All Souls' Day in November, they visit the cemeteries of Haag and Langenbruck. Toni Englhardt, born in Haag and former mayor of the training area villages of Langenbruck and Sorghof, had the idea to restore the cemetery in 1992. Since then, he has also organized the cemetery visits. Every year, priests from Vilseck, Schlicht, Sorghof and Grafenwoehr together with the families and visitors, remember the dead with songs and prayers on the cemeteries in the training area. The visits are escorted by Vilseck resident Franz Zeilmann, a U.S. Army Garrison Public Affairs Officer and EOD officers of the German Army.

Langenbruck Cemetery

During the trip, a prayer service is also held at the old cemetery of Langenbruck. It is located on the outskirts of Rose Barracks in Vilseck.

During the visit in 2005, Toni Englhardt reminded the visitors of U.S. Sergeant Abraham who was stationed in Vilseck 40 years ago and voluntarily took care of the preservation of the old cemetery in Langenbruck. Abraham's daughter, also a soldier, was stationed in Heidelberg in 2005 and delivered her father's greetings to Toni Englhardt.

Oberst Nils Christian Sorenson zeigt beim Gräbergang 2008 Interesse an der Geschichte des alten Ortes. Toni Englhardt gibt Erläuterungen. Englhardt war einer der Initiatoren der Friedhofsanierung und organisiert jährlich die Fahrten.

Col. Nils Christian Sorenson shows his interest in the history of the old village during the cemetery visit in 2008. Toni Englhardt provides explanations. Englhardt was one of the initiators of the restoration of the cemetery and organizes the visits every year.

Über Jahrzehnte lagen die Grabmäler im Erdreich.

For many decades, the headstones were buried in the earth.

Ein Grabstein mit Putte im Winterkleid

A snow-covered putto headstone

Eine Hand ragt aus dem Schlamm

Sergeant Abraham investierte damals sehr viel Zeit in die Pflege des alten Friedhofs. Er erneuerte die Friedhofsmauer und setzte neue Holzkreuze über die Grabstellen. Eines Tages, so berichtet Toni Englhardt, brachte er einen eisernen Christus-Korpus, der zufällig auf dem Gelände des Übungsplatzes gefunden wurde, weil eine Hand aus dem Schlamm des Straßengrabens ragte. Über die Herkunft des Korpus ist weiter nichts bekannt. Der Sergeant ließ ein Kreuz zimmern, das heute mit der alten Christus-Statue der Mittelpunkt des Friedhofs in Langenbruck ist.

Die Pflege der Anlage wird inzwischen von zivilen Angestellten der US-Armee in Vilseck erledigt.

A hand protruded from the mud

In those days, Sergeant Abraham invested much of his time in taking care of the old cemetery. He renewed the cemetery's wall and put new wooden crosses on the graves. One day, said Toni Englhardt, he brought an iron corpse of Jesus Christ. It had been found by chance on the training area because its hand had protruded from the mud of a ditch along the road. Where the corpse came from remains unknown. The sergeant had a cross made and today, the corpse on the cross is the center of Langenbruck Cemetery.

Today, civilian employees of the U.S. Army in Vilseck take care of the cemetery.

Andacht vor dem Friedhofskreuz in Langenbruck. Die eiserne Christusfigur wurde im Schlamm auf dem Gelände des Übungsplatzes gefunden.

Prayer service in front of the cemetery cross in Langenbruck. The iron corpse of Jesus Christ was found in the mud of the training area.

Auf Wiedersehen. Grabstein auf dem Haager Friedhof

Farewell. A headstone on Haag Cemetery

Gruß aus Hopfenohe vor 1935
Greeting from Hopfenohe before 1935

Hopfenohe

Die Ruinen von „St. Peter und Paul"

Nach den vielen Jahren der Nutzung des Übungsplatzes ist „Hopfenohe Church" für übende Soldaten aller Nationen zu einem festen Begriff geworden. Im Jahr 2005 konnte die Kirchenruine direkt auf der Höhe der Europäischen Hauptwasserscheide in ihrem Bestand gesichert werden. Der Turm und die Mauern der ehemaligen Pfarrkirche „St. Peter und Paul" von Hopfenohe sollen Besucher und Soldaten daran erinnern, dass das Übungsareal nicht immer unbewohnt war, sondern einst in den ehemaligen Dörfern und Weilern mit ihren Kirchen und Kapellen, kirchliches und gesellschaftliches Leben pulsierte.

Rittergut „Hopfenache"

Hopfenohe war eine der ältesten Siedlungen in der Gegend. Hervorgegangen aus dem alten Rittergut „Hopfenache" steht der Ort auch für die Geschichte der ehemaligen Besitz- und Lehensverhältnisse der Region.

Zur Pfarrgemeinde Hopfenohe gehörten 20 kleine Dörfer, Weiler und eine Mühle. Insgesamt zählte die Pfarrei im Jahr 1939 etwa 1000 Seelen. Das Dorf selbst hatte rund 200 Einwohner.

Die katholische Pfarrkirche „Peter und Paul" lag inmitten des Dorfes. Entstanden war sie aus einer schlichten Burgkapelle des früheren Rittersitzes wohl um das Jahr 800.

Die Kirche stand unter Denkmalschutz und ging in ihren gotischen Teilen bis in die Zeit um 1300 zurück. „St. Peter und Paul" bildete über mehrere Jahrhunderte den kirchlichen und geistlichen Mittelpunkt der Gemeinde.

The ruins of "St. Peter and Paul"

After many years of training, "Hopfenohe Church" has become a landmark for training soldiers from all nations. In 2005, the church ruin, located directly on the European watershed, was secured to preserve it. The tower and the walls of the former "St. Peter and Paul" church of Hopfenohe remind visitors and soldiers that the training area was once populated and that spiritual, religious, and social life once pulsated in the former villages and hamlets.

Manor "Hopfenache"

Hopfenohe was one of the oldest settlements in this region. The village, which developed around the old "Hopfenache" Manor, is also a symbol of the region's way of life and the feudal structures of those times. Hopfenohe parish consisted of 20 small villages, hamlets and a mill. In 1939, the parish had approximately 1,000 inhabitants. The actual village had approximately 200 residents.

"Peter and Paul" catholic church was located in the center of the village. It had been built from the remnants of the simple castle chapel of the former knights' manor dating back to the year 800.

The church was a protected monument and its gothic parts date back to the years around 1300. For many centuries, "St. Peter and Paul" was the religious and spiritual center of the village.

Sonnenuntergang über Hopfenohe
Sunset over Hopfenohe

1935, nur vier Jahre vor der Auflösung von Hopfenohe, zeigten Pfarrer Johann Ritter und die Gläubigen noch großen Einsatz bei der Erweiterung der Kirche „St. Peter und Paul".

In 1935, only four years before the displacement of Hopfenohe, Father Johann Ritter and his parishioners, showed a lot of commitment during the expansion of "St. Peter and Paul" church.

70 Jahre später: Der Verfall der Kirchenruine ist gestoppt. Johann Wittmann (†), Vorsitzender der Heimatfreunde Hopfenohe, freut sich auf der Baustelle über die Sicherung der Ruine. Als 16-Jähriger hatte er beim Kirchenneubau mitgeholfen.

70 years later: The decay of the church ruins has been stopped. Johann Wittmann (†), chairman of the Hopfenohe Historic Society is happy about the preservation of the ruins during a visit of the construction site. At age 16, he had helped during the church's expansion.

Kirchenausbau und Absiedelung

Im Jahre 1935 wurde das Gotteshaus unter dem sehr aktiven Pfarrer Johann Ritter aufwendig renoviert und erweitert. Die Pfarrangehörigen halfen mit Geldspenden, Hand- und Spanndiensten eifrig mit.

Der Kirchenausbau konnte die Ablösung der Gemeinde 1939 durch die Reichsumsiedlungsgesellschaft im Zuge der Erweiterung des Truppenübungsplatzes Grafenwöhr jedoch nicht abwenden. Die Kirche blieb dennoch bis zum Kriegsende 1945 unversehrt, danach musste sie endgültig aufgegeben werden. Die Altäre und die Inneneinrichtung wurden für das durch Kriegseinwirkung ausgebrannte Gotteshaus in Troschenreuth zur Verfügung gestellt. Dort sind sie heute noch zu bewundern.

Church extension and resettlement

In 1935, Father Johann Ritter, who was a very industrious priest, initiated an extensive renovation and extension of the church. The parishioners helped by donating money and their manpower. However, the extension of the church did not prevent the displacement of the village by the Reich's Resettlement Corporation in 1939 when Grafenwoehr Training Area was expanded. The church, however, remained undamaged until the end of the war in 1945 but then had to be abandoned for good. The altars and the interior were donated to the church in Troschenreuth who had been gutted by fire. There, they can still be admired today.

„Hopfenoh´ und Hohenzandt sind die höchsten Punkt´ im Land", hebt ein Spruch die exponierte Lage der ehemaligen Gemeinde an der Europäischen Wasserscheide heraus. Vom alten Kirchturm schweift der Blick über das weite Übungsareal.

"Hopfenoh´ and Hohenzandt are the highest locations in the country," explains a saying the exposed location of the former village at the European watershed. From the old church tower, one has an excellent view across the large training area.

1936　　　　　　　　1960　　　　　　　　2003　　　　　　　　2006

Das Kirchengebäude im Wandel der Zeit - *The church over the course of time*

Erhalt der Ruine

Die Heimatfreunde Hopfenohe und der Heimatverein Grafenwöhr stellten im Lauf der Jahre mehrere Anträge, um die Ruine der Kirche zu sichern. 2004 bewilligte die US-Armee unter Oberst Richard G. Jung, dem Kommandeur der 100. Gebietsunterstützungsgruppe (100th Area Support Group), die Geldmittel. Im Zuge der Erhaltungsmaßnahmen wurde der 1934 erstellte Anbau mit Zinkblechen gegen das Eindringen von Wasser abgedichtet. Umfangreich waren die Arbeiten an dem aus dem Jahr 1791 stammenden Kirchturm. Große Risse gingen durch die äußere Sandsteinmauer, an der Westseite war der Sandsteinsims bereits abgestürzt. Mit einem Ringanker wurde der obere Turm fixiert. Das Mauerwerk wurde mit Eisenverspannungen gegen weiteres Auseinanderdriften gesichert. Mit einem flachen Dach aus Zinkblech und Regenschutz an den Vorsprüngen wurde das Bauwerk wetterfest gemacht. Die Kirchturmfenster und Türen wurden mit Holz verschlagen. Ausgeführt wurden die Arbeiten von der Firma Prösl aus Eschenbach.

Preservation of the ruins

Over the years, the Historic Societies of Hopfenohe and Grafenwoehr requested many times that the ruins of the church be preserved. In 2004, Col. Richard G. Jung, the commander of the U.S. Army's 100th Area Support Group approved the funds. As part of the preservation measures, the nave which had been built in 1934 was sealed with zinc sheets to protect it from water. Extensive work was done on the tower that dates back to 1791. Large cracks ran through the tower's outer sandstone wall and on the western side, the sandstone ledge had already collapsed. The upper tower was stabilized with a circular beam. The walls were secured with iron braces to avoid their further drifting apart. The tower was made weather-proof with a flat roof made out of zinc sheets and rain protection on the ledges. The tower's windows and doors were closed off with wooden panels. The work was done by the Prösl Co. from Eschenbach.

Vor der beeindruckenden Kulisse der Hopfenoher Kirchenruine „St. Peter und Paul" feierten Gläubige am 11. September 2005 den Gedenkgottesdienst zum Abschluss der Sanierungs- und Sicherungsmaßnahmen an dem Mauerwerk.

Guests celebrate a memorial service to mark the end of the church's restoration and preservation measures on September 11, 2005 in front of the impressive backdrop of the ruins of Hopfenohe's "St. Peter and Paul" Church.

| 1936 | 1960 | 2003 | 2005 | 2006 |

Der Kirchturm geht auf das Jahr 1791 zurück. Der Verfall wurde durch die Sicherungsmaßnahmen gestoppt.
The tower dates back to 1791. The decay was stopped by preservation measures.

Feier an 9-11

Mit einem feierlichen Gottesdienst am deutschen Tag des Denkmals, dem 11. September 2005 – der symbolträchtig auch der Jahrestag des Anschlags auf die Twin-Towers in New York ist – wurde die Erhaltungsmaßnahme an der Ruine auch von kirchlicher Seite gewürdigt. Zusammen mit dem Auerbacher Stadtpfarrer Pater Dominik Sobolweski und weiteren Geistlichen zelebrierte Pfarrer Franz Schmidt, 1936 in Oberfrankenohe geboren, den Gottesdienst. Neben ehemaligen Hopfenohern nahmen 250 Gläubige, Gäste aus den Randgemeinden, Behördenvertreter und der Kommandeur der 100. Gebietsunterstützungsgruppe, Oberst Brian T. Boyle, an der Feier teil.

Symbol für aufgelassene Ortschaften

An der Südseite der Kirchenruine wurden an der Stelle des alten Friedhofskreuzes ein neues Kreuz und eine Gedenktafel angebracht. Die Tafel ist ein Beitrag des Erzbistums Bamberg. Mit Texten und Bildern wird die Geschichte der Pfarrei Hopfenohe und der Kirche skizziert. Verfasst wurde der Text von Gerald Morgenstern aus Grafenwöhr und Hans Jürgen Kugler aus Nitzlbuch, der als Herausgeber des Hopfenoher Heimatbuches auch die Bilder zur Verfügung gestellt hat. Kugler und Eckehart Griesbach haben sich in ihren Büchern detailliert mit der Geschichte von Hopfenohe befasst.

Die Kirchenruine in besonders exponierter Lage ist trotz des intensiven Übungsbetriebs meist zugänglich. Für Soldaten, Besucher und ehemalige Bewohner ist sie zu dem Symbol für die geräumten Ortschaften, Weiler und Gehöfte geworden.

Service on 9-11

With a festive service on the German Day of the Historic Monument on September 11, 2005, which is also the anniversary of the terrorist attack on the Twin-Towers in New-York, the preservation of the ruins was honored by the church. Father Franz Schmidt, born 1936 in Hopfenohe, along with the city of Auerbach's priest Father Dominik Sobolweski and other priests, performed the church service. Apart from former Hopfenohe residents, 250 guests from surrounding villages, local officials and the commander of the 100th Area Support Group, Col. Brian T. Boyle, attended the service.

Symbol of the abandoned villages

A new cross and a commemorative plaque were installed on the southern side of the church ruins where the old cemetery cross was formerly located. The plaque was donated by the Archbishop of Bamberg. Texts and pictures tell the story of the Hopfenohe parish. The text was written by Gerald Morgenstern from Grafenwoehr and Hans Jürgen Kugler from Nitzlbuch, the editor of the Hopfenohe Almanac, who also provided the pictures. In their books, Kugler and Eckehart Griesbach provided a detailed accord of the history of Hopfenohe.

Despite intensive training activities, the church ruins at its prominent location, is mostly accessible. For soldiers, visitors and former residents it has become THE symbol of all the abandoned villages, hamlets and farms.

11. September 2005: Oberst Brian T. Boyle dankte zusammen mit Pressesprecherin Susanne Bartsch den Priestern für die Gestaltung der Gedenkfeier. Geistlicher Rat Franz Schmidt (rechts) und der Auerbacher Stadtpfarrer Pater Dominik Sobolweski zelebrierten den Gottesdienst.
September 11, 2005: Col. Brian T. Boyle and public affairs officer Susanne Bartsch thank the priests for their celebration of the memorial service. Father Franz Schmidt (right) and Auerbach's priest Father Dominik Sobolweski celebrate the service.

Die gesicherte Kirchenruine mit dem 1791 erbauten Turm steht direkt an der Europäischen Wasserscheide auf 558 Metern Meereshöhe.

The secured church ruins with the church tower built in 1791 are directly located at the European watershed, 558 meters above sea level.

Berühmter Film: Zeit zu leben, Zeit zu sterben

Das verlassene Dorf Hopfenohe wurde nach 1945 zum Abbruch freigegeben. Vielfach wurde auch Baumaterial aus den Häusern und der Kirche entnommen. In den Folgejahren wurden die Gebäude in den Übungsbetrieb einbezogen und schließlich geschliffen. Die Kirche war dem Verfall preisgegeben.

Noch einmal stand sie im Blickpunkt: als Kulisse für den Kriegsfilm „Zeit zu leben, Zeit zu sterben" (A Time To Love And A Time To Die). Im Jahr 1958 verfilmte der berühmte Regisseur Douglas Sirk den gleichnamigen Roman von Erich Maria Remarque. Bekannte und internationale Schauspieler waren dabei. Als Drehort diente unter anderem die bereits halb verfallene Ortschaft Hopfenohe. Deutlich ist die Kirche noch mit ihrem Zwiebelturm und das Kirchenschiff, noch mit Dachstuhl, zu erkennen.

Famous movie: A Time To Love And A Time To Die

After 1945, the abandoned village of Hopfenohe was approved for demolition. Construction material was taken from the houses and the church. In the following years, the buildings became part of training operations and were then completely demolished. The church was left to decay.

But it became the center of attention once more as the backdrop for the war movie A Time To Love And A Time To Die. In 1958, the famous director Douglas Sirk made the novel of the same name by Erich Maria Remarque into a movie. Famous international actors played in the movie. One of the movie's location was the dilapidated village of Hopfenohe. The church, with its onion dome and the nave still with its distinctive roof, are easily recognizable.

Ein Obelisk markiert den Verlauf der Europäischen Hauptwasserscheide.

An obelisk marks the European watershed.

„Hopfenohe Church" ist inzwischen für die übenden Soldaten aller Nationen zu einem festen Begriff geworden.

"Hopfenohe Church" has become a well-known landmark for soldiers from all nations.

Netzaberg

Vom „Dorf Netzaberg" zur „Stadt Netzaberg"

Insgesamt 57 Ortschaften, Gehöfte und Weiler mit rund 3500 Bewohnern wurden bei der Erweiterung des Truppenübungsplatzes in den Jahren 1937-1939 aufgelöst, eine dieser betroffenen Ortschaften war das Dorf Netza-berg. Mit dem Bau der US-Wohnsiedlung Netzaberg in den Jahren 2006 bis 2008 kamen das Dorf Netzaberg und der „Gasthof zur schönen Aussicht" zu neuen Ehren. Die riesige Wohnsiedlung wurde benötigt wegen der Stationierung einer neuen US-Brigade auf dem Truppenübungsplatz Grafenwöhr.

From Netzaberg Village to the Town of Netzaberg

When the training area was expanded from 1937 through 1939, 58 villages, farms and hamlets with a total of 3,500 residents were disbanded. One of those villages was Netzaberg. Netzaberg Village and the restaurant „Zur schönen Aussicht" (beautiful view) came back to life when Netzaberg Housing Area was built from 2006 – 2008. The huge housing area was needed due to the stationing of a new U.S. brigade at Grafenwoehr Training Area.

Ursprünge bis zur keltischen Zeit

Das Dorf Netzaberg lag auf dem Höhenzug des gleichnamigen Netzaberges zwischen Grafenwöhr und Eschenbach. Die älteste bekannte Nennung steht als „Netzberg" im sogenannten „Böhmischen Saalbüchlein" des Kaisers Karl IV. aus dem Jahre 1366/68. Diese Erkenntnis teilte das Landesamt für Denkmalpflege mit. Bei Grabungen im Jahr 2006 stießen das Amt und die beauftragten Archäologen auf spektakuläre Funde. In Gruben wurden die Knochen eines beigesetzten Huftieres geborgen, die der keltischen Zeit zwischen 500 und 300 vor Christus zuzuordnen sind. Keramiken und Tonscherben deuten auf eine slawische Siedlung zwischen dem 9. und 10. Jahrhundert hin. Freigelegte Mauerreste sind auf die Zeitspanne Barock (1600 n. Chr.) bis in die heutige Zeit zu datieren. Es handelte sich in erster Linie um die Grundmauern des Dorfes Netzaberg.
Die Funde wurden geborgen und dokumentarisch festgehalten, so dass eine weitere Bebauung des Gebietes möglich war.

Origins can be traced back to the Celts

Netzaberg Village was located on Netzaberg mountain between the cities of Grafenwöhr and Eschenbach. The oldest historic mention appears as "Netzaberg" in the so-called "Bohemian Hall Book" of Emperor Karl IV. dated 1366/68.
Excavations by the Bavarian Office for Historic Monuments in 2005 revealed spectacular findings. Bones of a buried hoofed animal were found in a pit that can be traced back to Celtic times between 500 and 300 B.C. Unearthed ceramic and clay shards indicate a Slavic settlement between the 9th and 10th century. Uncovered foundations can be dated from the Baroque period (1600 A.C.) to modern times. They are predominantly foundations of Netzaberg Village.
The findings were dug up and documented so that a new settlement could be built in that area.

GRUSS AUS NETZABERG

Westlich des ehemaligen Dorfes Netzaberg und des „Gasthofs zur schönen Aussicht" wurden 12 Bereiche mit insgesamt 830 Wohneinheiten errichtet.

12 housing sections with 830 housing units were built west of the former Netzaberg Village on the location where the restaurant „Zur schönen Aussicht" once stood.

Soldatenromantik gibt die historische Postkarte am Netzaberg wieder: Ein Soldat des bayerischen Armeekorps trifft an der Wegegabelung vor dem „Gasthof zur schönen Aussicht" sein Mädchen. Die kolorierte Postkarte ist im Besitz des Sammlers Hermann Dietl.

A soldier's romance is depicted on this historic postcard of Netzaberg: A soldier of the Bavarian Army Corps meets his girlfriend at a fork in the road in front of the "Zur Schönen Aussicht" restaurant. This color postcard belongs to the collector Hermann Dietl.

„Gasthof zur schönen Aussicht"

Gleichzeitig mit der Eröffnung des Truppenübungsplatzes errichtete Franz Fichtl in den Jahren 1909/10 auf dem höchsten Punkt des Netzabergs, östlich des ursprünglichen Dorfes, den „Gasthof zur schönen Aussicht". Von hier aus konnte man fast den gesamten alten Platz überblicken und das Schießen der königlich-bayerischen Fußartillerie mitverfolgen. Die Schießübungen lösten seinerzeit bei der Bevölkerung rund um den Übungsplatz großes Interesse aus und wurden sogar als Werbemittel zum Anlocken von Besuchern benutzt. Im Garten des Gasthofes wurden Linden und Kastanien für einen Biergarten gepflanzt, die wie die Grundmauern des Gasthauses, heute noch zu sehen sind. Franz Fichtl verlor bald das Interesse an seinem Gasthof und richtete zwecks Verkauf schon 1911 ein Schreiben an das bayerische Kriegsministerium. Gleichzeitig beklagte er sich über Schäden am Haus, die durch Erschütterungen des Schießens entstanden sein sollen. Diese Erkenntnisse gibt die Literatur zum Truppenübungsplatz von Helmut Mädl und Eckehart Griesbach sowie die Ausgabe 2004 der „Heimat Eschenbach" in einem Artikel von Karlheinz Keck wieder.

„Restaurant zur schönen Aussicht" (Beautiful View)

In 1910, Grafenwoehr Training Area was opened south of Netzaberg for use by the Third Bavarian Army Corps. In 1909/1910, Franz Fichtl simultaneously built the „Restaurant zur schönen Aussicht" east of the village and located it on the highest elevation. From there you could see almost the entire original training area and view the training of the Bavarian artillery. In those days, the live fire exercises were met with great interest by the local population around the training area. They were even used as a means of advertisement to attract customers. Linden and chestnut trees were planted in the garden of the restaurant to build a beer garden. Just like the foundations of the restaurant, they can still be found there today. Soon, Franz Fichtl lost interest in his restaurant and offered to sell it in a letter he sent to the Bavarian War Ministry in 1911. In his letter, he also mentioned damages to the house as a result of the vibration from the shooting. This is documented in the books about the training area by Helmut Mädl and Eckehart Griesbach as well as in an article by Karlheinz Keck in the 2004 edition of the publication "Heimat Eschenbach."

Viel Grün und Kinderspielplätze sind in den Wohnbereichen zu finden.

Every housing section features lots of green space and a playground.

Alle Häuser haben einen Garten und eine Garage mit Abstellraum. Es gibt elf Haustypen mit einer Wohnfläche von 130 bis 180 Quadratmetern.

All houses have a garden and a garage with a storage room. The houses feature eleven different floor plans with a floor space of 130 to 180 square meters.

In den Jahren 2006 bis 2008 entstand die neue „Netzaberg Stadt". Mittelpunkt ist das Village-Center mit Schulen und Betreuungseinrichtungen. Vorne ist die östliche Siedlung mit den Wohnbereichen zu sehen. Links an der Straße, am bewaldeten Teil, liegt der Platz des alten Dorfes Netzaberg mit dem Biergarten des „Gasthofs zur schönen Aussicht".

Construction of the Netzaberg Housing Area started in August 2006 and was completed two years later. Its heart is the "Netzaberg Village Center" with schools and child care facilities. Pictured in front is the eastern part of Netzaberg Housing Area with the site of the former Netzaberg Village and the beer garden of the restaurant "Zur schönen Aussicht" (beautiful view) under the trees on the left.

Auf dem höchsten Punkt stand der „Gasthof zur schönen Aussicht". Hier konnte man das Schießen der königlich-bayerischen Fußartillerie mitverfolgen. Um 1910 wurden die Kastanien und Linden für den Biergarten gepflanzt, rechts war ein Schießstand für Luftgewehrwaffen. Der Gasthof wurde um 1948 abgebrochen.

The „Restaurant zur schönen Aussicht" was located on the highest elevation. From there, guests could observe the firing of the Royal Bavarian Foot Artillery. Around 1910, chestnut and linden trees were planted for a beer garden. A shooting range for air rifles was on the right. The restaurant was torn down in 1947.

Der Gasthof wechselte die Besitzer

Bei einer Übungsplatzrundfahrt im Jahr 1991 berichtete die ehemalige Bäuerin Anna Moosmüller vom Leben auf dem Netzaberg. Die bayerische Artillerie nutzte ihn als Beobachtungsstelle. Oft kehrten die Soldaten auch bei ihr in der Bauernstube ein. Bereits im Herbst 1933 wurden die ersten Erkundungen für die Erweiterung des Übungsplatzes vom Höhenpunkt Netzaberg aus durchgeführt.

Restaurant changes hands

During a training area tour in 1991, the former farmer Anna Moosmüller talked about her life on Netzaberg. The Bavarian artillery used it as an observation point and often came to her farm house for a drink and a snack. In the fall of 1933, the first reconnaissance missions for the expansion of the training area were conducted from Netzaberg.

Zu Ehren der heiligen Barbara, der Schutzpatronin der Artillerie und der Feuerwerker, wurde das Barbara-Marterl aufgestellt. Das Marterl und eine Informationstafel stehen im ehemaligen Biergarten des „Gasthofs zur schönen Aussicht", im Hintergrund sind noch die Grundmauern des Anwesens zu sehen.

The "Barbara Marterl" was put up to honor Saint Barbara, the patron saint of the artillery and EOD. The "Marterl" and a sign were put up in the former beer garden of the „Restaurant zur schönen Aussicht." The foundations of the former restaurant can be seen in the background.

Im September 2006 fiel der offizielle Startschuss für die Bauarbeiten auf dem Netzaberg.

Construction on Netzaberg officially started in September 2006.

Das Dorf Netzaberg wird aufgelöst

Bei der Auflösung im Jahr 1937 hatte der Ort fünf Hausnummern und gehörte zur politischen Gemeinde Thomasreuth und zur Pfarrei Eschenbach. Die Kinder gingen in Eschenbach zur Schule.

1937 wurde durch die Lagerkommandantur die Wirtin Anna Maier von Grünhund, einem Weiler im alten Platz, als Betreiberin des Gasthofs eingesetzt, der als „Kantine Netzaberg" auf einer Postkarte festgehalten ist. Zeitzeugen berichten, dass noch in den Jahren 1945/46 Veranstaltungen und Tänze auf dem Netzaberg stattfanden. Im folgenden Jahr wurde der Gasthof abgebrochen, Baumaterial und Ziegel wurden bei Baumaßnahmen in der Ortschaft Trag wieder verwendet. Auch in der Ortschaft Neurunkenreuth entstanden Häuser mit Baumaterial vom Netzaberg.

Militärische und zivile Nutzung

Das Gebiet um Netzaberg wurde im Truppenübungsplatz als Sicht- und Horchbeobachtungsstelle für das Artillerieschießen sowie später als Übungsfläche (Training Area 1) und Pulververnichtungsplatz genutzt. Mit Genehmigung der Kommandantur war es zeitweise auch Flugplatz für den Segelflugverein Grafenwöhr und Speedwaybahn des deutsch-amerikanischen Auto-Racing-Clubs.

Entlang der alten Steinbrüche und des Thumbachtals wurde die Netzaberg-Straße gebaut, im Hintergrund der Wasserturm.

Netzaberg Road was built along old quarries and Thumbach valley. The Water Tower can be seen in the background.

Netzaberg Village is disbanded

When Netzaberg village was disbanded in 1937, the village consisted of five houses and belonged to the town of Thomasreuth and the Eschenbach parish. The children attended school in Eschenbach.

In 1937, the training area command appointed Anna Maier from Grünhund as the new owner of the restaurant which was shown on a postcard as "Canteen Netzaberg." Contemporary witnesses report that as late as 1945/46 events and dances were held on Netzaberg. In the following year, the restaurant was demolished and construction material and bricks were used for buildings in the villages of Trag and Neurunkenreuth.

Military and civilian use

As part of the Grafenwoehr Training Area, the Netzaberg area was used as an observation point, training ground (Training Area 1) and explosive ordnance demolition area. With the approval of the commander it was also used for some time as a landing area by the Grafenwöhr Glider Flight Club and as a speedway track by the German-American Auto-Racing Clubs.

Auf der ehemaligen Panzer-Übungsfläche Training Area 1, entstand die Netzabergsiedlung.
Netzaberg Housing Area was constructed on the site of what used to be TA1, a tank maneuver site.

September 2006

Ein Heer von Bauarbeitern war beschäftigt, die Häuser aus Beton-Fertigteilen zu errichten.
An army of construction workers erects the houses from prefab concrete elements.

Netzaberg war das größte US-Wohnbau-Projekt in ganz Deutschland.
Netzaberg was the largest U.S. housing area construction project in Germany.

Die Häuser schießen wie Pilze aus dem Boden. Bereits im Juni 2006 begann der Bau der ersten Häuser.
Houses are growing like mushrooms. Construction of the first houses started in June 2006.

Die Netzaberg-Housing-Area wächst.
Netzberg Housing Area is growing.

April 2007

Im September 2008 wurden die letzten Häuser übergeben, hier das westliche Baufeld mit Blick zum Rauhen Kulm.

In September 2008, the last houses were turned over to the U.S. Army. View of the western part of Netzaberg with the "Rauhe Kulm" mountain in the background.

Die neue Stadt Netzaberg

2001 gab die US-Armee ihre Pläne für den Bau einer neuen Stadt (New-Town) auf dem Netzaberg bekannt. Die neue Stadt Netzaberg erstreckt sich westlich des ehemaligen Dorfes.

In einer Rekordzeit von nur zwei Jahren und zwei Monaten wurden durch den Generalunternehmer, die Firma Zapf aus Bayreuth, 830 Wohneinheiten errichtet. Die Gesamtkosten für dieses zivile Wohnungsbauprojekt betrugen rund 200 Millionen Euro. Es gibt 12 Wohnbereiche mit elf verschiedenen Haustypen, diese sind als Doppel- und Dreifachhäuser gegliedert. Die Wohnbereiche sind aufgelockert durch Kinderspielplätze und viele Grünanlagen. Die Häuser werden vom US-Wohnungsbauamt verwaltet, die Wohnbereiche gehören zur Stadt Eschenbach.

Netzaberg Housing Area

In 2001, the US Army announced plans to build a new town on Netzaberg. The new town is located west of the site of the former village. Zapf Construction Co. from Bayreuth, built the 830 housing units in the record time of only two years and two months. The total cost of this civilian construction project was 200 million Euro. There are twelve housing sections. The houses, duplexes or row houses, feature eleven different floor plans. The housing sections feature lots of green space and playgrounds. The housing area is part of the city of Eschenbach while the houses are assigned to the Soldiers by the garrison housing office.

Der Bau der Schulen im Village-Center im Mai 2005, das westliche Baufeld ist noch frei, im Hintergrund die Stadt Eschenbach.

May 2005: Construction of the schools in the Village Center. The western construction area is still empty. The city of Eschenbach can be seen in the background.

Netzaberg Village Center

Die Siedlung gibt Platz für rund 4000 Menschen, Mittelpunkt ist das „Netzaberg Village Center". Dort entstanden eine Grund- und Mittelschule für 1400 Schüler, ein Kinderbetreuungs- und Jugendzentrum sowie eine Tankstelle mit Einkaufsmöglichkeit.

Eine Straße entlang der alten Sandsteinbrüche und entlang des Thumbachtals verbindet den Netzaberg mit dem Lager Grafenwöhr.

Der Platz des ehemaligen „Gasthofs zur schönen Aussicht" mit einigen Mauerresten, dem alten Biergarten und alten Obstbäumen wurde als schützenswerter Naturbereich erhalten. Bundeswehr, Bundesforst und US-Armee stellten dort das Barbara-Marterl auf. Initiatoren waren Revierförster Andreas Irle und Stabsfeldwebel Gerald Morgenstern. Eine Tafel berichtet in Deutsch und Englisch von der Geschichte des Netzabergs.

Netzaberg Village Center

The housing area provides room for 4,000 inhabitants. Its center is the Netzaberg Village Center with an elementary and middle school for 1,400 students, a child development center, a youth services center and a gas station with a shoppette.

A newly constructed road along the sandstone quarries and Thumbach valley connects Netzaberg with the Grafenwoehr Training Area.

The land of the former restaurant "Zur Schönen Aussicht" with some foundation stones, the old beer garden and fruit trees, was preserved as a natural protection area.

The German Army, the German Federal Forest Office and the U.S. Army put up the "Barbara Marterl", a historic religious road monument. The project was initiated by Forest Ranger Andreas Irle and Sergeants Major Gerald Morgenstern. A sign tells visitors about the history of Netzaberg in German and in English.

Der Bau der Mittelschule im April 2007, der Blick reicht bis zum Kloster Speinshart.
April 2007: Construction of the Middle School. The Speinshart Monastery can be seen in the background.

Mittelschule - *Middle School*

Netzaberg Chapel

Die Größe und Allmacht Gottes wird in der Dimension der neuen Chapel auf dem Netzaberg zum Ausdruck gebracht. Von weitem ist der riesige Kirchenbau mit seinem Turm sichtbar. Neben den Schulen, dem Kindergarten und dem Jugendzentrum im Village Center des Netzaberg, ist das religiöse Multifunktionszentrum mit einer Investitionssumme von rund 12 Millionen Euro das letzte Projekt des EB-G Standortausbauprogramms.

Das Design der Netzaberg Chapel stammt von den Architekten Brückner & Brückner. Gebaut wurde von der Arbeitsgemeinschaft Mickan/Gross. Baubeginn war im März 2014, über zwei Jahre wurde an der Chapel gebaut.

Die Kirche ist eine Rundbogenkonstruktion mit zum Turm ansteigender Höhe. Die Bögen im Innenraum wirken wie Himmelspforten und sollen auch das Oberpfälzer Hügelland symbolisieren. Ein Spanndeckensystem ermöglicht eine indirekte Beleuchtung. Der große Hauptinnenraum kann durch eine Trennwand in ein Worship Center (Andachtsraum) und Activity Center (Veranstaltungsraum) aufgeteilt werden. Die maximale Bestuhlung im Kirchenschiff, einschließlich der gegenüber dem Turm liegenden Bühne, beträgt 672 Plätze. Vom Taufbecken der Baptisten hinter dem Altar ist der Blick in den 33 Meter hohen Turm frei.

The dimensions of the new chapel on Netzaberg reflect God's magnitude and divine omnipotence. The large church building and its tower can easily be seen from a distance. In addition to the schools, child care facility, and youth center on Netzaberg Village Center, this religious multi-purpose center, with a total cost of about 12 million Euro, is the final project of the garrison's EB-G construction program.

Netzaberg Chapel was designed by Brückner & Brückner Architects. It was built by the Mickan/Gross consortium. Construction of the chapel started in March 2014 and took more than two years.

The church features an arch construction with a gradual rise of the nave towards the altar. The interior arches look like Pearly Gates and reflect the hills of the Oberpfalz region. The suspended ceiling allows for indirect illumination. The large interior can be divided by a partition into a worship and an activity center. The entire nave, including the stage located across from the tower, has room for a maximum of 672 seats. Visitors have an unobstructed view of the 33-meter-high tower from the baptistery behind the altar.

Der Innenraum der Netzaberg Chapel
The interior of the Netzaberg Chapel

Netzaberg Chapel im Oktober 2015
Netzaberg Chapel im Oktober 2015

Seminar- und Schulungsräume, Sakristei, Büros, eine Bibliothek, Räume für Kinderbetreuung, Multifunktionsräume, Umkleiden, Küche und sanitäre Anlagen liegen in den Seitenschiffen. Runde 3000 Quadratmeter beträgt die gesamte Gebäudefläche. Sehr ausgefeilt sind die Gebäudeleittechnik und die Medienausstattung des Zentrums. Zum Kirchenkomplex gehört auch ein Amphitheater für Freiluftgottesdienste.

Im Mai 2015 besichtigte der Bischof der Diözese Regensburg, Rudolf Voderholzer, die Baustelle. Der katholische Bischof zeigte sich vom Stil, der Ausführung und der Funktionalität des neuen Gotteshauses sehr beeindruckt. Zum Anblick des Turms mit Gerüsten und Kran, hatte der Bischof mit einem Schmunzeln den Vergleich mit einer Raketenrampe von Cape Canaveral parat.

The aisles with classrooms, vestry, offices, library, child care facilities, multi-purpose rooms, changing rooms, kitchen and rest rooms are attached to the nave. The entire building has a floor space of 3,000 square meters. The central building control systems and the media equipment are very sophisticated. The church complex also includes an amphitheater for outdoor church services.

In May 2015, Rudolf Voderholzer, bishop of the Regensburg diocese, visited the construction site. The catholic bishop was very impressed by the design, workmanship and functionality of the new church. Looking at the tower with the scaffolding and crane, he commented with a smile that it reminded him of a rocket launch pad at Cape Canaveral.

Die Main Post Chapel am Wasserturm ist längst zu klein für das religiöse Leben der Militärgemeinde
The chapel near the Water Tower on main post became too small for religious activities on post

Bischof Rudolf Voderholzer besuchte die Baustelle im Mai 2015
Bishop Rudolf Voderholzer visited the construction site in May 2015

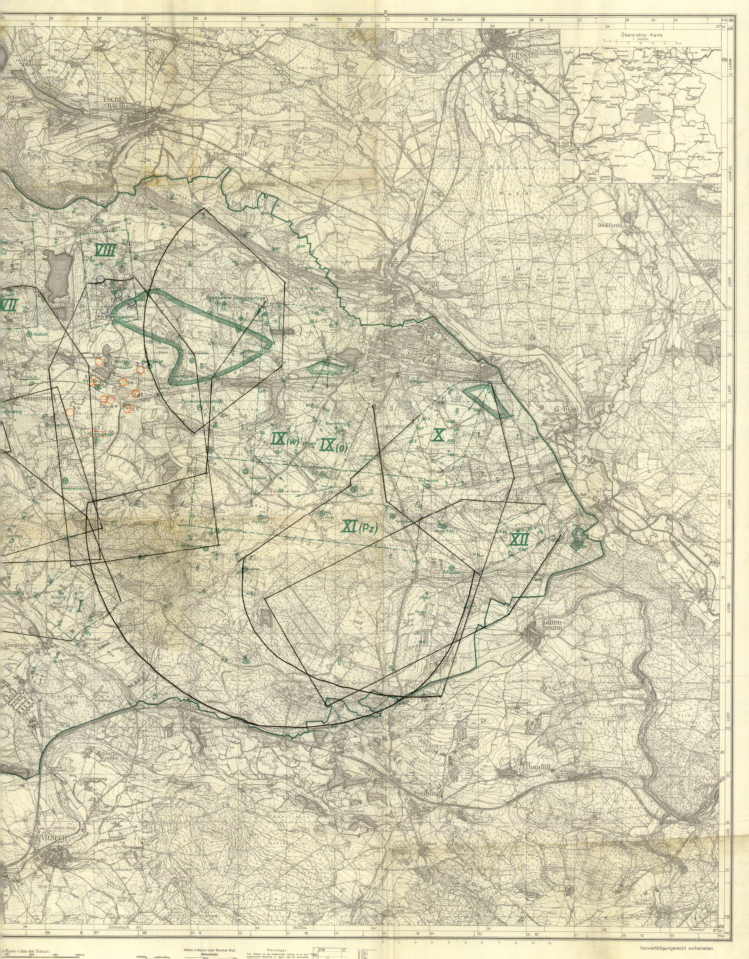

Karte / Map 1939

Westwallbunker

„Festungskampffeld Grafenwöhr"

Bunkerruinen aus meterdickem Beton, bewehrt mit Unmengen von Eisen, säumen Geländeabschnitte und Panzerstraßen auf dem Übungsplatz. Sie sind Zeugen jener unseligen Zeit, als Adolf Hitler Bunkertypen des Westwalls im „Festungskampffeld Grafenwöhr" bauen ließ. Während der original Westwall an der Grenze zu Frankreich mit seinen mehr als 22000 Bunkern und Sperren entstand, wurde 1938 auf dem Übungsplatz eine verkleinerte Ausgabe mit maßstabsgerechten Bunkertypen gebaut. Ein Heer von Arbeitern war notwendig, um die Bunker in kurzer Zeit fertigzustellen. Als junger Mann arbeitete der mittlerweile verstorbene Maurermeister Georg Brunner mit. Für den Transport von Sand, Kies, Zement, Eisen und anderem Material wurden Lkw angemietet sowie Bauern mit Pferde- und Ochsengespannen verpflichtet, wusste Brunner zu berichten. Tag und Nacht waren die Handwerker und Helfer des Reichsarbeitsdienstes auf den Baustellen und es lief die Motormischmaschine. Es wurden Gruppenunterstände, Kasematten, Artilleriebeobachtungsstände, Regimentsgefechtsstände, Nachrichtentürme, Geschützstände und weitere Bunkertypen gebaut. Tonnenschwere Stahlglocken, Beobachtungskuppen, stählerne Schartenstände und Türme wurden in die verschiedenen Betonbunker eingelassen. Im Verteidigungsfeld vor Pappenberg waren meterhohe trockene und nasse Panzergräben, Linien aus Pfahlhindernissen, spanischen Reitern, Betonhöckern und Drahtverhauen den Bunkern vorgelagert. Auch Brückenbauwerke wurden dort errichtet.

"Fortress fighting area Grafenwoehr"

Bunker ruins, several meters thick, reinforced with lots of iron, line open areas and tank roads on the training area. They are witnesses of the disastrous time when Adolf Hitler directed that the bunker types of the West Wall be built on the "Fortress fighting area Grafenwoehr." While the original West Wall with its more than 22,000 bunkers and barricades was built along the border of France, a miniature version with bunkers true to scale was built on the training area in 1938. A large number of workers was necessary to finish the bunkers in a short amount of time. When he was a young man, the deceased mason Georg Brunner was one of the workers. Trucks were rented and farmers with their horse and oxen carriages were hired to transport sand, gravel, concrete, iron and other materials, Brunner reported. The motorized concrete mixers ran and the craftsmen and helpers of the Reich's Work Service worked day and night on the construction sites. Group shelters, casemates, artillery observation posts, regimental fighting positions, communication towers, shooting positions and other types of bunkers were built. Several tons of heavy steel caps, observation domes, steel notches and towers were built into the various bunkers. Several tall dry and wet tank ditches, lines of wooden posts, chevaux-de-frise, concrete bumps and hay-wire circuits were located in front of the bunkers on the Pappenberg defense area. Bridges were built there as well.

Bunkerruinen mit meterdicken Betonwänden sind überall im Gelände zu finden. Die Anlagen wurden 1945 von den Amerikanern gesprengt.

Bunker ruins with several meters thick walls can be found everywhere on the training area. The bunkers were demolished by the Americans in 1945.

Westwallübung fand nie statt

Im Juni 1938 besichtigte Hitler die Baustellen der Bunker. Zu dieser Zeit fanden auf dem Übungsplatz Manöver in einer bisher noch nicht dagewesenen Vielzahl statt. Für August 1939 wurde dann die große Westwallübung mit der Bezeichnung „Festungskriegsübung Grafenwöhr" angesetzt. Die große Bunkerübung fand jedoch nie statt, da nur einige Wochen später mit dem Angriff auf Polen der Zweite Weltkrieg begann. In den Kriegsjahren wurden die Bunker noch für verschiedene Versuche sowie als Zielbaubunker und Stände für die Artilleriebeobachter verwendet, berichtete einst Franz Felten, der 1938 als Soldat bei der Artillerie in Grafenwöhr Dienst tat.

Nach dem Einmarsch der Amerikaner wurden die Anlagen mit Unmengen von Sprengstoff zerstört. Von den 34 Bauwerken sind nur zwei ungesprengt geblieben. Der Aufbau der Westwallanlage lässt sich mit den überall liegenden Bunkerruinen und Hindernislinien auch heute noch gut nachvollziehen.

West Wall exercise never took place

Hitler toured the construction sites of the bunkers in June 1938. An unprecedented number of maneuvers took place on the training area during that time. The large West Wall exercise entitled "Fortress War Exercise Grafenwoehr" was scheduled for August 1939. But the huge bunker exercise never took place because World War II started only a few weeks later with the attack on Poland. During the war, the bunkers were used for various tests and as target construction bunkers and artillery observation posts, reported Franz Felten, an artillery soldier stationed in Grafenwoehr in 1938.

The facilities were destroyed with vast amounts of explosives after the invasion of the Americans. Only two of the 34 structures were not demolished. The construction of the West Wall system can still be retraced today by following the bunker ruins and defense lines that are located everywhere.

Drehkranz des Beobachtungsturms in einem gesprengten Bunker
Swing bearing of an obersevation tower in a blown bunker

Tonnenschwere, stählerne Kuppeln und Türme sind in die Bunker eingelassen
Steel domes and towers weighing several tons were built into the bunkers

Eingänge zu den Bunkern
Entrance to the bunkers

Beschriftung in einer Beobachtungsglocke
Marking in an observation tower

Ein Sechs-Scharten-Turm für einen Artilleriebeobachter
A six-notch tower for artillery observers

Drahtverhaue, Pfahlhindernisse, Panzergräben und Spanische Reiter liegen vor den Bunkern bei Pappenberg.
Hay-wire circuits, pole barricades, tank ditches and dragon teeth are located in front of the bunkers near Pappenberg.

Bombardierung
Air Raids

Bomben auf die „Festung Grafenwöhr"

„Bombenteppiche fielen auf Grafenwöhr, zerstörten Leben und hinterließen Verwüstung weit umher. Es war Grafenwöhrs schwärzester Tag vor genau 60 Jahren, möge Gott uns vor einer Wiederholung bewahren", heißt es in einem Gedicht, das die Lehrerin Anna Mock 2005 zum 60. Jahrestag der Bombardierung schrieb. Am 5. und 8. April 1945 erlebten die Stadt und das Lager bei den Luftangriffen ihr Inferno.

Giftgaslager verfehlt

Am Donnerstag, 5. April 1945, wurde das Lager, das damals vom Kommandanten zur „Festung Grafenwöhr" erklärt worden war, von alliierten Flugzeugverbänden das erste Mal angegriffen. Gegen 11 Uhr flogen die Bomber von Osten her an und warfen ihre Last - beginnend bei Bruckendorfgmünd - in das Waldgebiet Mark. Im Wald versteckt befand sich das größte Giftgaslager der Wehrmacht. Drei Millionen Gasgranaten und Gasgeschosse hätten ausgereicht, um das Leben in der gesamten Nordoberpfalz auszulöschen. Das Giftgaslager wurde bei dem Angriff nur knapp verfehlt.
Der Bombenteppich zog sich anschließend weiter über die Creußenwiesen und richtete im Nordteil des Hauptlagers verheerende Schäden an. Schwer getroffen wurden die Panzerwerkstätten und die angrenzenden Gartenanlagen. Dort wurden zehn Menschen, darunter allein fünf Kinder, getötet. Die Menschenverluste am 5. April wurden mit 74 Toten, darunter 15 Zivilisten, angegeben, wie der Historiker des Heimatvereins, Olaf Meiler, in seinen Recherchen festhielt.

Bombs on the "Grafenwoehr Fortress"

"Bomb carpets fell on Grafenwoehr, destroyed lives and left behind a lot of destruction. It was Grafenwoehr's worst day exactly sixty years ago, may God save us from a recurrence," writes the teacher Anna Mock in a 2005 poem to commemorate the 60th anniversary of the air raids. On April 5 and 8, 1945 the city and the training area experienced its inferno.

Poison gas depot missed

On Thursday, April 5, 1945, the training area, which the commander had declared to be the "Grafenwoehr Fortress ," was attacked by allied aircraft for the first time. Around 11 a.m. aircraft approached from the east and dropped their bombs into the Mark Forest, starting in Bruckendorfgmünd. The largest poison gas depot of the German Army was hidden in that forest. Three million gas grenades and gas projectiles would have been enough to destroy all life in the entire Northern Oberpfalz region. The attack missed the depot by a narrow margin. The bomb carpet then covered the Creussen meadows and caused severe destruction in the northern part of the main camp. Many people were killed. The tank repair shops and the adjacent gardens were heavily hit and ten people, among them five children, were killed. Olaf Meiler, Historic Society historian, recorded that a total of 74 people, 15 of them civilians, were killed on April 5.

„Grafenwöhr in Flammen" heißt das Gemälde von Norbert Richter-Scrobinhusen. Der geborene Grafenwöhrer malte das Bild aus seinen Kindheitserinnerungen und Schilderungen über den 8. April 1945. Es hängt im Sitzungssaal des Rathauses Grafenwöhr.

"Grafenwoehr in flames" is the name of the painting by Norbert Richter-Scrobinhusen. The painter, who was born in Grafenwoehr, painted the picture based on his childhood memories and the reports of April 8, 1945. It hangs in the conference room of the Grafenwoehr Town Hall.

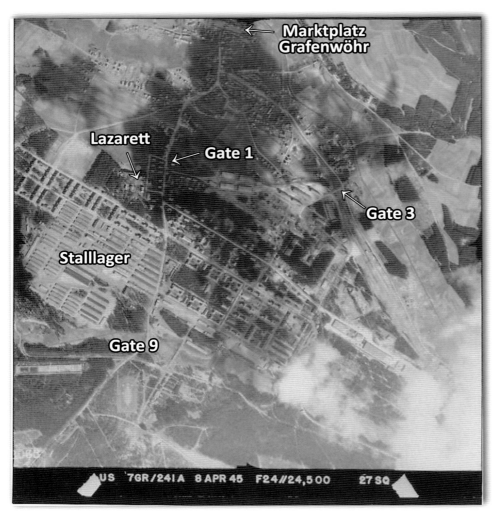

Sonnig klares Wetter mit leichten Wolken (großer Schatten) herrschte am Weißen Sonntag 1945. In den Morgenstunden hielten die Aufklärungsflugzeuge das Ziel „Festung Grafenwöhr" bereits im Bild fest. Einige Stunden später folgten die Bomber. Am rechten Rand sind die Bombentrichter des Angriffs vom 5. April auszumachen

On Low Sunday 1945 the weather was sunny and clear with light clouds (large shadow). In the morning hours, the reconnaissance aircraft had taken pictures of their destination, the "Grafenwöhr Fortress." The bombers followed several hours later. The bomb craters from the April 5 attack can be seen on the right.

Schwarzer Tag am Weißen Sonntag

Weit verheerender wirkte sich der Angriff am 8. April, dem Weißen Sonntag, aus. Gegen 11.30 Uhr ertönten die Sirenen und kündigten das Herannahen von 203 amerikanischen B-17-Bombern an. Grafenwöhrs Bewohner flüchteten in die als Schutzräume deklarierten Felsenkeller am Annaberg. Einige vertrauten sich dem Schutz ihrer durch Holzbalken abgestützten Hauskeller an.

Low Sunday – a disastrous day

The attack on Low Sunday, April 8, was even more disastrous. The sirens sounded around 11:30 a.m. and announced the approach of 203 American B-17 bombers. While some of Grafenwoehr's residents fled into the rock cellars of the Annaberg mountain which were used as bunkers, others entrusted their lives to the protection of their basements, which were supported by wooden beams.

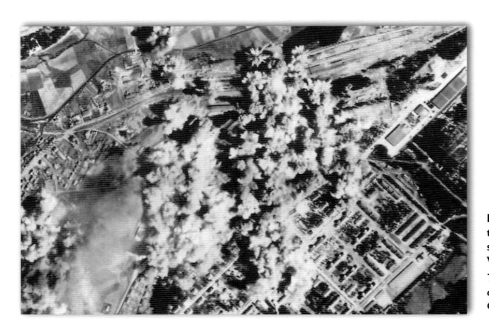

Die Bombardierung am Weißen Sonntag 1945: Brand- und Rauchwolken steigen über dem Lagerbahnhof an der Wache 3 auf.

The air raid on Low Sunday 1945: Fire and smoke raise from the train station at Gate 3.

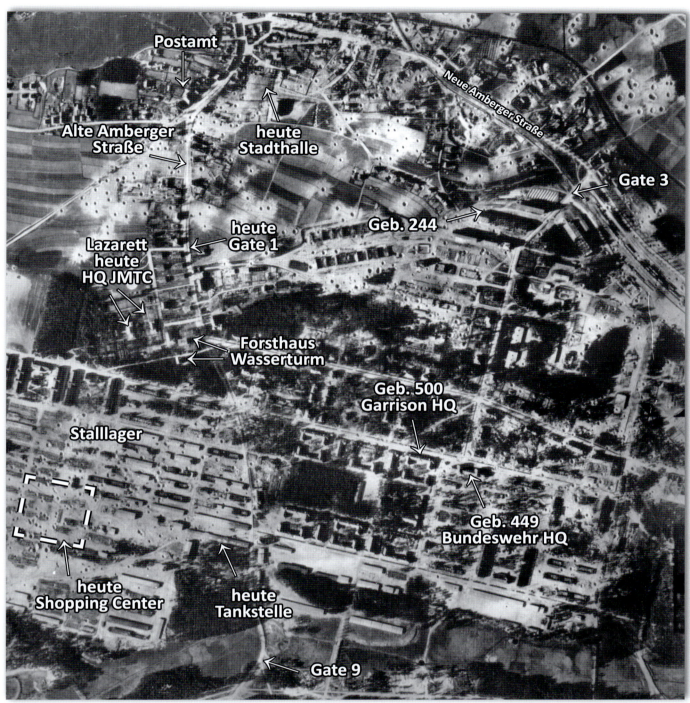

Am 16. April 1945 machten amerikanische Aufklärungsflugzeuge Luftaufnahmen von den Bombentrichtern und Zerstörungen.

American reconnaissance aircraft took aerial photos of the bomb craters and destructions on April 16, 1945.

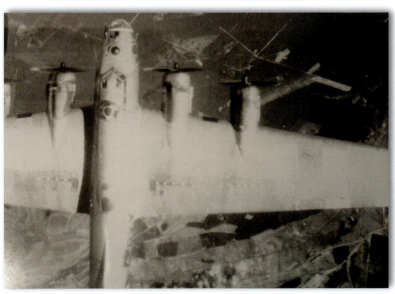

Ein B-17-Bomber direkt beim Angriff am 8. April 1945. Unten rechts sind die Klärteiche am Geismannskeller zu sehen.

A B-17 bomber during the attack on April 8, 1945. The sedimentation ponds at Geismannskeller are seen on the bottom right.

203 Bomber vom Typ B-17 „Flying Fortress" warfen am 8. April 1945 ihre todbringende und zerstörende Last an Spreng- und Brandbomben ab. Am 60. Jahrestag im April 2005 schilderte Engelbert Reiter seine Erlebnisse als damals 16-Jähriger.

203 B-17 "Flying Fortress" bombers dropped their deadly and destructive load of bombs and fire bombs on April 8, 1945. Engelbert Reiter tells about his experiences as a sixteen-year-old at the 60th anniversary in April 2005.

Die nördliche Oberpfalz blieb von einer Katastrophe verschont. Das riesige Lager der Wehrmacht mit mehr als drei Millionen Giftgasgranaten im Waldgebiet Mark wurde von den Bomben im April 1945 nur knapp verfehlt.

The Northern Oberpfalz region was spared from a catastrophe. The large depot of the German Army with more than three million poison gas grenades in the Mark Forest was barely missed by the bombs of April 1945.

Augenzeugen berichten

Dramatische Szenen spielten sich ab. Am 60. Jahrestag schilderten Augenzeugen ihre Erlebnisse: „Annähernd zwei Stunden dauerte das Bombardement", erzählte Anna Mock. Sie war damals 19 Jahre alt.
Im abgestützten Keller seines Elternhauses überlebte Engelbert Reiter die beiden Angriffe. „Mit den Bombenangriffen war der ´totale Krieg´ auf einmal total nahe gekommen", erinnert er sich. Nur um fünf Meter verfehlte eine 1000-Pfund-Bombe das Wohnhaus und Ladengeschäft Reiter in der Neuen Amberger Straße. Im Keller spürte man direkt wie die Mauern „dicke Backen bekamen", so der Erzähler. Zwischen den Angriffswellen musste der damals 16-Jährige mit seinem Vater und Bruder in die oberen Stockwerke, um die Stabbrandbomben zu entfernen, die das Dach durchschlagen hatten. Gedrängt vom dumpfen Brummen der erneut herannahenden Bomber wurden das bereits brennende Mobiliar und die Bettwäsche aus den Fenstern geworfen. Auf der anderen Straßenseite standen die Stallungen der Schreinerei Kraus, in der auch die landwirtschaftliche Betreuungsstelle des Übungsplatzes untergebracht war, lichterloh in Flammen. Das brennende Stroh war wie ein Feuerball, fast alles Vieh kam in den Flammen um.
„Mit blanken Händen haben die Leute im Trümmer- und Steinhaufen des zerbombten Horschelt-Hauses gewühlt, um die Verschütteten zu befreien. Die Hilfe kam jedoch zu spät. Die gesamte Familie ist jämmerlich im Keller der Trümmerruine erstickt", schilderte Martin Hößl (†) seine beklemmenden Erlebnisse als damals Zwölfjähriger.

Eyewitness reports

The scenery was dramatic. At the 60th anniversary, eyewitnesses reported their experiences: "The air raids lasted nearly two hours," reports Anna Mock. She was 19 years old at the time. Engelbert Reiter survived both attacks in the basement of his parents' house. "With the air raids, the ´total war´ had all of a sudden come very close," he remembers. A 1,000 pound bomb only missed the Reiters' home and business at Neue Amberger Strasse by five meters. Reiter reports that you could feel how the basement "expanded." In-between the air raids, the 16-year-old, his father and brother went upstairs to remove the fire bombs which had cut through the roof. Pressed by the sound of the approaching aircraft, burning furniture and linens were simply thrown out of the windows. Across the street, the stables of the Kraus family's carpenter shop, which was also responsible for the agricultural support of the training area, also burned. The burning hay was like a fireball. Nearly all the animals were killed in the fire.
"With their bare hands, people tried to free the buried victims from the debris of the bombed house of the Horschelt family. But their help came too late. The entire family horribly suffocated in the ruins of the basement," remembers Martin Hößl (†), an eyewitness who was twelve years old at the time of the nightmarish experience.

Blick vom Wasserturm auf die zerbombten Artillerie-Kasernen und das Stalllager

A view from the Water Tower of the bombed artillery barracks and stables

„Sehr gute - vermutlich ausgezeichnete Ergebnisse"

„427,5 Tonnen Sprengbomben und 178,5 Tonnen Brandbomben wurden von den Flugzeugen in mehreren Wellen auf die Stadt und das Hauptlager abgeladen", heißt es detailliert in dem mittlerweile vorliegenden Bericht der 3. Air Division. Die Ergebnisse werden darin als „Very good - possibly excellent results" bezeichnet.
Spätere Auswertungsflüge der Alliierten ließen das gesamte Ausmaß der Zerstörung erkennen.
Nahezu das gesamte Hauptlager war von Bombentreffern übersät. In der Stadt selbst hatte es vor allem die Häuser entlang der Neuen und der Alten Amberger Straße sowie in der Gartenstraße und am Alten Weg getroffen. Nach amtlicher Aufstellung waren 210 Gebäude, darunter 105 Wohnhäuser, zerstört oder beschädigt. 3000 Menschen waren obdachlos geworden. Elf zivile Opfer waren am 8. April 1945 in der Stadt zu beklagen. Über die Anzahl weiterer Todesopfer im Lager gibt es keine präzisen Angaben. Die Stadtchronik berichtet, dass bei beiden Angriffen mehrere Hundert Wehrmachtsangehörige und Kriegsgefangene ums Leben kamen.

Trauer, Entsetzen und Ratlosigkeit herrschten nach der Bombardierung bis zum Einmarsch der Amerikaner am 19. April. Viele obdachlose Bewohner hatten die Stadt verlassen. Das deutsche Militärpersonal war orientierungslos. Die Bombenangriffe hatten ihre Wirkung nicht verfehlt und die „Festung Grafenwöhr" zu Fall gebracht.

"Very good – possibly excellent results"

"427.5 tons of bombs and 178.5 tons of fire bombs were dropped from the aircraft on the town and the training area during multiple air raids," states the report of the 3rd Air Division which is now publicly available. The report classifies the results as "very good - possibly excellent". Reconnaissance flights by the allied forces after the attacks show the extent of the destruction.

Nearly the entire main camp was covered with bomb hits. In the city, most of the houses that were hit were located on Neue and Alte Amberger Straße, Gartenstraße and Am Alten Weg. According to official records, 210 buildings, among them 105 residential buildings, were destroyed or damaged. 3,000 people became homeless. Eleven civilians were killed on April 8, 1945. There are no precise records about the number of people killed in the training area. The city chronicle states that several hundred German soldiers and prisoners of war were killed.

Sorrow, horror and helplessness dominated the scene after the air raids until the Americans invaded Grafenwoehr on April 19. Many of the homeless people had left the city and the German soldiers were left without guidance. The air raids had accomplished their goals and destroyed the "Grafenwoehr Fortress."

Relikte der Bombardierung. 2004 wurde bei den Bauarbeiten im Hauptlager dieser Blindgänger, eine 250-Kilo-Sprengbombe, gefunden. Feuerwerker bei ihrer riskanten Arbeit: Sie entfernen den Zünder und machen den brisanten Fund unschädlich.

Relics of the air attacks. A piece of unexploded ordnance, a 250-kilo bomb, was found in 2004 during construction work on main post. EOD officers performing their dangerous work. They remove the fuse and disarm the bomb.

Zerstörte Häuser in der Alten Amberger Straße. Rechts im Hintergrund der Wasserturm. Er war damals mit einer Tarnfarbe gestrichen.
Destroyed houses on Alte Amberger Strasse. The Water Tower is seen in the background on the right. It was painted in camouflage color then.

Die Alte Amberger Straße heute
Alte Amberger Strasse today

Einmarsch der Amerikaner
Arrival of the Americans

Die Eroberung von Grafenwöhr war für die amerikanischen Streitkräfte ein zentraler Punkt im Schlachtplan für die Oberpfalz. Am 19. April 1945 rückte die 11. Panzerdivision mit zwei Kampfgruppen auf Grafenwöhr vor. Die anrückenden Amerikaner verspürten nur wenig Gegenwehr. Gegen 16.30 Uhr vermeldete die Division die Einnahme Grafenwöhrs. Am Morgen des 20. April 1945 kam es auch zur formellen Übergabe des Truppenübungsplatzes durch den letzten deutschen Lagerkommandanten, General Rupprecht.

The capture of Grafenwoehr was a major objective in the Oberpfalz battle plan of the American forces. On April 19, 1945, 11th Armor Division advanced on Grafenwoehr with two brigade troops. The advancing Americans encountered little resistance. The division reported the taking of Grafenwoehr around 4.30 p.m. On the morning of April 20, 1945, Grafenwoehr Training Area was formally turned over by General Rupprecht, the last German training area commander.

Die Kampfgruppe B der II. US-Panzerdivision rückte vom Südwesten her in das Lager Grafenwöhr ein und postierte sich mit ihren Sherman-Panzern im zerstörten Stalllager vor dem Wasserturm.

Brigade Troop B of 11th Armor Division advanced on Grafenwoehr Training Area from the southwest, positioning its Sherman tanks in the destroyed stable complex in front of the Water Tower.

70. Jahrestag der Bombardierung
70th Anniversary of the Air Raids

Mit vielen Emotionen schilderten Zeitzeugen im Museum ihre Erinnerungen an die Bombenangriffe auf die Stadt vor 70 Jahren.

At the museum, eye witnesses, charged with emotions, shared memories of the air raids on the city 70 years ago.

„Zum Gedenken an die Opfer der Fliegerangriffe im April 1945" lautet die Inschrift auf dem Boden vor dem Kriegerdenkmal am Rathaus. Im April 2015 wurde der Opfer der Bombenangriffe gedacht. Gemeinsam mit Oberst Mark Colbrook und Oberstleutnant Hans Joachim Gehrlein legte Bürgermeister Edgar Knobloch einen Kranz nieder. Dazu läuteten die Glocken der Grafenwöhrer Kirchen.
Mit vielen Emotionen schilderten Zeitzeugen im Museum ihre Erinnerungen an die Bombenangriffe auf die Stadt vor 70 Jahren.

The floor inscription of the town hall war memorial reads „Commemorating the victims of the air raids in April 1945." In April 2015, a commemoration ceremony was held. Mayor Edgar Knobloch laid a wreath with Col. Mark Colbrook and Lt. Col. Hans Joachim Gehrlein while the bells of Grafenwoehr churches rang.
At the museum, eye witnesses, charged with emotions, shared memories of the air raids on the city 70 years ago.

Die Verneigung vor den Opfern, Mahnung und Verpflichtung unserer Generation zum Erhalt des Friedens standen im April 2015 bei der gemeinsamen Gedenkfeier zum 70. Jahrestag der Bombardierung im Mittelpunkt.

The joint ceremony in April 2015 commemorated the 70th anniversary of the air raids, and focused on remembering the victims - a warning to our generation to preserve peace.

DORA

Hitlers Monstrum „starb" bei Metzenhof

Eine gewaltige Detonation ließ am 19. April 1945 gegen 13.30 Uhr die Region erzittern. Auf der Eisenbahnstrecke zwischen Eschenbach und Kirchenthumbach am nördlichen Rand des Übungsplatzes wurde bei Metzenhof das „größte Geschütz aller Zeiten" gesprengt. Auf Hitlers Befehl zerstörten die deutschen Landser das riesige Artillerie-Geschütz. Es sollte dem Feind keinesfalls im funktionsfähigen Zustand in die Hände fallen.

Hitler's monster "died" near Metzenhof

A huge detonation on April 19, 1945 around 1:30 p.m. shook the region. The "largest cannon of all times" was demolished on the railroad track between Eschenbach and Kirchenthumbach, on the northern border of the training area near Metzenhof. The German soldiers destroyed the huge artillery cannon upon Hitler's orders to prevent it from falling into the enemy's hands fully functional.

Das Model der Dora im Militärmuseum mit einem Originalstück des Rohres.
The "Dora" model with an original part of its muzzle

Hitler und sein Stab inspizieren die Wunderwaffe Dora beim Erprobungsschießen in Rügenwalde.
Hitler and his staff inspected the Dora weapons system during a proving live-fire exercise at Rügenwalde.

Die größten Geschütze der Welt

1937 wurden auf ausdrücklichen Wunsch Hitlers in der Waffenschmiede Krupp in Essen neben anderen Artillerie-Geschützen zwei 80-Zentimeter-Kanonen entwickelt. Die Eisenbahngeschütze trugen die formelle Wehrmachtsbezeichnung „Schwerer Gustav 1 und 2". In Rügenwalde in Hinterpommern wurde die Riesenwaffe montiert und getestet. Bei der Übergabezeremonie erhielt das erste Geschütz den Namen „Dora".

Vier Eisenbahnzüge und vier Bauzüge waren nötig für die Verlegung der Waffe und der Mannschaften. Die Schießstellung war zweigleisig. 4120 Eisenbahnpioniere wurden zum Aufbau der Stellung und 1500 Artilleristen für die Feuerleitung und Bedienung von „Dora" benötigt. Das Gewicht des Monstrums betrug 1350 Tonnen. Allein das Rohr mit einer Länge von über 32 Metern wog 400 Tonnen. Die Geschosse wogen bis zu 7000 Kilogramm (Panzergranate), eine Sprenggranate hatte eine Höhe von 5,40 Metern. Die größte Schussentfernung betrug 48 Kilometer. Zweifelsohne war die Entwicklung ein Meisterstück deutscher Ingenieurkunst, aber der Aufwand stand besonders in Anbetracht der Weiterentwicklung von modernen Raketen nicht im Verhältnis zur Wirkung – die war mehr eine psychologische.

The largest cannons of the world

In 1937, based upon Hitler's explicit request, the Krupp weapons factory in Essen developed two 80 caliber cannons along with other artillery guns. The railroad cannons were formally called "Heavy Gustav 1 and 2." The large weapon was assembled and tested in Rügenwalde in Outer Pommerania. When it was officially turned over to the Army, the first cannon was named "Dora."

Four trains and four track maintenance trains were necessary to move the weapon and the crews. The shooting position consisted of two tracks. 4,120 combat engineers were needed to build the shooting position and 1,500 artillery men to load and fire the "Dora." The monster weighed 1,350 tons. The cannon alone weighed 400 tons and was more than 32 meters long. The projectiles weighed up to 7,000 kilograms (armor-piercing grenade). An artillery shell was 5.4 meters high. The largest shooting distance was 48 kilometers. There is no doubt that the development of the weapon was a masterpiece of German engineering but the effort, especially in the light of the further development of modern rockets, did not justify the gains which were more psychological in nature.

Hitlers vermeintliche Wunderwaffe nach der Sprengung auf einem Bahngleis am nördlichen Rand des Truppenübungsplatzes
Hitler's alleged "magic" weapon after its detonation on a railroad track on the northern border of the training area

„Dora" vor der Festung Sewastopol

Als einziges Geschütz der Gustav-Geräte war „Dora" im Juni 1942 im Kampfeinsatz während der Schlacht bei Sewastopol. 48 panzerbrechende Granaten wurden auf die Festungsanlagen der Stadt abgefeuert. Die verursachten Schäden waren immens. Ein weiterer Kampfeinsatz der „Dora" erfolgte nicht. Sie wurde zurück nach Rügenwalde gebracht und dort in Hitlers Anwesenheit nur noch bei einem Vorführungsschießen abgefeuert. Im September 1943 gelangte „Dora" ins Heeres-Neben-Zeugamt nach Auerswalde bei Chemnitz (Sachsen). Dort strandete im Februar 1945 auch das zweite Geschütz „Gustav". Vor der herannahenden Roten Armee aus dem Osten und den Amerikanern aus dem Westen irrten die Geschützzüge durch das zusammenbrechende Reich Richtung Süden.

"Dora" in front of the fortress Sevastopol

"Dora" was the only Gustav-type cannon that was deployed during combat in June 1942 during the attack on Sewastopol. Forty-eight armor-piercing grenades were fired on the fortified walls of the city. The damages were heavy. The "Dora" was not deployed again. It was taken back to Rügenwalde and only fired in Hitler's presence during a demonstration of the weapon. In September 1943, "Dora" was taken to the Army's secondary depot in Auerswalde near Chemnitz (Saxony). In February 1945, the second cannon "Gustav" arrived there as well. Fleeing from the Red Army that was approaching from the east and the Americans, coming from the west, the railroad cannons were sent on an odyssey south through the collapsing Reich.

Die Munition der „Dora". Die Sprenggranate hatte eine Höhe von 5,40 Metern.

The ammunition of the "Dora." The artillery shell was 5.4 meters high.

1350 Tonnen brachte „Dora" auf die Waage. Das Rohr wog 400 Tonnen, war 32,48 Meter lang und hatte einen Innendurchmesser (Kaliber) von 80 Zentimetern.

The "Dora" weighed 1,350 tons. The cannon weighed 400 tons, was 32.48 meters long and had a caliber of 80 centimeters.

„Dora" oder „Gustav"?

Unterschiedlich waren lange Zeit die Aussagen darüber, welches Geschütz nun wirklich am Nordrand der Truppenübungsplatzes Grafenwöhr gesprengt wurde. Nach neuesten Erkenntnissen, unter anderem nachzulesen im Buch von Gerhard Taube, war es aller Wahrscheinlichkeit nach „Gustav". Das baugleiche Schwestergeschütz „Dora" ereilte bei Auerswalde das gleiche Schicksal.

Aufgrund der Tatsache, dass nur „Dora" im Kampfeinsatz war und somit legendären Ruhm erlangte, lebte in der verbreiteten Literatur, im allgemeinen Sprachgebrauch und in den Köpfen der Menschen auch nur der Name „Dora" weiter. In Berichten werden Augenzeugen zitiert, die von der Bewachung des Geschützzuges und der Sprengung bei der Metzenmühle berichten: „Es hat mächtig gescheppert, zentnerschwere Eisenteile flogen bis zu drei Kilometer durch die Luft, acht Tage hat es im Sprenggebiet noch gebrannt."

"Dora" or "Gustav"?

For a long time, the statements about which cannon was demolished on the northern border of the Grafenwoehr Training Area varied. The latest research, to be found for example in the book by Gerhard Taube, reveals that it was most likely "Gustav." The identically constructed "Dora" met the same fate near Auerswalde.

Based on the fact that only "Dora" was deployed during the war and came to legendary fame, the only name that survived in common literature, in every day conversation and in the minds of people was "Dora." Eyewitness reports talk about the guarding of the railroad cannon and its demolition near Metzenmühle: "It was a very loud noise and tons of iron pieces flew up to three kilometers through the air. The fire in the detonation area burned for eight days."

Im Rohr der Dora
Inside the "Dora" muzzle

Auch US-General Patton besichtigte im Sommer 1945 die Reste der „Dora".
Even U.S. General Patton visited the remains of "Dora" in the summer of 1945.

General Patton besichtigt „Dora"

Nach Kriegsende setzte ein regelrechter Pilgerstrom nach Metzenhof zum gesprengten Eisenbahngeschütz ein. Vor allem amerikanische GIs wollten einen Schnappschuss von Hitlers Monster-Geschütz, zahlreiche Zivilisten setzten sich in das Rohr der Dora. Im Sommer 1945 war auch General George S. Patton in Metzenhof. In einem Filmdokument wurde festgehalten, wie der legendäre US-General das Krupp-Typenschild der Dora als Souvenir mitnahm. Zur Aufrechterhaltung des Schienenverkehrs wurde ein Ausweichgleis um die Waggons mit den riesigen Schrottteilen der Dora gebaut. Erst 1950 zerlegte ein Montagetrupp die großen Eisenteile und transportierte sie ab.

„Dora" lebt als Modell weiter

Der Unternehmer Gerhard Seemann hat als gelernter Feinmechaniker den Bausatz aus Amerika besorgt. Im Maßstab 1:35 hat er die „Dora Super Heavy Railway Gun" in filigraner Kleinarbeit zusammengebaut. Man kann die gewaltigen Dimensionen heute noch erahnen: Schon das Modell bringt es auf eine Länge von knapp zwei Metern. Das Modell steht heute im Kultur- und Militärmuseum Grafenwöhr.

General Patton visits the "Dora"

After the end of the war, a lot of people went on a pilgrimage to Metzenhof to see the debris of the detonated railroad cannon. American GIs especially wanted to get a snapshot of Hitler's monster cannon. A lot of civilians sat down in the cannon. General George S. Patton visited Metzenhof in the summer of 1945. A video shows that the legendary U.S. general took the Krupp type plate and kept it as a souvenir. A passing track was built around the wagons with the huge scrap metal pieces of the "Dora" to ensure continuing railroad traffic. Not until 1950 did an assembly crew take the large iron pieces apart and transport them away.

The "Dora" survives as a model

The entrepreneur and precision engineer Gerhard Seemann bought the model kit in the United States. On a scale of 1 to 35, he painstakingly put together the "Dora Super Heavy Railway Gun." Even today, one can easily get an idea of its vast dimensions: the model is two meters long. The model is on display at the Grafenwoehr Military Museum.

Elvis GI

Elvis im Camp Algier

„Wir Jungen mochten Elvis eigentlich nicht, weil uns die Mädchen mit ihrer Schwärmerei für Elvis auf die Nerven gegangen sind", gestand Martin Hößl ein, der den King of Rock´n Roll auch wirklich getroffen hat. Und dennoch besorgte Martin Hößl reihenweise Autogramme für seine Frau und deren Freundinnen. Einige Wochen war Elvis Presley als Soldat 1958 und zu einem Manöver 1960 auch auf dem Truppenübungsplatz in Grafenwöhr. Martin Hößl hatte als Maler in der Nähe von Elvis' Baracke im Camp Algier zu tun und erzählt heute noch gern von einem freundlich lächelnden, jungen Elvis.
Reminiszenz gibt dem Weltstar das Militärmuseum mit einer Elvis' Ecke. Sonderausstellungen im Museum, Schriften und gar ein Buch, „Sergeant Elvis Presley in Grafenwöhr", von Peter Heigl halten den Mythos Elvis in der Oberpfalz am Leben.

Elvis in Camp Algiers

„We boys did not like Elvis because the girls got on our nerves with their puppy love for Elvis," admitted Martin Hößl who actually met the King of Rock'n' Roll. Yet, Martin Hößl obtained lots of autographs for his wife and her girlfriends. As a soldier, Elvis Presley was stationed at Grafenwoehr Training Area for several weeks in 1958 and for a maneuver in 1960. Martin Hößl worked as a painter near his barracks in Camp Algiers and still loves to tell people about a friendly smiling young Elvis. The military museum remembers the superstar with a special Elvis corner. Special exhibitions, articles and even a book "Sergeant Elvis Presley in Grafenwöhr" by Peter Heigl keep the myth of Elvis in the Oberpfalz region alive.

Vor seiner Baracke im Camp Algier
In front of his barracks at Camp Algiers

Elvis GI – eingeritzt am Bleidorn-Turm
Elvis GI – scratched into Bleidorn Tower

Für Gastleute und Belegschaft gab Elvis ein Konzert in der Micky- Bar.
Elvis gave a concert for his hosts and their employees at the Micky Bar.

Elvis mit Bundeswehrsoldaten aus Amberg
Elvis with German soldiers from Amberg

Konzert in der Micky-Bar

Einmalig ist auch das Konzert, das Elvis in der Micky Bar gab. Die legendäre Bar bot täglich Tanzkapellen internationalen Formats und Mädchen, die mit Striptease die Besucher erfreuten. In den Privaträumen der Familie Feiner hielten sich Elvis' Vater und sein Begleiter auf, bei einem Besuch von Elvis, abgeschirmt von der Öffentlichkeit. Das Lokal hatte noch geschlossen, als sich Elvis an den Flügel setzte und für die Gastgeber und das Personal ein paar Lieder sang.

Greifbare Kultstätte zur Erinnerung an Elvis ist auch der Backstein am Bleidorn Tower. „Elvis GI" ist eingeritzt, angeblich vom King selbst.

Concert at the Micky Bar

The concert that Elvis performed at the Micky Bar is unique. Every day, the legendary bar offered performances by bands of an international caliber and girls that delighted visitors with striptease shows. Protected from the public, Elvis' father and his companions stayed in the apartment of the Feiner Family during one of Elvis' visits. The bar was still closed when Elvis sat down at the piano and sang a few songs for the hosts and their employees. Another location that commemorates Elvis is the brick on Bleidorn Tower. "Elvis GI" is scratched into it, allegedly written by the King himself.

Ironie des Schicksals und der Geschichte: Aus dem Vergnügungslokal wurde eine Kirche.
Irony of fate and history: The bar was turned into a church.

Lächelnd beim Konzert für die Kameraden
Smiling during a concert for his comrades

Kevin Costner – lächelnd beim Konzert für die Soldaten
Kevin Costner – smiling during a concert for the soldiers

Von Elvis bis Costner

Kevin Costner war kein GI. Er hat nur im Film Uniform getragen und mit dem Wolf getanzt. Nicht ganz hat Kevin den Weltruhm von Elvis aber als Superstar ging auch er mit den GIs auf Tuchfühlung. Costner und seine Band gaben im März 2010 ein Konzert für die Soldaten. Elvis und Costner sind nicht die einzigen Stars, die in Grafenwöhr auf der Bühne standen. „Truppenbetreuung" leisteten schon viele Show-Größen.

From Elvis to Costner

Kevin Costner never was a GI but he wore a uniform in the movies and danced with wolves. Kevin has not gained the fame of Elvis but he also met up close and personal with the GIs. Costner and his band gave a concert for the soldiers in March 2010. Elvis and Costner aren't the only stars that took the stage in Grafenwoehr. Many show stars provided entertainment to the troops.

Elvis-Ecke im Museum. Martin Hößl (†) war Autogrammjäger bei Elvis.
Elvis corner in the museum. Martin Hößl (†) was an Elvis autograph hunter.

Ein Original-Autogramm
An original autograph

Elvis in Grafenwöhr 1960 / Costner in Grafenwöhr 2010
Elvis in Grafenwoehr 1960 / Costner in Grafenwoehr 2010

Fesselballons und Luftschiffe wurden um 1910 zur Aufklärung und als Artilleriebeobachter eingesetzt.

Tethered balloons and blimps were used circa 1910 for reconnaissance purposes and as artillery observers.

Vom Fesselballon zum Kampfjet
Aviation

Fesselballons

Die Fliegerei hielt auf dem Truppenübungsplatz Grafenwöhr schon vor dem Ersten Weltkrieg Einzug. Im Juni 1912 fand eine große Übung im Verbund mit Luftschiffen auf dem Truppenübungsplatz statt. Die Luftschiffer mit ihren starren oder halbstarren Fluggeräten und Fesselballons waren als Beobachter der Artillerie eingesetzt. Die riesigen Luftschiffe am Himmel über dem Lager gehörten zum Tagesbild, zahlreiche Luftaufnahmen der Kasernen wurden mit ihrer Hilfe fotografiert.

Tethered balloons

Flight operations at Grafenwoehr Training Area started before World War I. A large exercise with blimps took place on the training area in June 1912. The blimp pilots who served as artillery observers used fixed and semi-rigid blimps as well as captive balloons. The large blimps in the sky over the training area were an everyday occurrence, many pictures of the barracks were taken from the blimps.

Chinook CH-47
Chinook CH-47

Das Grafenwoehr Army Airfield
The Grafenwoehr Army Airfield

Das Flugfeld Hammergmünd aus der Luft gesehen. Deutlich können Hangars und Doppeldeckemaschinen erkannt werden. Oben verläuft die Amberger Straße, die heutige B-299.

Aerial photo of the Hammergmünd airfield. Hangars and biplanes can easily be recognized. Amberger Straße, today known as B-299, is seen on top.

Flugfeld Hammergmünd

1913 wurden erstmals bei Hammergmünd, wo auch heute das Airfield liegt, zwei Doppeldecker in einem eigenen Flugzeugschuppen stationiert.

Der Ausbruch des Ersten Weltkrieges forcierte die Fliegerei. Mit dem Kriegseintritt der USA 1917 musste auch Deutschland seine fliegerischen Kapazitäten ausweiten. 1917 kam der Beschluss den Flugstützpunkt Hammergmünd zu einer provisorischen Artillerie-Flieger-Station aufzustufen. Schon 1918 wurde sie zu einer Artillerie-Beobachter-Schule ausgebaut.

Nach dem Ersten Weltkrieg war Deutschland die militärische Fliegerei verboten, sämtliche Anlagen wurden abgerissen. Erst in den 1930er Jahren wurde die Nutzung des Flugfeldes wieder aufgenommen. Der Flugplatz wurde in der Wehrmachtszeit weiter ausgebaut. Mit dem Bau des Südlagers Vilseck entstand auch bei Heringnohe eine Start- und Landebahn. Zeitweise unterhielt die Firma Messerschmitt dort eine eigene Außenstelle.

Hammergmünd Airfield

In 1913, the first two biplanes were stationed in an aircraft hangar near Hammergmünd where the airfield is still located today. The start of World War I sped up aviation. When the U.S. entered the war in 1917, Germany had to expand its aviation capacities. In 1917 it was decided to turn Hammergmünd airfield into a provisional artillery flight station. The station was expanded into an artillery observer school in 1918.

After World War I, German was forced to stop military flight operations and the buildings were demolished. Operations at the airfield resumed in the 1930s and the airfield was expanded during the Wehrmacht period. A runway was also built near Heringnohe when the south camp was built in Vilseck. For a while, the Messerschmitt Co. built some of its aircraft at Heringnohe.

Doppeldecker auf dem Flugfeld Hammergmünd
Biplanes on Hammergmünd airfield

Im Flugzeughangar um 1913
Inside an aircraft hangar circa 1913

US-Airfield

Seit 1945 steht der Grafenwöhrer Flugplatz unter der Verwaltung der amerikanischen Truppen. Auch unter ihrer Regie wurde er modernisiert. Bei der letzten größeren Umbaumaßnahme wurde der Tower verlegt, ein größerer Vorplatz geschaffen, die Startbahn neu asphaltiert und Umweltsanierungen durchgeführt. Der Grafenwöhrer Flugplatz ist für Sicht- und Instrumentenflug geeignet und hat somit volle Nachtflugtauglichkeit. Ausgestattet ist der Militärflugplatz mit modernsten technischen Geräten. Eine Flugfeldfeuerwehr steht für den Notfall bereit. Seit Jahrzehnten wird der Flugplatz unfallfrei betrieben. Ständig sind auf dem Airfield auch zwei Ambulanz-Hubschrauber stationiert.

U.S. Airfield

Since 1945 the Grafenwoehr airfield has been used by the American forces. The military airfield was continually expanded and modernized. The tower was moved, a larger apron was built, the runway received a new blacktop, and environmental projects were completed during the last renoration. Grafenwoehr airfield is certified for VFR, IFR and night flight operations. The military airfield is equipped with state-of-the-art technology and an airfield fire crew is on stand-by for emergencies. The airfield has been operated for decades without any accidents. Two medevac helicopters are stationed at the airfield at all times.

Auf dem Airfield Grafenwöhr: Fallschirmspringer besteigen eine C-130 Hercules.
On Grafenwoehr airfield. Paratroopers board a C-130 Hercules.

Luftlandeübung: Fallschirmspringer werden über der Drop Zone abgesetzt.
Airborne training: Paratroopers are launched on the drop zone.

Hercules und Fallschirmspringer

Auf der zirka 1000 Meter langen Landebahn können Propellerflugzeuge bis zur Größe des US-Militärtransporters C-130 Hercules landen und starten. Eine Nutzung von Strahlflugzeugen ist nur für Lear Jets möglich und vorgesehen. Für Kampfjets ist die Startbahn zu kurz. Ein in den 1960er Jahren notgelandeter Starfighter musste per Tieflader wieder abtransportiert werden.

In Grafenwöhr landende und startende Hercules-Maschinen nehmen vielfach Fallschirmspringer auf, die für ihre Ausbildung die zirka drei Quadratkilometer große Drop Zone westlich Hütten oder freies Gelände außerhalb des Platzes nutzen. Fast jeden Abend ziehen die Hercules-Transporter von der US-Luftwaffenbasis Ramstein her kommend ihre Kreise und üben das Absetzen militärischer Lasten in der Drop Zone.

Hercules and paratroopers

Propeller aircraft up to the size of a C-130 Hercules U.S. military transport aircraft are certified to take off and land at the approximately one kilometer-long runway. The only jet aircraft that are authorized to land are Lear jets. The runway is too short for fighter aircraft. A Starfighter aircraft that performed an emergency landing in the 1960s had to be removed with a flat bed truck.

Hercules aircraft taking off and landing in Grafenwoehr often pick up paratroopers who use the approximetely three square kilometer-wide drop zone or open land outside the training area for their training. Coming from Ramstein, the Hercules transport aircraft circle almost every evening over the training area and release their military loads on the drop zone.

Fallschirmspringer werden über der Drop Zone abgesetzt. - *Paratroopers are launched on the drop zone.*

Chinook CH-47

F-16 Jet

Drohne auf der Startrampe - *Drone on the launch pad*

Tiger beim Raketenschießen - *An Tiger helicopter fires rockets*

Panzerknacker A-10 „Warzenschwein" über der Impact Area - *A tank-breaking A-10 Warthog over the impact area*

Hubschrauber, Drohnen und Jets

Hubschrauber gewinnen in militärischen Einsätzen einen immer größeren Stellenwert. Für sie ist in der Nähe des Airfields ein Feldflugplatz angelegt. Große Schießbahnen verfügen über markierte Landeplätze. Apache-Kampfhubschrauber nutzen die Ranges für ihre Ausbildung und für Schießübungen.

Für den Flugbetrieb innerhalb des Platzes gelten strenge Regularien, die bestimmte Flugrouten und Flughöhen vorschreiben, um Kollisionen mit anderen Waffen und Sicherheitsbereichen auszuschließen.

Für Aufklärungszwecke werden ebenso häufig unbemannte Fluggeräte eingesetzt, die Ausbildung mit diesen Drohnen gehört inzwischen zum Standard. Ausbildungs- und Einsatzzeit wird in Grafenwöhr auch der Luftwaffe eingeräumt. Die Impact Area dient dann als Zielgebiet für Kampfjets der verschiedensten Nationen.

Helicopters, UAVs and jet aircraft

The importance of helicopters in military operations continues to increase. There is an additional airfield for helicopters near the airfield and large ranges are supplied with marked helicopter pads. Apache attack helicopters use the ranges for maneuver training and live fire exercises. Strict rules govern flight routes and aircraft altitudes within the training area to avoid any interference with other weapon systems. UAVs (unmanned aerial vehicles) are often used for reconnaissance purposes. Training with those aircraft is a regular part of training activities. Training and operating times at Grafenwoehr are also provided to the Air Force. Fighter jets from various nations use the impact area as their target area.

Apache beim Raketenschießen - *An Apache helicopter fires rockets*

D.U.S.T.O.F.F.

Dedicated Unhesitating Service To Our Fighting Force
Engagierter, unverzüglicher Dienst für unsere Einsatztruppen

Die amerikanischen Rettungsflieger

„Ich brauche einen Dustoff!" wurde über den Funkverkehr zu einem vertrauten Notruf in vielen Kriegen. Die Besatzungen der MEDEVAC-Hubschrauber rücken aus, um verwundete Soldaten auf dem Gefechtsfeld zu versorgen und ihr Leben zu retten. Dabei geraten sie oft selbst unter Feindbeschuss.

1968 wurde die Einheit in Fort Polk aufgestellt und nach umfangreicher Schulung als 236. Medizinische Abteilung im Vietnam-Krieg meist mit der legendären „Huey", der Bell UH-1D, eingesetzt. Für die Evakuierung von 41.000 Patienten in unzähligen Missionen und Flugstunden wurden die Rettungsflieger nach der Rückverlegung in San Antonio in Texas ausgezeichnet.

Mehrmals wurde die Einheit umbenannt und wechselte die Unterstellungsverhältnisse. Weitere Stationierungsorte der Dustoffs waren Augsburg, Nellingen und Landstuhl in Deutschland. Es folgten Einsätze in Südwestasien während der Operation Desert Storm, in Tuzla, Bosnien, im Rahmen der Operation Joint Endeavor sowie weitere Einsätze in Bosnien, Ungarn und Kroatien und während der Operation Iraqi Freedom. 2014 verlegte die Einheit im Rahmen der Operation Enduring Freedom nach Kuwait.

The American MEDEVAC unit

„I need Dustoff!" became a familiar radio emergency call during many wars. The crews on MEDEVAC helicopters fly to the aid of wounded soldiers on the battlefield, and saving lives while often subjecting themselves to hostile fire.

In 1968, the unit was activated at Fort Polk, La., and after extensive training deployed with the legendary „Huey" Bell UH-1D in the Vietnam War as the 236th Medical Detachment. For the evacuation of 41,000 patients during numerous missions and flight hours, the unit was awarded the Meritorious Unit Citation for exceptionally meritorious service after its redeployment to San Antonio, Texas.

The unit was renamed several times and put under various commands. It was stationed in Augsburg, Nellingen and Landstuhl, Germany. It was deployed to Southwest Asia in support of Operation Desert Storm, to Tuzla, Bosnia, during Operation Joint Endeavor and on support missions in Bosnia, Hungary and Croatia, and Operation Iraqi Freedom. In 2014, it deployed to Kuwait in support of Operation Enduring Freedom.

Dustoff-Soldaten mit der Blackhawk im Einsatz
Dustoff soldiers during an operation with a Blackhawk

UH-60 Blackhawk und die legendäre „Huey" des Sammlers Frank Heinrich vor dem Hangar auf dem Airfield Grafenwöhr
UH-60 „Blackhawk" and the legendary „Huey" of collector Frank Heinrich in front of a hangar at Grafenwoehr Army Airfield

Charlie Kompanie, 1-214th Aviation Regiment

Im Mai 2014 kam die Charlie-Kompanie der 1-214th nach Grafenwöhr. Mit sechs Hubschraubern vom Typ UH-60 „Blackhawk" steht die Kompanie dem JMTC in Grafenwöhr, dem JMRC in Hohenfels und den trainierenden Einheiten aller Nationen für den Notfall und die medizinische Evakuierung sowie für Schulung und Ausbildung zur Verfügung. Die mit dem Roten Kreuz gekennzeichneten Helikopter sind mit Tragen und medizinischem Notfallgerät ausgestattet. Die Besatzung besteht aus für den Rettungseinsatz ausgebildeten Soldaten und einem Flugrettungssanitäter. Sie führen die lebensrettende Erstversorgung durch und versorgen den Patienten während des Transports. Die Charlie-Kompanie steht bereit für die nächste Mission um jederzeit, jedermann von überall zu evakuieren.

Charlie Company, 1-214th Aviation Regiment

In May 2014, Charlie Co., 1-214th Aviation Regiment moved to Grafenwoehr with six UH-60 "Blackhawk" helicopters to provide training and MEDEVAC support for JMTC in Grafenwoehr, JMRC in Hohenfels and training units of all nations. The helicopters, marked with the Red Cross, are equipped with stretchers and medical emergency equipment. Flying with medically trained crewmembers and a flight medic, they provide life-saving first aid and enroute care to the patients. C Company readily awaits its next world mission, prepared to evacuate anyone, anywhere, at anytime!

Schüler besuchen die Dustoffs auf dem Airfield.
Students visit the Dustoffs on the Airfield.

Blackhawk und das neue Flugfeldlöschfahrzeug Panther.
Blackhawk and the new airfield rescue and firefighting vehicle Panther.

Apache-Kampfhubschrauber
Apache attack helicopter

Tiger-Kampfhubschrauber - *Tiger attack helicopter*

Bundeswehr
German Army

Schwieriger Start im Jahre 1956

Schon zwei Tage nach dem Eintreffen der ersten Bundeswehrangehörigen im Juli 1956 auf dem Truppenübungsplatz wurden die Mitarbeiter der neuen deutschen Streitkräfte von der amerikanischen Kommandantur wieder des Platzes verwiesen. Grund dafür war, dass keine offizielle Order zum Einzug der Bundeswehr auf dem Truppenübungsplatz vorlag. Trotz dieses nicht gerade reibungslosen Anfangs entwickelten sich die Dienststellen der Bundeswehr in Grafenwöhr sehr schnell zu verlässlichen Partnern der Amerikaner und zu ständigen Mitbenutzern des Übungsareals.

Unter der Bezeichnung „Der Bundesminister der Verteidigung - Verwaltungsstelle Grafenwöhr" trat die Bundeswehr am 16. Juli 1956 erstmals auf dem Übungsplatz in Erscheinung.

Erstes Domizil im Gebäude 449

Zur Erfüllung ihrer Aufgaben in Grafenwöhr wurde den Männern der ersten Stunde das vollkommen verwahrloste Gebäude 449 zur Verfügung gestellt, das sie aber bereits zwei Tage später wieder räumen mussten. Quartier fand die Dienststelle vorläufig im privaten Anwesen Hausmann gegenüber der Micky Bar. Wichtigste Aufgabe der Verwaltungsbeamten war es zunächst, erste zivile Mitarbeiter aus der Region einzustellen. Am 3. August 1956 trafen Major Werner von Detten als Kommandant der kleinen Standortkommandantur und zwei Feldwebel in Grafenwöhr ein. Gleich darauf wurde endgültig das Gebäude 449 bezogen und der volle Dienstbetrieb aufgenommen.

Difficult start in 1956

Only two days after the first employees of the new German Armed Forces arrived at the training area in July 1956, they were expelled from the training area by the American headquarters because no official order had been received regarding the stationing of German Armed Forces on the training area. Despite this rocky start, the offices of the German Army in Grafenwoehr quickly became reliable partners and permanent co-users of the training area.

The first German Armed Forces office on the training area opened on July 16, 1956 and was known as "The Federal Minister of Defense – Administration Office Grafenwoehr."

First offices in building 449

The members of the first group of soldiers were given the completely run-down building 449, which they had to vacate again after only two days. As a result, the office found its first home in the private quarters of the Hausmann family across from the Micky Bar. The most important task of the civil servants was to recruit the first civilian employees in the region. Major Werner von Detten, the first commander of the small headquarters and two non-commissioned officers arrived in Grafenwoehr on August 3, 1956. Soon thereafter, they moved into building 449 and began work.

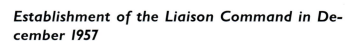

Antreten im Scheibenhof zum 10-jährigen Bestehen des Verbindungskommandos im Jahr 1967

Roll call in the target machine shop celebrating the 10th anniversary of the liaison command in 1967

40-jähriges Jubiläum des damaligen Verbindungs- und Truppenübungsplatzkommandos.

40th anniversary of the liaison and training command.

Gründung des Verbindungskommandos im Dezember 1957

Im Februar 1957 fand das erste Schießen der Bundeswehr auf dem Truppenübungsplatz statt. Um die Belange der übenden Truppe bezüglich der Schießbahnen und Übungsraumverteilung gegenüber der US-Kommandantur besser vertreten zu können, wurde am 1. Dezember 1957 eine „Verbindungsstelle" im Gebäude 621 geschaffen. Dies war gleichzeitig die offizielle Gründung des „Verbindungskommandos".

Establishment of the Liaison Command in December 1957

In February 1957, the first live-fire training of the German Army took place on the training area. On December 1, 1957 the liaison office was established in Building 621 to better represent German training troops' needs regarding use of ranges and training space against the U.S. headquarters. This was also the official establishment of the "liaison command."

Bereits zur Gründungszeit entstand im östlichen Mannschaftslager der Block 72. Heute trägt er die Gebäudenummer 449 und ist Domizil der Bundeswehr.

Block 72 was built as part of the eastern barracks complex when the training area was established. Today, it is known as building 449 and is the local headquarters of the German Army.

April 2010: Soldaten und zivile Mitarbeiter des DMV. Mit der Einführung des optimierten Betriebsmodells erfuhr die militärische Dienststelle eine erhebliche Personalreduzierung.

April 2010: Soldiers and civilian employees of the DMV. The implementation of the optimized operations plan led to a severe personnel reduction.

Aufbau mit eigenem Werkzeug

Teilweise mit Werkzeug, das sie von zu Hause mitbrachten, bauten die ersten zivilen Mitarbeiter dieser Dienststelle den Scheibenhof auf. Die Jahre 1958 und 1959 waren geprägt von ständig wechselnden Übungstruppenteilen der Bundeswehr und auch des Bundesgrenzschutzes. Grafenwöhr war außerdem der Ort der Erstaufstellung weiterer Bundeswehreinheiten.

1960 wurde die vertragliche Übernahme von Unterkunftsgebäuden und Großküchen im Lager Normandie für die dauernde Nutzung durch die Bundeswehr und eine Betreuung durch die eigene Standortverwaltung festgeschrieben. Im April 1962 wurden die ersten Schießbahnen speziell für die Bundeswehr ausgebaut und bald darauf auch mit beweglichen Zielanlagen ausgestattet. Es folgten weitere Personalaufstockungen. Überschattet wurde das erfolgreiche Wirken des Verbindungskommandos 1969 von einem tragischen Schießunfall, bei dem der Schießbahnarbeiter Hans Heindl ums Leben kam.

1978 zog das Kommando mit seinen Diensträumen in das Gebäude 500 um. Seit Februar 1995 ist das Quartier wieder dort, wo alles seinen Anfang genommen hatte: Im alten Standortverwaltungsgebäude 449.

Build-up with personally-owned tools

The first civilian employees of the command partly built up the target machine shop with their personally-owned tools which they had brought from home. The first two years (1958 and 1959) of training activities were dominated by changing German Army and border police units. Additionally, other German Army units were initially deployed to Grafenwoehr.

In 1960, the German Army signed the contract for the permanent use of barracks buildings and kitchens at Camp Normandy and their administration by an independent German Army installation command. In April 1962, the first ranges were built especially for the German Army and soon thereafter equipped with moving targets. Several personnel increases followed. The successful work of the liaison command was overshadowed by a tragic shooting accident in 1969 which killed range worker Hans Heindl.

In 1978, the command moved its offices into building 500. Since February 1995, the command has been located again where everything once started: In building 449, the command's former administration building.

Soldaten und zivile Mitarbeiter im März 2014
Soldiers and civilian employees in March 2014

Der DMV im April 2012 mit den neuen Kontrollfahrzeugen Widder
The DMV team in April 2012 with the new Widder range control vehicles

Suchen und Räumen von Blindgängern und Munitionsschrott
Searching and removing unexploded ordnance

Überwachung einer Blindgängersprengung aus sicherer Distanz
Observing the detonation of unexploded ordnance from a safe distance

Strukturelle Veränderungen

1993 erreichte das Verbindungskommando die Hiobsbotschaft von der geplanten Auflösung. Nur durch einen politischen Kraftakt gelang der Erhalt der Bundeswehr in Grafenwöhr, wenn auch mit deutlich reduzierter Personalstärke. Durch die Neuregelung der Abkommen zum NATO-Truppenstatut wurde im Herbst 1997 durch die Einrichtung der Dienststelle des "Deutschen Militärischen Vertreters" (DMV), das bisherige Verbindungs- und Truppenübungsplatzkommando umbenannt und umgegliedert.

DMV Truppenübungsplatzkommandantur Grafenwöhr

Seit Januar 2015 gehört die Bundeswehr in Grafenwöhr zum „Bereich Truppenübungsplatzkommandantur Süd" und verlor somit ihre Selbständigkeit. Dem Bereich Süd unterliegen die bayerischen Übungsplätze Wildflecken und Hammelburg sowie Heuberg in Baden-Württemberg und Baumholder in Rheinland-Pfalz. Die Bezeichnung der Dienststelle lautet nun „DMV Truppenübungsplatzkommandantur Grafenwöhr".

In der Kommandantur Grafenwöhr verrichten sechs zivile Mitarbeiter und 24 Soldaten, davon 11 Feuerwerker, ihren Dienst. Sie stellen in der neuen Struktur auch künftig einen uneingeschränkten Service für die übende Bundeswehrtruppe sicher.

Structural changes

In 1993, the liaison command was notified of its disbandment. Thanks to a significant political intervention, the German Army's presence in Grafenwoehr with a severely reduced amount of troops was achieved. The revision of the NATO Status of Forces Agreement in the fall of 1997 led to a reorganization of the German Army and the establishment of the Office of the German Military Representative (DMV) which replaced the former liaison and training command.

DMV German Army Commander's Office

Since January 2015, Grafenwoehr's German Army unit belongs to "Major Training Area Headquarters, SOUTH," losing its independence. The headquarters is responsible for the Bavarian training areas in Wildflecken and Hammelburg, Heuberg in Baden-Württemberg and Baumholder in Rhineland-Palatinate. The new name of the unit is "DMV German Army Commander's Office Grafenwoehr."

The Grafenwoehr unit is comprised of six civilian employees and 24 soldiers, including 11 explosive ordnance specialists. They continue to provide unrestricted service to the training German Army units within the new structure.

Schießbahnkontrolle - *Range Control*

Planen - Schießen - Überwachen   Planing - Shooting - Controlling

Einplanung und Beratung der Truppe im Innendienst
Scheduling and advising troops in the scheduling office

Dienst im Kontrollraum bei Range Control
On-duty at the range control office

Leopard und Tiger in Deckung auf der Schießbahn 301 - *Leopard and Tiger taking cover on Range 301*

Spezialkräfte beim Sturmangriff mit dem Schlauchboot
Special Forces during an assault from a rubber boat

Scheibenfertigung
Target production

Das Zielbaupersonal stellt Hilfsziele im Einschussgebiet auf.
Range support personnel put up targets in the impact area.

Neubau des Scheibenhofs

In den 1980er Jahren ging der Neubau des Scheibenhofs in Planung. Die modernen und großzügig errichteten Gebäude wurden in den Jahren 1983 bis 1987 übergeben. Vertraglich wurde festgelegt, dass das Zielbaupersonal des Kommandos außerhalb der Bundeswehrprioritäten auch US-Truppen und Soldaten anderer Nationen auf fest zugeteilten Bahnen betreut.

Bundeswehr Service Center

Eng verknüpft mit der Geschichte des Verbindungskommandos und der jetzigen Kommandantur, ist die Entwicklung der einst selbständigen Standortverwaltung Grafenwöhr. Sie entwickelte sich aus der 1956 eröffneten Verwaltungsstelle. Seit 1995 gehört die im Personalumfang reduzierte Außenstelle der Standortverwaltung Amberg an. Sie trägt heute den Namen „Bundeswehrdienstleistungszentrum Amberg - Servicecenter Grafenwöhr".
Zivile Mitarbeiter gewährleisten die Liegenschaftsverwaltung und den Küchenbetrieb, Gebäude- und Materialerhaltung, die Geländebetreuung sowie den Betrieb eines Geräte-, Verpflegungs- und Wäschelagers.
2007 wurden mit der Einführung eines „Optimierten Betriebsmodells" Bereiche der Kommandantur und des Standortservice zusammengefasst. Fast alle zivilen Mitarbeiter (derzeit 100 Mann) und deren Aufgabengebiete mit den Werkstätten und der Scheibenfertigung einschließlich des Zielbaus und der Fahrbereitschaft unterstehen nun der zivilen Verwaltung. Als neue Aufgabe kam die Fertigung von Ziel- und Schießscheiben für alle Standort-Schießanlagen im süddeutschen Raum dazu.

Construction of the new target machine shop

Construction of the new target machine shop began in the 1980s. The large, modern buildings were opened between 1983 and 1987. A contract was signed which stipulates that German range personnel will also support U.S. troops and soldiers from other nations on ranges that are permanently assigned to the German Army during non-German Army training priority times.

German Army service center

The development of the former installation management command Grafenwoehr is closely related to the history of the training command. It was developed out of the administration office that was opened in 1956. In 1995, its personnel strength was reduced and it was attached to the installation command in Amberg. Today it is called "German Army Service Center Amberg – Installation Service center Grafenwoehr."
Civilian employees perform the following tasks: Property administration, food operations, building maintenance, supply services, infrastructure maintenance and the operation of an equipment, food and linen supply center.
In 2007 runs the implementation of the "Optimized Operations Plan." Operational areas of the training command and the installation service branch were combined. Nearly all civilian employees (currently 100) and their operational areas with repair shops, drivers, target machine shop and range support operations now belong to the civilian administration. Constructing targets for all garrison ranges in southern Germany is one of the new tasks.

Die Mitarbeiter des Service Center Grafenwöhr 2010
The employees of Service Center Grafenwoehr in 2010

Oberstleutnant Anton Kussinger (rechts) ist der 16. Dienststellenleiter der Bundeswehr in Grafenwöhr. Der Kommandowechsel im August 2015 wurde auch zum Treffen mit seinen Vorgängern: (von links) die ehemaligen Oberstleutnante Ludwig Widmann, Gerhard Mühln, Otto Glaser, Dieter Kargl und Hans Joachim Gehrlein.

Lt. Col. Anton Kussinger (right) is the 16th commander of the German Army unit in Grafenwoehr. The change of command in August 2015 was also a meeting of his predeccessors: Former Lt. Cols. Ludwig Widmann, Gerhard Mühln, Otto Glaser, Dieter Kargl and Hans Joachim Gehrlein (from left).

Leiter der Bundeswehrdienststellen und Kommandanten (ab 1986)
Directors and commanders of the local German Army office and unit (from 1986)

Oberstleutnant Ludwig Widmann	April 1986 - September 1993
Oberstleutnant Gerhard Mühln	Oktober 1993 - Februar 1996
Oberstleutnant Otto Glaser	März 1996 - Dezember 2002
Oberstleutnant Franz Lienert	Dezember 2002 - März 2006
Oberstleutnant Dieter Kargl	März 2006 - Juli 2012
Oberstleutnant Hans Joachim Gehrlein	Juli 2012 - August 2015
Oberstleutnant Anton Kussinger	seit August 2015

Die Leiter der Standortverwaltung Grafenwöhr (ab 1984)
Directors of the local German Army office (from 1984)

Regierungsamtsrat Gerhard Werzinger	Dezember 1984 - Januar 1989
Regierungsamtsrat Horst Pfeffer	Februar 1989 - Dezember 1994

Leiter der Außenstelle, Service Center
Chiefs of the branch office, Service Center

Regierungsamtmann Otto Vilsmeier	Januar 1995 - April 1997
Regierungsoberinspektor Reinhard Mulzer	Mai 1997 - August 2000
Regierungsamtmann Hans Konheiser	Oktober 2000 - Juli 2003
Regierungsamtmann Karl-Heinz Holzer	August 2003 - April 2007
Regierungsamtsrat Heinz Seitz	seit April 2008

Zitat aus einer Grußkarte eines Soldaten aus früheren Zeiten: „Liebe Eltern! Bin gut in diesem Staub- und Sandnest angekommen, eine öde und traurige Gegend, wie man sie nicht so leicht wiedersieht ...".

Aus diesen Anfängen hat sich der modernste Übungsplatz in Europa entwickelt, der viele Arbeitsplätze und hervorragende Möglichkeiten für die Bundeswehr zur Ausbildung und zur Zusammenarbeit mit anderen Nationen bietet.

Ich wünsche den Soldaten aller Nationalitäten eine unfallfreie Zeit während ihres Aufenthaltes in Grafenwöhr.

Anton Kussinger, Oberstleutnant und Kommandant seit August 2015

Quote from a soldier's postcard of the past: „Dear parents! Have arrived safely in this dusty and sandy neck of the woods, a barren and sad area that you don't see very often ..."
These were the beginnings of Europe's most modern training area which provides many jobs and offers the German Armed Forces excellent training opportunities and possibilities to cooperate with other nations.
I wish the soldiers of all nations an accident-free time during their stay in Grafenwoehr.

LTC Anton Kussinger, German Military Representative and Commander since August 2015

Partnerschaft mit Soldaten aus Österreich:
Partnership with Soldiers from Austria:
Vizeleutnant Karl Ecklberger, die Oberstleutnante Dieter Kargl und Franz Lienert; Oberst Elmar Rosenauer (von links)

Regelmäßiger Austausch mit der Reservisten Kameradschaft Grafenwöhr
Regular partnership activities with German Army Reserve associations

Deutsch-Amerikanische Weiterbildung an der ehemaligen Grenze zur DDR in Mödlareuth, Klein-Berlin genannt
German-American training at the former GDR border in Mödlareuth, also known as Little Berlin

Hunderte von Gästen werfen jedes Jahr bei Besucherrundfahrten einen Blick hinter die Kulissen. Die Bundeswehr arbeiten dabei eng mit der US-Armee zusammen.
Every year, hundreds of guests catch a glimpse "behind the scenes" during visitors' and range tours. The German Army work closely with the U.S. Army to accomplish that.

Die Heilige Barbara ist die Schutzpatronin der Feuerwerker und Artilleristen. Mit amerikanischen Soldaten, Kameraden aus Österreich und zivilen Gästen wird am Barbara-Marterl der Gedenktag gefeiert.
Saint Barbara, the patron saint of EOD officers and artillerymen. The saint's day is celebrated at the Barbara wayside cross with American soldiers, comrades from Austria and civilian guests.

Partnerschaft und Zusammenarbeit

In Zusammenarbeit mit der US-Kommandantur, Range Control, Range Operations und dem Service Center schafft die Kommandantur die optimalen Voraussetzungen für einen reibungslosen Schieß- und Übungsbetrieb. Vor allem die Einplanung sowie die Überwachung der Schießsicherheit auf den Einrichtungen des Platzes zählt zu den Hauptaufgaben der Kommandantur. Munitionsfachkundige nehmen als Feuerwerker Aufgaben im Schießsicherheitsbereich wahr. Dazu gehört auch das Suchen und Räumen von Blindgängern auf den Schießbahnen.

Die Bundeswehr leistet darüber hinaus einen wesentlichen Beitrag zur Darstellung des Truppenübungsplatzes in der Öffentlichkeit. Bei Besucherführungen und Rundfahrten werfen jedes Jahr hunderte von Gästen einen Blick hinter die Kulissen des Truppenübungsplatzes. Die Feuerwerker arbeiten dabei eng mit der US-Armee Garnison Grafenwöhr zusammen. Es bestehen Patenschaften mit der Reservistenkameradschaft, dem Soldaten-, Reservisten- und Kameradschaftsbund Grafenwöhr und der 702. Kampfmittelbeseitigungskompanie. Gute Kontakte bestehen zum Militärkommando Oberösterreich.

Partnership and cooperation

In cooperation with the U.S. garrison command, range control, range operations and the service center, the training command provides the optimal preconditions for smooth shooting and training operations. Range scheduling and supervising range safety on the training area's facilities are the main operational tasks of the DMV office. Ammunition specialists and explosive ordnance officers work in range safety to include the removal and destruction of unexploded ordnance on the ranges.

The German Army also significantly contributes to the public image of the training area. Every year, hundreds of guests catch a glimpse "behind the scenes" during visitors' and range tours. The EOD officers work closely with the U.S. Army Garrison Grafenwoehr to accomplish that. A partnership has been established between the Soldiers, Reservists and Comradeship Association Grafenwoehr and the U.S. Army's 702nd Explosive Ordnance Disposal company. Good contacts also exist with Upper Austrian Military Command.

Deutsch-Amerikanisches Vergleichsschießen
German-American shooting competition

Übergabe der erworbenen Schießauszeichnungen
Presentation of the shooting awards

Militär und Politik
Military and Politics

Seit seiner Gründung zu Zeiten der königlich bayerischen Armee bis in die heutigen Tage, hat der Übungsplatz mit seiner internationalen Truppenbelegung eine herausragende Bedeutung. Immer wieder zieht er prominente Besucher an.

Since its foundation during the times of the Royal Bavarian Army until today, the training area has been of great importance because of the allocation of international troops. Time and again it attracts distinguished visitors.

Der scheidende Bayerische Ministerpräsident Dr. Edmund Stoiber lud im Juli 2007 Soldaten aus ganz Bayern zum Empfang in das Physical Fitness Center ein. Eine polierte Messingkartusche sollte das Geschenk der Grafenwöhrer Bundeswehrsoldaten sein.

In July 2007, outgoing Bavarian Minister President Dr. Edmund Stoiber invited soldiers from all over Bavaria to a reception at the Physical Fitness Center. A polished brass cartridge was supposed to be the gift from the German Army soldiers stationed in Grafenwoehr.

Hoch zu Roß inspizierte Seine Königliche Hoheit Prinz Leopold von Bayern im Juni 1912 die bayerischen Soldaten.

On horseback, His Royal Highness Prince Leopold of Bavaria inspected Bavarian soldiers in June 1912.

1984: US-Verteidigungsminister Caspar Weinberger (von rechts) mit dem damaligen Bundeskanzler Helmut Kohl und Verteidigungsminister Manfred Wörner auf dem Grafenwöhr Army Airfield.

1984: U.S. Secretary of Defense Caspar Weinberger (from right) with former German Chancellor Helmut Kohl and German Secretary of Defense Manfred Wörner on Grafenwoehr Army Airfield.

Am Steuer eines Lear Jet landete Ministerpräsident Franz Josef Strauß in den 1980er Jahren auf dem Grafenwöhr Army Airfield. 1958 war er als Bundesverteidigungsminister bei einem Truppenbesuch auf dem Platz.

In 1980, Bavarian Minister President Franz Josef Strauß landed on Grafenwoehr Army Airfield at the helm of a Lear Jet. In 1958, during his tenure as German Secretary of Defense, he visited the troops on the training area.

1926 besuchte der damalige Reichspräsident Paul von Hindenburg den Truppenübungsplatz Grafenwöhr.

in 1926, Paul von Hindenburg, former president of the German Reich, visited Grafenwoehr Training Area.

Informationen für den US-Botschafter in Deutschland, John B. Emerson, im November 2013.

Briefing John B. Emerson, U.S. ambassador to Germany, in November 2013.

US-Verteidigungsminister Ashton Carter besuchte das JMTC im September 2015.

In September 2015, U.S. Secretary of Defense Ashton Carter visited JMTC.

Truppenbesuch beim **DMV**: Im September 2009 kam der Bundesminister der Verteidigung Dr. Franz-Josef Jung (November 2005 – Oktober 2009)

Troop visit with DMV: In September 2009, German Secretary of Defense Dr. Franz-Josef Jung (November 2005 – October 2009) visited the DMV soldiers

Der ehemalige Staatssekretär im Bundesministerium der Verteidigung Christian Schmidt zusammen mit dem Bundestagsabgeordneten Albert Rupprecht zu Besuch bei Range Control im September 2006

Christian Schmidt, former State Secretary in the German Federal Ministry of Defense and Federal Parliamentarian Albert Rupprecht visit Range Control in September 2006

Besuch in Grafenwöhr im August 2010: Bundesverteidigungsminister Karl-Theodor zu Guttenberg (Oktober 2009 – März 2011) und der amerikanische Botschafter in Deutschland, Philip D. Murphy, im Informationsaustausch mit deutschen und amerikanischen Soldaten.

Visit to Grafenwoehr in August 2010: German Secretary of Defense Karl-Theodor zu Guttenberg (Oct. 2009 – March 2010) and the American Ambassador to Germany, Philip D. Murphy, exchange information with German and American soldiers.

Ein Buch für den Minister - *A book for the Secretary of Defense*

Gemeinsames Multinationales Ausbildungskommando der 7. US-Armee

Das Gemeinsame Multinationale Ausbildungskommando der 7. US-Armee (JMTC) ist das größte Ausbildungskommando außerhalb der Vereinigten Staaten. Seinen Hauptsitz hat es in Grafenwöhr, den Dienst nahm es am 1. Juli 1976 auf.

Die zentrale Aufgabe des Kommandos ist die Ausbildung der Soldaten für Operationen und Einsätze im Verbund mit den anderen Teilstreitkräften sowie mit anderen NATO- und Partnernationen. Dafür stellt JMTC moderne und realistische Trainingbedingungen und Einrichtungen zur Verfügung. Regelmässige Ausbildung gemeinsam mit multinationalen Partnern schafft Vertrauen, entwickelt Kompatibilität und legt den Grundstein für erfolgreiche Koalitionen bei zukünftigen Einsätzen.

7th Army Joint Multinational Training Command

The 7th Army's Joint Multinational Training Command (JMTC) is the largest training command outside the continental United States. It is headquartered in Grafenwoehr and was commissioned on July 1, 1976.

The command's central mission is to train soldiers for operations and contingencies in a joint and multinational environment with other NATO- and partner nations. JMTC provides modern and realistic training conditions and facilities to accomplish that. Routinely training with multinational partners builds trust, develops interoperability and sets the conditions for creating strong military coalitions for future missions.

Regenbogen vom JMTC Hauptquartier bis zum alten Hauptquartiersgebäude 621
Rainbow from the JMTC headquarters building to the old headquarter building 621

Die Abteilungen des Joint Multinational Training Command
The Directorates of Joint Multinational Training Command

Truppenübungsplatz Grafenwöhr
Grafenwoehr Training Area

Gemeinsames Multinationales Simulationszentrum
Joint Multinational Simulation Center Simulation

Gemeinsames Multinationales Zentrum zur Einsatzvorbereitung
Joint Multinational Readiness Center

Waffenausbildungszentrum
Combined Arms Training Center

International Zentrum für die Ausbildung von Spezialkräften
Special Training Centre Special Forces

Unteroffiziersschule des Heeres
Noncommissioned Officers Academy

Übungsunterstützungszentrum - Europa
Training Support Activity Europe

Kommandeure des JMTC (vormals 7th ATC)
JMTC Commanders (formerly 7th ATC)

Brigadegeneral John H. Tilelli
Mai 1988 - Juli 1990

*Brigadier General John H. Tilelli
May 1988 to July 1990*

Brigadegeneral Richard E. Davis
Juli 1990 - Oktober 1991

*Brigadier General Richard E. Davis
July 1990 to October 1991*

Brigadegeneral Montgomery C. Meigs
Oktober 1991 - Mai 1993

*Brigadier General Montgomery C. Meigs
October 1991 to May 1993*

Brigadegeneral Charles H. Baumann
Mai 1993 - Juni 1995

*Brigadier General Charles H. Baumann
May 1993 to June 1995*

Generalmajor George H. Harmeyer
Juni 1995 - Oktober 1996

*Major General George H. Harmeyer
June 1995 to October 1996*

Brigadegeneral John T.D. Casey
Oktober 1996 - August 1999

*Brigadier General John T.D. Casey
October 1996 to August 1999*

Brigadegeneral Bantz J. Craddock
August 1999 - September 2000

*Brigadier General Bantz J. Craddock
August 1999 to September 2000*

Brigadegeneral Guy C. Swan III
September 2000 - August 2002

*Brigadier General Guy C. Swan III
September 2000 to August 2002*

Brigadegeneral Robert M. Williams
November 2002 - September 2004

*Brigadier General Robert M. Williams
November 2002 to September 2004*

Brigadegeneral Mark P. Hertling
September 2004 - August 2005

*Brigadier General Mark P. Hertling
September 2004 to August 2005*

Brigadegeneral David G. Perkins
August 2005 - April 2007

*Brigadier General David G. Perkins
August 2005 to April 2007*

Brigadegeneral David P. Hogg
April 2007 - Mai 2009

*Brigadier General David P. Hogg
April 2007 to May 2009*

Brigadegeneral Steven L. Salazar
Mai 2009 - Juli 2011

*Brigadier General Steven L. Salazar
May 2009 to July 2011*

Oberst Bryan L. Rudacille
Juli 2011 - Juni 2013

*Colonel Bryan L. Rudacille
July 2011 - June 2013*

Brigadegeneral Walter E. Piatt,
Juni 2013 - Juli 2014

*Brigadier General Walter E. Piatt,
June 2013 - July 2014*

Es ist eine Ehre für mich, ein Mitglied dieser Gemeinde und der Kommandeur des 7th Army Joint Multinational Training Command sein zu dürfen!

Der Erfolg dieses Kommandos und des Truppenübungsplatzes Grafenwöhr beruht auf der Unterstützung der ihn umgebenden Gemeinschaft. Wir geniessen die Freundschaft der Gemeinden rund um die Truppenübungsplätze Grafenwöhr und Hohenfels.

Wir begreifen uns heute als wahrhaftigen Teil dieser freundlichen Gemeinden, die unsere Soldaten und ihre Familien willkommen heißen, von denen die meisten in den umliegenden Gemeinden in diesem wunderschönen Teil Bayerns wohnen.

Der Truppenübungsplatz Grafenwöhr ist eines der besten Trainingszentren in Europa. Seit seiner Gründung 1910 setzt der Truppenübungsplatz die Standards. Und durch Innovation, Technologie und die Anstrengungen derer, die hier leben und arbeiten, verbessert der Übungsplatz ständig sein Ausbildungspotential.

Brigadegeneral Christopher G.Cavoli
Brigadier General Christopher G.Cavoli

Der Truppenübungsplatz Grafenwöhr ist von entscheidender Bedeutung für die Zukunft unserer Streitkräfte in Europa. Sein zentraler Standort macht ihn zum idealen Trainingsort für die Soldaten vieler Nationen. Es liegt in unserer Verantwortung sicher zu stellen, dass wir die qualitativ hochwertigste Ausbildung anbieten können. Die Vergangenheit hat uns gelehrt, dass die Zukunft ungewiss ist, darum trainieren wir, um einsatzbereit zu sein.

Dieses Buch wird Sie lehren, dass es bei diesem Truppenübungsplatz um mehr geht, als um Streitkräfte. Die Geschichte dieses Truppenübungsplatzes ist auch eine, die sich um Menschen und Familien, um das Land und die Ortschaften, die Ruinen und um das Gedeihen und den Erhalt der Natur dreht.

Wenn Sie dieses Buch lesen, denken Sie daran, dass in den vergangenen hundert Jahren abertausend Soldaten hier gelebt haben und ausgebildet wurden. Jeder dieser Soldaten und viele Familienangehörige sind mit schönen Erinnerungen an Bayern und Grafenwöhr von hier weggegangen. „Bereit durch Training!"

Christopher G. Cavoli, Brigadegeneral, US-Armee
Kommandeur, 7th Army Joint Multinational Training Command, seit Juli 2014

Die oben geäußerte Meinung ist meine eigene und stellt nicht die offizielle Politik oder Auffassung der US-Armee, des US-Verteidigungsministeriums oder der US-Regierung dar.

I am honored to be a member of this community and the commander of the 7th Army Joint Multinational Training Command!

The success of this command, and the Grafenwoehr Training Area lies in the support given by the community around it. We have enjoyed a great friendship with the communities that surround the Grafenwoehr and Hohenfels Training Areas.

Today, we truly feel part of this friendly community, which welcomes our soldiers and their families, many of which live in the surroundings of this beautiful part of Bavaria.

Grafenwoehr Training Area remains one of the premier training centers in Europe. Since its inauguration in 1910, GTA has stayed at the forefront of military training. GTA continues to improve its capabilities through innovation, technology and the efforts of those who live and work here.

The Grafenwoehr Training Area is vital to the future of our armies in Europe. Its central location makes it ideal for soldiers of many nations to train here. It is our responsibility to ensure that we provide the highest quality of training possible. The past has taught us that the future is uncertain, so we train to remain ready.

In this book, you will learn that this training area is not just about militaries. The history of this training area is one of people and families, land and villages, ruins and prosperity and preservation of nature.

As you read this book, remember that over the last 100 years, thousands and thousands of soldiers have lived and trained here. Each of those Soldiers, and many family members left with warm memories of Bavaria and Grafenwoehr. "Ready thru Training!"

Christopher G. Cavoli, Brigadier General, U.S. Army
Commander, 7th Army Joint Multinational Training Command, since July 2014

The views expressed above are my own and do not reflect the official position of the U.S. Army, Department of Defense, or the U.S. Government.

Unteroffiziersschule der 7. US-ARMEE
Pattons Schreibtisch
7TH ARMY NCO ACADEMY
Patton´s Desk

Die NCO-Akademie der 7. US-Armee (Noncommissioned Officer Academy/Unteroffiziersschule) ist eine der ältesten Einrichtungen der US-Armee dieser Art und die einzige dieser Größe außerhalb der Vereinigten Staaten. 1949 wurde die Schule in München gegründet und trägt deshalb das Münchner Kindl in ihrem Wappen. 1958 zog die NCO-Akademie in die Flint Barracks nach Bad Tölz, 1990 kam die Ausbildungseinrichtung nach Grafenwöhr. Im Zuge des EB-G Bauprogramms fand die Schule im umgebauten Camp Normandy ihren Platz.

Das Motto der Schule ist „Leaders training Leaders". Die Akademie hält pro Jahr neun Lehrgänge ab, an denen rund 300 Soldaten teilnehmen. Ein Lehrgang dauert 22 Tage. In Grafenwöhr werden nicht nur angehende US-Unteroffiziere ausgebildet, sondern auch Soldaten von US-Bündnispartnern aus Europa und Afrika. Die NCO-Akademie unterhält eine offizielle Partnerschaft mit der Unteroffiziersschule des Heeres in Delitzsch.

The 7th Army NCO Academy is one of the oldest schools of its kind in the U.S. Army and the only one of its size outside the United States. The school was founded in Munich in 1949 and therefore carries the "Münchner Kindl", the figure in the coat of arms of the city of Munich, in its crest. In 1958, the NCO Academy moved to Flint Kaserne in Bad Tölz and to Grafenwoehr in 1990. Here, the school was relocated to Camp Normandy as a result of the EB-G construction program.

The school motto is "Leaders training Leaders." Every year, the academy offers nine course cycles, training about 300 soldiers. A course lasts 22 days. The academy provides training for U.S. noncommissioned officers as well as soldiers from U.S. allies in Europe and Africa. The NCO Academy enjoys an official partnership with the German Army's NCO Academy in Delitzsch.

Soldaten bei der Ausbildung in der NCO-Akademie
Soldiers during their training at the NCO Academy

Die NCO-Akademie im Camp Normandy
The NCO Academy at Camp Normandy

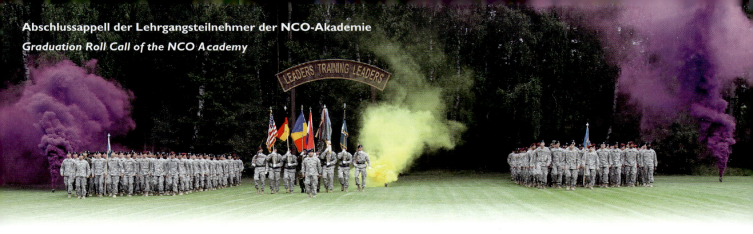

Abschlussappell der Lehrgangsteilnehmer der NCO-Akademie
Graduation Roll Call of the NCO Academy

Rommel und Patton

Im Stabsgebäude der NCO-Akademie im Camp Normandy ist auch der Schreibtisch des legendären US-Generals George S. Patton zu finden. Der Schreibtisch, Stuhl und der Teppich stammen aus dem Schloss La Rochefoucauld in Frankreich. An ihm saß einst der bekannte Generalfeldmarschall der Deutschen Wehrmacht, Erwin Rommel. Er ging unter anderem als „Wüstenfuchs" in die Militärgeschichte ein. Der Schreibtisch wurde von General Patton annektiert und weitergenutzt. Er stand zuletzt in Pattons Hauptquartier in Bad Tölz. Später fand der Tisch Verwendung bei den Kommandeuren der NCO-Akademie.

Rommel and Patton

The desk of the legendary U.S. General George S. Patton can be seen in the headquarters' building of the NCO Academy at Camp Normandy. Desk, chair and carpet came from La Rochefoucauld palace in France. Once the famous general field marshal of the German Wehrmacht, Erwin Rommel, also known in military history as the "Desert Fox," sat at this desk. The desk was annexed and used by General Patton and was previously located in Patton's headquarters in Bad Tölz. Later, the desk was used by the commanders of the NCO Academy.

Der Schreibtisch an dem einst Wüstenfuchs Erwin Rommel und dann US-General George S. Patton saß.
The desk that was once used by "Desert Fox" Erwin Rommel and then by U.S. General George S. Patton.

Gefechtssituationen im Gruppentrainer
Battlefield scenarios in the group trainer

JMSC Simulation Center

Joint Multinational Simulation Center (JMSC)

Bereits seit Jahren werden für die militärische Ausbildung Simulatoranlagen eingesetzt, um Natur und Ressourcen zu schonen. Neue Maßstäbe setzt die jüngste Modifizierung des Joint Multinational Simulation Center (JMSC). Über 1000 Computer-Arbeitsplätze stehen bereit, um das Arbeiten in einer Operationszentrale, das Zusammenwirken einzelner Zellen und Verbände, die logistische Versorgung im Einsatz sowie das Arbeiten mit Netzwerken und Kommunikationssystemen zu üben. Große Übungen mit NATO-Soldaten und Teilnehmern weiterer Nationen finden dazu in Grafenwöhr statt.

Training Support Activity, Europe (TSAE)

Im TSAE stellen zum Teil Vertragsfirmen der US-Armee in großen Containern weitere Simulator-Übungsanlagen bereit, an denen sehr realitätsnah der Umgang mit Waffen und Fahrzeugen geübt werden kann. Verschiedene Situationen auf dem Gefechtsfeld, der Überschlag von Fahrzeugen oder auch die Erste Hilfe an Kameraden können unter anderem trainiert werden. 120 verschiedene Szenarien in Wald, Wüste oder Ortschaften bietet ein Gruppentrainer. Fahrzeuge vom Schützenpanzer Bradley, Kampfpanzer Abrams über den Hummer bis zum Kampfmittelbeseitigungsfahrzeug Buffalo können in mit Beamern projektierten Landschaften fahren und ihre Waffen und Systeme anwenden.

Joint Multinational Simulation Center (JMSC)

Simulators have been used for military training for many years to protect nature and natural resources. The latest modification of the Joint Multinational Simulation Center (JMSC) sets new standards. More than 1,000 computers are available to train working in a headquarters' control room, conducting joint operations between individual cells and formations, providing logistical support during military operations, and working with networks and communication systems. Large exercises with NATO soldiers and participants from other nations are held in Grafenwoehr.

Training Support Activity, Europe (TSAE)

At TSAE, the U.S. Army and civilian contractors of the U.S. Army provide additional training simulators in large containers where the use of weapons and vehicles can be trained in a very realistic way. Different scenarios on the battlefield, the rollover of vehicles, or first aid for a comrade and other scenarios can be trained there. A group trainer provides 120 different scenarios in a forest, desert, or urban setting. Vehicles ranging from the Bradley fighting vehicle, Abrams tank, Humvee to the Buffalo can be driven and use their weapons and systems in beamer-projected landscapes.

After Action Review im Container
After Action Review in the container

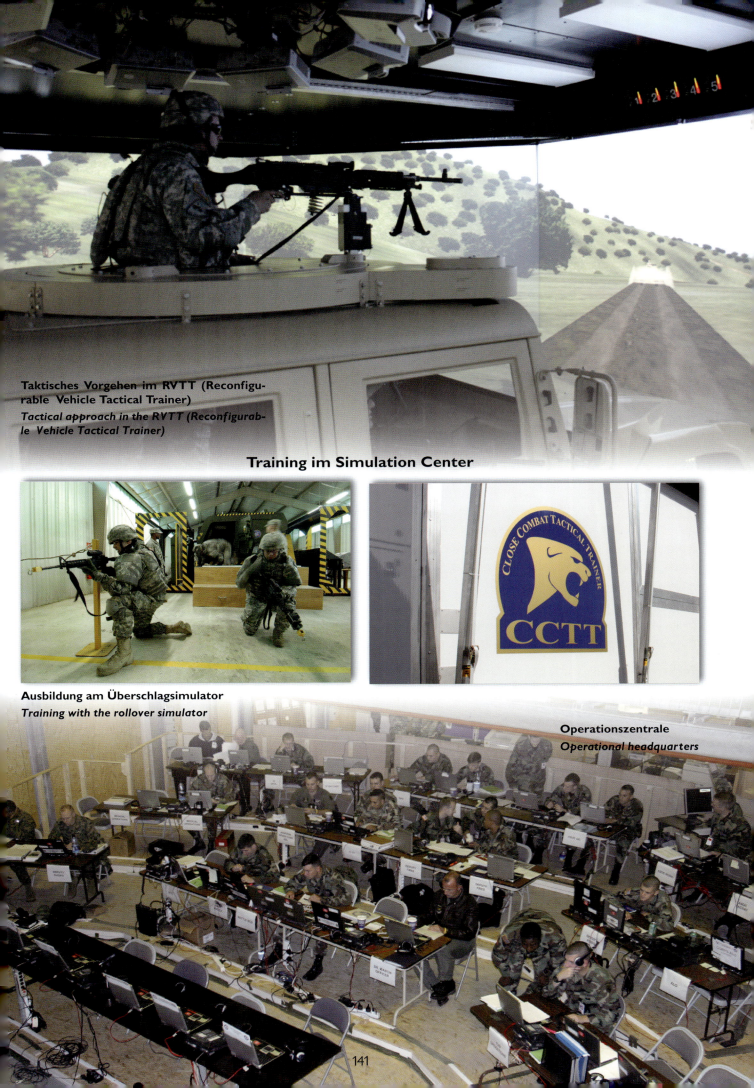

Taktisches Vorgehen im RVTT (Reconfigurable Vehicle Tactical Trainer)
Tactical approach in the RVTT (Reconfigurable Vehicle Tactical Trainer)

Training im Simulation Center

Ausbildung am Überschlagsimulator
Training with the rollover simulator

Operationszentrale
Operational headquarters

GTA Range Operations

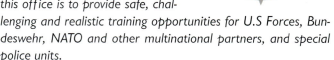

GTA Range Operations mit dem „Firing Desk" ist das Herzstück beim Betrieb des Truppenübungsplatzes. Sichere, anspruchsvolle und realistische Voraussetzungen beim Schieß- und Übungsbetrieb für die US-Streitkräfte, die Bundeswehr, die Partner in der NATO und der multinationalen Truppen sowie für spezielle Polizeieinheiten zu schaffen, dies ist die Aufgabe von GTA Range Operations."

Rund 200 Mitarbeiter von Range-Support stellen den technischen Betrieb auf den über 40 Schießbahnen und den Übungseinrichtungen sicher. In einer Schreinerei und Lackiererei werden die Holzzielscheiben und weiteren Ausstattungen für die Bahnen gefertigt. Eine Elektronikabteilung wartet die 4700 Scheiben-Lifter die auf den Schießbahnen eingebaut sind. Deutsches Zivilpersonal arbeitet auf den Rangen im Schichtdienst und bietet der übenden Truppe den optimalen Service.

Chef von Range-Operations ist ein Oberstleutnant der US-Armee. Er hat einen zivilen Stellvertreter und einen Operationschef, Offiziere, Sergeants sowie deutsche und amerikanische zivile Mitarbeiter. Insgesamt 40 Personen bilden den Stab von Range Operations.

In Verteilerkonferenzen werden die Schießbahnen und Übungseinrichtungen vergeben. Abteilungen für die verschiedenen Waffengattungen beraten die Truppe und legen die Gefahrenbereiche fest. Täglich wird von der Abteilung Range Safety das Range Bulletin, der Schießbefehl, herausgegeben und regelt den Betrieb.

GTA Range Operations with its firing desk is the core of the training area where all operations are coordinated. The purpose of this office is to provide safe, challenging and realistic training opportunities for U.S Forces, Bundeswehr, NATO and other multinational partners, and special police units.

About 200 employees in the Range Support Section support all technical operations on more than 40 ranges and training facilities. The wooden targets and other range equipment are produced in the target machine shop and paint shop. The electronic department maintains 4,700 target machines located on the ranges. German civilian employees work in shifts on the ranges and provide optimal service to units training on GTA.

Range Operations is headed by a U.S. Army lieutenant colonel. He has a civilian deputy, an operations chief and a staff of about 40 officers, sergeants and U.S. and German civilian employees. Training on the ranges and training facilities is assigned to troops in special conferences. Departments for the various types of weapons systems advice the troops and determine danger zones. The range bulletin is published daily by range safety and regulates range operations. The firing desk is responsible for safety and security on ranges and controls live fire and all other types of training. It is continuously manned by U.S range control personnel.

Ziviles und militärisches Personal bilden den Stab von Range Operations, hier zusammen mit den Mitarbeitern von JMTC Safety
The staff of Range Operations consists of civilian and military personnel, seen here together with the employees of JMTC Safety

Scheibenfertigung - *Target production*

Als Sicherheitsorgan steuert der „Firing Desk" den Schieß- und Übungsbetrieb. Er ist ständig mit US-Range-Control Soldaten besetzt. Bei Nutzung durch Bundeswehreinheiten setzt der DMV für seinen Kontrollraum Sicherheitspersonal ein. Streifen überprüfen den sicheren Ablauf auf den Schießbahnen und sorgen für die äußere Sicherheit. Bei Bränden, Unfällen und Notsituationen werden Lösch- und Hilfseinsätze über den Firing Desk gesteuert.

Räumlich ist Range Operations die Abteilung JMTC Safety angegliedert. Militärische und zivile Mitarbeiter überwachen die Einhaltung der Arbeitsschutzvorschriften. Sie beraten den Kommandeur von JMTC in Sachen Schießsicherheit und Lagerung von Munition und Explosivstoffen. Sie stellen übergeordnet auch die Schießsicherheit auf dem Übungsplatz und im gesamten Verantwortungsbereich der US-Armee in Europa sicher.

Durch die hohe technische Ausstattung der Schießbahnen und Übungseinrichtungen, die Professionalität des militärischen und zivilen Personals sowie durch die gute Zusammenarbeit mit der Bundeswehr, der US-Armee-Garnison Bavaria und dem Bundesforst steht der Truppenübungsplatz Grafenwöhr an der Spitze aller Übungsplätze in den USA und im Ausland.

Der „Firing Desk", der Kontrollraum, ist die Sicherheitszentrale für den Schieß- und Übungsbetrieb auf dem Platz.
The firing desk serves as the control and safety center for all live-fire and training operations on the training area.

When ranges are used by Bundeswehr units, the German military unit on post mans its firing desk with range safety personnel. Range patrols control and ensure safe and secure operations on ranges and surrounding areas. Fire-fighting and rescue missions are also coordinated by the firing desk in the event of fire, accidents or emergency situations.

The Joint Multinational Training Command safety department is co-located with Range Operations. Military and civilian employees control the compliance with occupational safety regulations and advice the JMTC commander regarding firing safety and storage of ammunition and explosives. They have overall responsibility for firing safety on the training area and in the entire area of responsibility of U.S. Army in Europe.

Grafenwoehr Training Area continues to hold the top position among all training areas in the United States and abroad due to the high-quality of its technical equipment on the ranges and in its training facilities, the professionalism of its military and civilian personnel, and the excellent cooperation with the Bundeswehr, U.S. Army Garrison Bavaria and the Bundesforst.

Zielbau auf den Ranges
Target assembly on the ranges

Panzerabwehrlenkwaffe JAVELINE
Medium Antitank Weapon System

Schießen und Üben
Training

Modernster Platz in Europa

Der Truppenübungsplatz Grafenwöhr ist der modernste Übungsplatz in Europa. Unter der amerikanischen Verwaltung und zu einem kleinen Teil auch von der Bundeswehr wurden die Einrichtungen des Platzes in den vergangenen Jahrzehnten ständig erweitert, ausgebaut und modernisiert. Für das Schießen und Üben der Truppe stehen eine Vielzahl von Ausbildungseinrichtungen und Schießbahnen zur Verfügung. Der Schwerpunkt liegt in der Ausbildung der Kampf- und Kampfunterstützungstruppen. Für Artillerie, Mörser und Raketen sind Feuerstellungen und Feuerstellungsräume mit den zwei großen Hauptzielgebieten vorgesehen. Als Artilleriezielgebiet wird in erster Linie die A-Impact Area genutzt. Sie ist auch Zielraum für Kampfflugzeuge und –hubschrauber bei Luft-Boden-Einsätzen.

Most modern training area in Europe

Grafenwoehr Training Area is the most modern training area in Europe. The American administration, and for a small part also the German Army, have continuously expanded, developed and modernized the training area during the past decades. A variety of training facilities and ranges are available to the troops for shooting and training. Emphasis is put on the training of combat and combat support troops. Artillery positions and assembly areas with two main impact areas are available for the firing of artillery rounds, mortars and rockets. The artillery mainly uses impact area A. It is also the impact area for fighter jets and attack helicopters during surface-to-air missions.

An der Feldhaubitze um 1915
At the field howitzer circa 1915

US-Feldhaubitze im direkten Richten
U.S. field howitzer during direct fire

Sprengung im Zielgebiet
Demolition in the impact area

Artillerie-Geschosse
Artillery projectiles

Geschützdienst an der M 777 Tripple-Seven
Duty at the M 777-Tripple-Seven

Im Schießhaus - *Inside the shoot house*

Drohne
UAV

Ausgefeilte Technik

Sprengplätze, Handgranatenwurfstände und Anlagen für den Orts- und Häuserkampf ergänzen die Anzahl der Schießbahnen für Flachfeuerwaffen. Diese liegt bei rund 40 Einrichtungen, große Ranges können von Kampfpanzern bis zu einem Kaliber von 120 Millimeter genutzt werden. Die Schießbahnen und Einrichtungen wurden im Laufe der Jahre weitgehend auch um das neue Einsatzspektrum zur Konvoi-, Checkpoint- und Häuserkampfausbildung erweitert. Netzstromversorgung, insgesamt über 4600 computergesteuerte Zielanlagen (Fahrzeuge, Personenziele sowie bewegliche Fahrzeug- und Infanterieanlagen), Zielbeheizung für Nachtsicht- und Wärmebildgeräte, Videoüberwachung des Ablaufs, Trefferlageauswertung wie auch Wärmebildgeräte auf den Kontrolltürmen gehören zur technisch ausgefeilten Ausstattung. Bedient und gewartet werden die Anlagen von zivilem Zielbaupersonal. Vertragsfirmen der US-Armee sind für neue Einrichtungen wie Schießhaus oder Häuserkampffelder zuständig, immer mehr hält auch die computerunterstützte Simulation Einzug. Alle Anlagen dienen dazu den Soldaten eine möglichst realistische Ausbildung zu gewährleisten.

Elaborated technique

Demolition areas, hand grenade ranges and MOUT (Military Operations Urban Terrain) sites complete the number of ranges for artillery weapons. There are 40 of those ranges; large ranges can be used by tanks equipped with weapons up to a caliber of 120 millimeters. Over the past years, the ranges and training facilities were expanded to meet the demands of new mission requirements such as convoy, checkpoint- and MOUT training. Electric power supply, more than 4,600 computerized targets (vehicle, personal and moving targets as wells moving vehicle and infantry facilities), heated targets for night vision - and infrared equipment, video control of training activities, strike analysis as well as infrared equipment on the control towers are part of the technically elaborate equipment. The facilities are operated and maintained by civilian range maintenance personnel. U.S. Army contractors are responsible for operating the shoot house and the MOUT sites. Computer-aided simulation exercises are on the rise. All facilities have been developed to provide the soldiers with as realistic a training environment as possible.

Grenadiere mit Schützenpanzer Marder im Einsatz
Tank crew with a Marder tank during deployment

Panzerabwehrlenkflugkörper MILAN
Guided anti-tank missile MILAN

Häuserkampfanlage
MOUT site

Gemeinsames Üben von Bundeswehr und US-Army
Joint training of the German and the U.S. Army

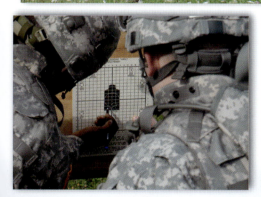

Auf der Schießbahn - *On the range*

Feuerzauber beim Nachtschießen
Fire sparkles during a night-firing exercise

Kampfpanzer Abrams M1
Combat tank Abrams M1

Der Panzerabwehrhubschrauber Bo-105 beim Abfeuern einer HOT-Rakete
An anti-tank helicopter Bo-105 fires a HOT-rocket

Kampfpanzer M60
Combat tank M60

Kampfpanzer Leopard
Combat tank Leopard

Die Panzerhaubitze 2000 in der Feuerstellung
A howitzer 2000 in a firing position

Panzerattrappen aus der Reichswehrzeit im Gegensatz zum Kleinpanzer Wiesel der Bundeswehr – klein – luftverladbar und feuergewaltig

Tank dummies dating back to the so-called Reichswehrzeit next to a "Wiesel" tank of the German Army – small – transportable by air and equipped with a lot of fire power.

Humvee
Humvee

Transport früher und heute: CH-53 der Bundeswehr
Transportation yesterday and today – a CH-53 of the German Army

Raketenartillerie, MLRS
Rocket artillery, MLRS

Sanitäter im Einsatz
Medics during training

Gemeinsame Multinationale Ausbildung
Joint Multinational Training

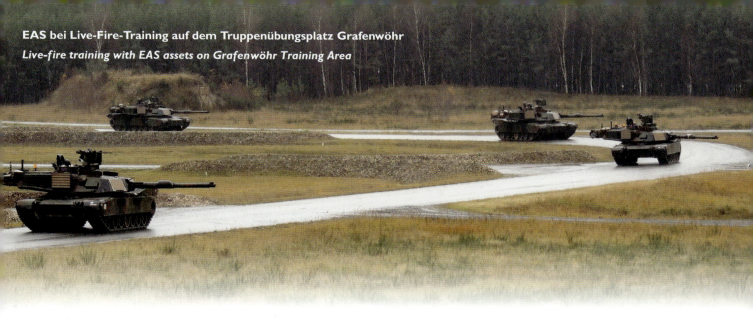

EAS bei Live-Fire-Training auf dem Truppenübungsplatz Grafenwöhr
Live-fire training with EAS assets on Grafenwöhr Training Area

Europäische Einsatzausstattung (EAS)

Zwei Jahre nachdem die letzten US-Panzerbrigaden Europa verlassen haben, kehrte 2014 das schwere Gerät nach Grafenwöhr zurück. Im European Activity Set (EAS - Europäische Einsatzausstattung) sind Abrams- Kampfpanzer sowie Bradley-Schützenpanzer. Einem Rotationsprinzip folgend werden Soldaten aus den USA für drei bis vier Monate ohne ihre Familien nach Europa verlegt, um gemeinsam mit NATO-Partnern und verbündeten Armeen zu trainieren.

European Activity Set (EAS)

In 2014, two years after the last U.S. tank brigades had left Europe, heavy armor returned to Grafenwoehr. The European Activity Set (EAS) includes Abrams tanks and Bradley fighting vehicles. Rotational forces deploy without their families for three to four months from the United States to Europe to train together with NATO- and other allied forces.

Live-Fire-Training Abrams M1
Live-fire training Abrams M1

EAS Bradley M2
EAS Bradley M2

Vilseck

Der Vogelturm ist das Wahrzeichen der Stadt Vilseck.
The Bird Tower Vilseck's landmark.

1185 wurde Vilseck erstmals urkundlich erwähnt. Die Ursprünge der Siedlung gehen jedoch weiter zurück. Über die Stadt ragt der Bergfried der Burg Dagestein. Zusammen mit der Stadtbefestigung, die aus Mauern, Türmen, vier Toren und einem Wassergraben bestand, sollte die Burg eine Schutzfunktion für die Handelsstraße Nürnberg – Prag haben. Die Burg Dagestein ist heute ein Zentrum für gesellschaftliche und kulturelle Veranstaltungen sowie für Seminare. Ein Tor der ehemaligen Stadtbefestigung, der Vogelturm, ist das Wahrzeichen von Vilseck. Dort befindet sich das "1. Deutsche Türmermuseum", in dem ein Stück Oberpfälzer Geschichte lebendig bleibt.

Vilseck was first mentioned in an official document in 1185 but the origins of the settlement go back even farther. The donjon of Dagestein Castle towers over the city. The castle, together with the city fortification which consists of walls, towers, four gates and a moat, was built to protect the trading route from Nuremberg to Prague. Today, Dagestein Castle is a center of social and cultural life and seminars. The Bird Tower, one of the towers of the city fortification, is Vilseck's landmark. It is the home of the first German tower keeper museum which keeps a piece of Upper Palatine history alive.

www.vilseck.de

„Der Truppenübungsplatz bestimmt seit Jahrzehnten den Pulsschlag in unserer Region. Amerikanische Soldaten in Uniform und ihre Familien gehören seit langer Zeit nicht nur zum Straßenbild in den Städten Vilseck und Grafenwöhr, sondern es haben sich vielfältige Kontakte und beste Freundschaften entwickelt. Hoffen wir alle, dass sowohl der Übungsplatz und die amerikanische Präsenz noch lange in dieser Form erhalten bleiben und auch das partnerschaftliche Miteinander weiter bestehen wird."

Hans-Martin Schertl, Bürgermeister der Stadt Vilseck, Mai 2011

"For decades, Grafenwoehr Training Area has determined the heartbeat of our region. American Soldiers in uniform and their families have not only been regulars in the streets of the cities of Vilseck and Grafenwoehr for a long time, but various contacts and best friendships have developed. Let's all hope that the training area as well as this type of American presence and the cooperative partnership will remain here for a long time."

Hans-Martin Schertl, Mayor of the City of Vilseck, Mai 2011

Einzug der Stryker mit dem Nachtwächter "Tschung" von Vilseck
Stryker arrival accompanied by the Vilseck night watchman called "Tschung"

Stadt Vilseck

Die Stadt zählte im Jahr 2009 rund 6500 Einwohner. 35 Dörfer und Ortsteile gehören zur Stadt. Viele amerikanische Familien leben in Vilseck und nutzen die gastronomische Infrastruktur und Freizeiteinrichtungen wie beispielsweise das Höhenschwimmbad.

City of Vilseck

In 2009, the city had approximately 6,500 inhabitants. Thirty-five villages and subdivisions belong to the city. South camp is located in Vilseck. Many American families live in Vilseck and use the local restaurants and recreational facilities such as the town's outdoor pool.

Die Burg Dagestein ist heute ein Zentrum für gesellschaftliche und kulturelle Veranstaltungen

Today, Dagestein Castle is a center of social and cultural life

Landkreis Amberg-Sulzbach
Amberg-Sulzbach County

Landkreis Amberg-Sulzbach

Die Stadt Vilseck liegt im Landkreis Amberg-Sulzbach, der südlich und westlich an den Übungsplatz angrenzt. Vielfältig und abwechslungsreich sind nicht nur die Landschaft, Natur und Kultur des Landkreises, auch touristisch hat die Region Amberg-Sulzbach einiges zu bieten. Als höchster Sandberg Europas ragt bei Hirschau der „Monte Kaolino" in die Höhe. Die weiße Düne inmitten der grünen Oberpfälzer Landschaft wartet mit einzigartigem Freizeitspaß auf. Zentrum des Landkreises ist die Fürstenstadt Amberg mit ihrer fast tausendjährigen Geschichte, Alt und Neu greifen dort eng ineinander.

Amberg-Sulzbach County

The city of Vilseck is located in Amberg-Sulzbach County which borders the training area in the south and the west. The county's landscape, nature and culture are versatile and diversified but the Amberg-Sulzbach region also has a lot to offer for tourists. "Monte Kaolino," Europe's highest sand mountain, is rising in the air near Hirschau. The white dune in the middle of the green Upper Palatine landscape offers unique recreational fun. Amberg, a former princes' residence town with a thousand-year-old history, is the center of the county. Old and new mix very well there.

www.amberg-sulzbach.de

Monte Kaolino, Hirschau

Sand-Boarding und Freizeitspaß am Monte Kaolino - *Sand boarding and leisure fun at Monte Kaolino*

bach am westlichen Rand des penübungsplatzes
bach located on the western bor- f the training area

Südlager - South Camp
Rose Barracks

Die Geschichte des Südlagers begann mit der Erweiterung des Truppenübungsplatzes Grafenwöhr in den Jahren 1937/38. Für den Lagerbau mussten Ortschaften geräumt werden. Die heutigen US-Wohnsiedlungen im Südlager sind nach den ehemaligen Dörfern Kittenberg, Grünwald, Altneuhaus und Langenbruck benannt. In nur elf Monaten wurde beginnend im Juli 1937 das "Lager Altneuhaus" gebaut. Die Aufstellung von Fronttruppen sowie der spanischen "Blauen Division" und der italienischen Division "San Marco" erfolgte während des Zweiten Weltkrieges. Auch der "Arbeitsstab Panzer" von General Heinz Guderian war zeitweise in Vilseck einquartiert. Am 8. April 1945 fielen Bomben auf das Südlager, zwölf Soldaten starben. Am 21. April 1945 besetzten schließlich Einheiten der 71. Infantriedivision der 3. US-Armee ohne Widerstand das Südlager.

The history of South Camp began in 1937/38 with the expansion of the Grafenwoehr Training Area. Villages had to be resettled to build the camp. The U.S. housing areas located in South Camp are named after the former villages of Kittenberg, Grünwald, Altneuhaus and Langenbruck. "Camp Altneuhaus," as South Camp was originally called, was built in only eleven months, starting in July 1937. During World War II, front troops and the Spanish "Blue Division" and the Italian „San Marco" division were deployed here. General Heinz Guderian's "Task Force Panzer," was also temporarily located in Vilseck. On April 8, 1945 South Camp was bombarded and 12 soldiers were killed. Units of the 71st Infantry Division, 3rd U.S. Army, occupied South Camp on April 21, 1945 and did not meet any resistance.

Das „Truppenlager Altneuhaus" wurde nach einem ehemaligen Dorf benannt.
The "Troop Camp Altneuhaus" was named after a former village

Der "Duce" Benito Mussolini besichtigte im April 1944 zusammen mit Generalfeldmarschall Wilhelm Keitel seine Truppen.
The "Duce", Benito Mussolini, visited his troops with General Field Marshal Wilhelm Keitel in April 1944.

In den Jahren 1981 bis 1991 wurde die Garnison Vilseck ausgebaut.
The Vilseck garrison was expanded from 1981 to 1991.

Panzerausbildungszentrum und Garnison

Kriegsgefangenen- und Flüchtlingslager nach 1945, Panzerausbildungszentrum, Umbenennung in „Rose Barracks", Ausbildungszentrum und Schule für kombinierte Waffen und Hauptwaffensysteme der US-Armee sind nur einige Schlagworte aus der Geschichte des Standorts Vilseck. Wichtige Ereignisse und Daten sind auf der Zeittafel in diesem Buch festgehalten.

Eine Milliarde Mark

Ein ebenso prägendes Ereignis wie die Gründung des Südlagers 1937 war für Vilseck, den Übungsplatz und die Region der Ausbau der „Rose Barracks". In den Jahren 1981 bis 1991 investierte die US-Armee rund eine Milliarde Mark in die Garnison Vilseck. Kasernen, technische Bereiche, Fahrzeugabstellflächen, Infrastruktureinrichtungen sowie Wohnbereiche für die Soldaten und ihre Familien wurden gebaut. Die Wohnhäuser sind alle Fertigbauten, die aus den Staaten nach Vilseck gebracht wurden. Neben dem militärischen Nutzen ist der Wirtschafts- und Beschäftigungsfaktor für die Region Vilseck ein enormes Plus. 4500 Soldaten sind heute in Vilseck stationiert. Die größte Einheit ist das´Kavallerieregiment, hinzukommen das Medizinische und Zahnmedizinische Kommando sowie die US-Waffenschule.

Tank training center and garrison

Prisoner of war and refugee camp after 1945, tank training center, "Rose Barracks" and Combined Arms Training Center of the U.S. Army are just some of the buzzwords describing the history of the military installation at Vilseck. Important events and dates are listed in this book's chronology.

One billion mark

The expansion of "Rose Barracks" was just as important an event for Vilseck, the training area and the region as the establishment of South Camp in 1937. The U.S. Army invested one billion mark in the garrison from 1981 to 1991. Barracks, maintenance facilities, motor pools, infrastructure as well as housing for the soldiers and their families were built. The houses were made of prefabricated parts that were transported from the United States to Vilseck. Apart from the military use, the economic impact and the employment opportunities were an enormous plus for the region. Today, 4,500 soldiers are stationed in Vilseck. The largest unit is the 2nd Cavalry Regiment. Also stationed in Vilseck are the Bavarian Medical Activity and Dental Command as well as the Combined Arms Training Center.

Die heutigen US-Wohnsiedlungen im Südlager sind nach den ehemaligen Dörfern benannt.

The U.S. housing areas located in South Camp are named after the former villages.

Zeilmann Linde in Grünwald

Linden tree named by Zeilmann in former village Grünwald

Neu gebauter Block für alleinstehende Soldaten - *New Single Soldier Barracks in Vilseck*

Vilseck-Lagereingang

Vilsecks alter Lagereingang
Vilsecks former main gate

MP-Station - DES
Abteilung für Notfalldienste
Directorate of Emergency Services (DES)

Am heutigen Standort der MP-Station in den Rose Barracks lag früher die alte Wache von Vilseck. Im Gebäude 2099 befindet sich das Directorate of Emergency Services, kurz DES, die Abteilung für Notfalldienste der USAG Bavaria. Unter den Notrufen 114 für die Militärpolizei und 112 für Feuerwehr und Rettungsdienst, wird für Hilfe und Sicherheit gesorgt. Die MP-Station ist auch Sitz des Provost Marshal, der als oberster Militärpolizist Hüter über Gesetz und Ordnung in der Garnison ist. Ein deutscher Kontaktbeamter hält die Verbindung zwischen den Amerikanern und der deutschen Polizei und den Sicherheitsbehörden.

MP station - DES
Directorate of Emergency Services (DES)

The MP station on Rose Barracks is located where Vilseck's former main gate once stood. Building 2099 houses the USAG Bavaria Directorate of Emergency Services (DES). When dialing 114 for the military police and 112 for fire and medical emergencies, help and security will be provided. Located at the MP station, the provost marshal is the chief of all garrison military police activities. A German police liaison officer is responsible for maintaining relations between the Americans and German police and security agencies.

DES Vilseck MP Station

AFN-Bavaria

1943 geht der amerikanische Soldatensender „American Forces Network" (AFN) in London erstmals auf Sendung. Er sollte die amerikanischen Boys in Europa bei Laune halten. Mehrere Sendestationen waren nach dem Krieg in Deutschland verteilt. 1995 kommt der US-Militärsender AFN Nürnberg in die Rose Barracks und wird in AFN Bavaria umbenannt. Fritz Egner der prominente bayerische Radio- und Fernsehmoderator machte 1974 seine ersten Radio-Schritte bei AFN-Munich und startete dort seine Karriere. Zum 70. Geburtstag von AFN besuchte Egner im April 2013 in Vilseck seine ehemaligen Kollegen des „American Forces Network".

AFN-Bavaria

In 1943, the American military radio station „American Forces Network" (AFN) first went on the air. It was intended to keep up the American troops' spirits. After the war, several transmitting stations were spread across Germany. In 1995, AFN Nuremberg was moved to Rose Barracks and renamed as AFN Bavaria. Fritz Egner, the famous German radio and television host, started his career in 1974 at AFN Munich. When AFN celebrated its 70th anniversary, Egner came to Vilseck in April 2013 to visit his former AFN colleagues.

Fritz Egner bei AFN Bavaria
Fritz Egner at AFN Bavaria

Gesundheitswesen
Health Care

Vom Lazarett zum Bavarian Health Command (BHC)

From a military hospital to Bavarian Health Command

Die Geschichte der medizinischen Versorgung auf dem Truppenübungsplatz begann mit der Königlich Bayerischen Armee im Jahre 1910. Neben dem Wasserturm wurde das „Lazarett" gebaut. Der Komplex umfasste mehrere Gebäude und ist heute Teil des Hauptquartiers des Joint Multinational Training Command. Nach dem Zweiten Weltkrieg wurde das Lazarett von den Amerikanern als „Health Clinic" weiterbenutzt und mit einem Gebäude für die Zahnärzte erweitert. Der Neubau der Health- und Dental Clinic an der heutigen Stelle erfolgte um 1985. Im Zuge des Standortausbauprogramms (2003-2010) wurde der Bau auf die heutige Größe erweitert.

The history of medial care on the training area began with the Royal Bavarian Army in 1910 when a military hospital called „Lazarett" was built next to the Water Tower. The complex consisted of several buildings. Today, they are part of Headquarters, Joint Multinational Training Command. After WWII, the military hospital was used by Americans as their health clinic and a building was added for dentists. The current health and dental clinic was built around 1985. The clinic complex was expanded to its current size as part of the Efficient Basing - Grafenwoehr construction program (2003-2010).

Das alte Lazarett von 1910 wurde nach 1945 als US-Army Health Clinic Grafenwöhr genutzt. Heute ist das Gebäude Teil des JMTC-Hauptquartiers

The old military hospital built in 1910. After 1945, it was used by the U.S. Army as the Health Clinic Grafenwoehr. Today, the building is part of JMTC Headquarters

Die Health- und Dental Clinic in den Tower Barracks

The Health and Dental Clinic on Tower Barracks

Bavaria Dental Activity (BDENTAC)

In Vilseck entstand 1938 das Südlager, die heutigen Rose Barracks. Das Gebäude 301 wurde von den Amerikanern ab 1956 als Sanitätsbereich genutzt und gehörte zum General Hospital in Nürnberg. 1989 wurde für einen Preis von 3,8 Millionen US-Dollar die Vilseck Health Clinic gebaut. Ein Teil dieses Gebäudes wird heute als Zahnklinik genutzt. Im Januar 2015 war Einweihung der Vilseck Dental Clinic, deren Sanierung und Erweiterung rund 4,5 Millionen Euro kostete. Auf 25 Behandlungsstühlen und in Fachräumen bieten die militärischen Ärzte und Helfer den Soldaten und Familien beste zahnmedizinische Versorgung. Vilseck ist auch das Hauptquartier der „Bavaria Dental Activity" (BDENTAC)

Ein Gesamtbudget von 21,7 Millionen Euro hat der Neu- und Umbau der Vilseck Health Clinic in den Rose Barracks. Auf einer Geschossfläche von 5500 Quadratmetern entsteht ein komplexes Gesundheitszentrum, das mit anspruchsvoller moderner Technik ausgestattet wird. Fertiggestellt wurde der zweigeschossige Neubau im August 2015, nun erfolgt die Sanierung und der Umbau des alten Klinikgebäudes von 1989. Bis zum Mai 2016 soll die Vilseck Health Clinic mit modernsten Standards im Hinblick auf medizinische Gerätschaften, Technik, Sicherheit und Umwelt komplett fertiggestellt sein.

BHC

Mit der Schließung der Kaserne in Würzburg wurde Vilseck 2006 zum Hauptquartier der „United States Army Medical Department Activity-Bavaria", kurz BMEDDAC genannt. Im September 2015 erfolgte die Umbenennung in Bavaria Health Command (BHC). Diesem Kommando unterstehen alle medizinischen Einrichtungen der US-Armee in Bayern. Die Ärzte des BHC arbeiten eng mit den zivilen Fachärzten und Krankenhäusern in der Region zusammen. Jährlich werden tausende von Überweisungen ausgestellt.

Das BHC unterhält Partnerschaften mit der Gemeinde Edelsfeld und BDENTAC mit der Gemeinde Weiherhammer.

Bavaria Dental Activity (BDENTAC)

Rose Barracks in Vilseck was built in 1938. In 1956, the Americans starting using building 301 as their health clinic. It belonged to the Nuremberg General Hospital. In 1989, the Vilseck Health Clinic was built at a cost of $3.8 million. Today, a part of the building is used as dental clinic. In January 2015, the Vilseck Dental Clinic, whose renovation and expansion cost nearly 4.5 million Euro, was opened. The military dentists and other medical personnel provide high-quality dental care for soldiers and their families. Vilseck also is the headquarters of the Bavaria Dental Activity (BDENTAC).

The new construction and renovation of the Vilseck Health Clinic on Rose Barracks has a total budget of 21.7 million Euro. A complex health center, equipped with sophisticated modern technology, is built on a floor area of 5,500 square meters. The new, two-story building was finished in August 2015. Now the old health clinic, built in 1989, is undergoing renovation and reconstruction. The new Vilseck Health Clinic, equipped with the most modern medical equipment, technology, safety and environmental standards is scheduled to be finished in May 2016.

BHC

When the U.S. Army installation in Würzburg was closed in 2006, Headquarters, United States Army Medical Department Activity-Bavaria, short BMEDDAC, moved to Vilseck. In September 2015, it was rededicated as Bavaria Health Command (BHC). It is responsible for all medical facilities of the U.S. Army in Bavaria. The doctors of BHC work closely together with regional civilian specialists and hospitals. Every year, thousands of referrals are made.

BHC has a partnership with the town of Edelsfeld and BDENTAC with the town of Weiherhammer.

Gäste bei der Eröffnung der Zahnklinik Vilseck
Guestws at the opening of the Vilseck Dental Clinic

Der Neubau der Vilseck Health Clinic
The new building of the Vilseck Health Clinic

2 CR — 2nd Cavalry Regiment / 2. Kavallerieregiment

2. Kavallerieregiment

Das 2. Kavallerieregiment ist in der US-Armee das traditionsreichste, älteste noch aktive Kavallerieregiment. Die Soldaten werden auch als Dragoons (Dragoner) bezeichnet. Die Geschichte des Regiments beginnt 1836, als die Einheit zur Befriedung der Indianer in Florida aufgestellt wurde. Die Dragooner kämpften in vielen Kriegen auf dem amerikanischen Kontinent, auf Kuba und den Phillipinen sowie im Ersten und Zweiten Weltkrieg. Unter der Führung von Oberst Charles H. Reed retteten sie Ende des Zweiten Weltkriegs auch die berühmten Lipizzaner Pferde hinter den sowjetischen Linien. Mit Hauptquartier in Nürnberg und Standorten in Bindlach, Bamberg, Hof, Feucht, Weiden und Amberg sicherten sie unter dem Namen 2. Gepanzertes Kavallerieregiment während des Kalten Krieges die westdeutsche Grenze zum Eisernen Vorhang. Es folgten Einsätze während der Befreiung von Kuwait, in Bosnien und im Irak.

Willkommen in Vilseck

Im Sommer 2006 wurde die Einheit als 2. Stryker-Kavallerieregiment aus Fort Lewis im US-Bundesstaat Washington nach Vilseck verlegt.

2nd Cavalry Regiment

The 2nd Cavalry Regiment is the U.S. Army's oldest, active cavalry regiment and has the longest tradition. The soldiers are also called Dragoons. The regiment's history starts in 1836 when the unit was deployed to pacify the Native Americans in Florida. The Dragoons fought in many wars on the American continent, on Cuba, the Philippines and in World Wars I and II. At the end of WWII, commanded by Col. Charles H. Reed, they also rescued the famous Lipizzaner horses behind the Soviet lines. Under the name 2nd Armored Cavalry Regiment, headquartered in Nuremberg and with installations in Bindlach, Bamberg, Hof, Feucht, Weiden and Amberg, the unit protected the West German border at the Iron Curtain during the Cold War. Deployments during the liberation of Kuwait, to Bosnia and Iraq followed.

Welcome to Vilseck

The 2nd Stryker Cavalry Regiment was relocated from Fort Lewis, Washington, to Vilseck in the summer of 2006.

Dragoons

Das Motto der Stryker „Toujours Prêt – Allzeit bereit" schallte bei der Parade im September 2006 über das Flugfeld bei Vilseck.
The Stryker's motto "Toujours Prêt – Always Ready" sounded across the airfield in Vilseck during a parade in September 2006.

Zum Gedenken an die Gefallenen traten im Juli 2011 die Schwadrone des 2. Stryker-Kavallerieregiments im Ehrenhain in den Rose Barracks an.

In July 2011, the squadrons of the 2nd Stryker Cavalry Regiment assembled in the regiment's memorial grove on Rose Barracks to commemorate their fallen comrades.

Einsatz im Irak

Bereits 2007 wurde die Truppe zum Irakeinsatz gerufen, von dem sie im November 2008 zurückkehrte. Die rund 4000 Soldaten des Regiments waren im Bereich Bagdad sowie im Nordirak eingesetzt. Die Rückkehr des 2. Stryker-Kavallerieregiments aus dem 15-monatigen Einsatz wurde im November 2008 mit einer großen „Welcome Home Ceremony" gefeiert.

Leider musste die Einheit auch schmerzliche Verluste während des Einsatzes hinnehmen. 26 Soldaten sind im Irak ums Leben gekommen und kehrten nicht zu ihren Familien, Kameraden, Freunden und Bekannten zurück.

Afghanistan fordert Opfer

Im Juni 2010 trat das Regiment zu einem weiteren Einsatz, diesmal in Afghanistan, an. Die 4000 Soldaten des 2. Stryker-Kavallerieregiments wurden im südöstlichen Afghanistan eingesetzt. Der Kampf gegen Terroristen forderte erneut Opfer.

Trauer um 20 gefallene Soldaten dämpfte im Juli 2011 die Freude über die Rückkehr des Regiments in die Oberpfälzer Heimat Vilseck. Für jeden der toten Soldaten steht im Ehrenhain des Regiments ein Ahornbaum.

Deployment to Iraq

In 2007, the regiment was deployed to Iraq and returned in November 2008. The regiment's approximately 4,000 soldiers were stationed in Baghdad and in northern Iraq. The return of the 2nd Stryker Cavalry Regiment from its 15-month-deployment was celebrated in November 2008 with a large "Welcome Home Ceremony."

Unfortunately, the unit suffered painful losses during the deployment. 26 soldiers were killed in Iraq and did not return to their families, comrades, friends and acquaintances.

Deployment to Afghanistan claims victims

In June 2010, the regiment deployed again, this time to Afghanistan. The 4,000 soldiers of the 2nd Stryker Cavalry Regiment were stationed in south-eastern Afghanistan. The fight against terrorits claimed additional victims. In July 2011, mourning the loss of 20 fallen soldiers outweighed the happiness that accompanied the regiment's return to its Upper Palatine home of Vilseck. A maple tree was planted in the regiment's memorial grove for each soldier killed in action.

Die Gedenkstätte in der Vilsecker Militärgemeinde erinnert an die gefallenen Soldaten des 2. Stryker Kavallerieregiments.

The memorial at Rose Barracks commemorates the fallen soldiers of the 2nd Stryker Cavalry Regiment.

„Dragoon Ritt" und NATO-Einsätze

2015 war die 3. Schwadron „Wolfpack", 2CR, drei Monate in Estland, Lettland, Litauen und Polen im Einsatz. Als Teil der Operation Atlantic Resolve Nord übten sie dort gemeinsam mit den Truppen der NATO-Verbündeten. Das „Wolfpack" führte einen strategischen Landmarsch durch das Baltikum und die Tschechische Republik zur Rückkehr nach Vilseck durch. Mit einer Länge von 1,800 Kilometern war es der längste Marsch des US-Heeres in Europa seit dem Ende des Zweiten Weltkriegs. Die Soldaten des „Dragoon Ritt" wurden am 1. April 2015 in den Rose Barracks feierlich empfangen.

Die 2. Schwadron „Cougars", 2CR, verlegte im März 2015 im Rahmen der Operation Atlantic Resolve South nach Rumänien, um die Beziehungen mit dem rumänischen Heer durch bilaterales und multilaterales Training zu stärken. Der Landmarsch der 4. Schwadron „Sabers", 2CR, durch die Tschechische und Slowakische Republik endete in Ungarn mit einem taktischen Brückenschlag unter Verwendung von Material der ungarischen Pioniere.

"Dragoon Ride" and NATO missions

In 2015, 3rd Squadron "Wolfpack", 2CR, deployed to Estonia, Latvia, Lithuania and Poland as part of Operation Atlantic Resolve North and simultaneously trained with their NATO Allies in all four countries for three months. The "Wolfpack" conducted a strategic road march through the Baltic states and Czech Republic to return to Vilseck. With a length of 1,800 km, it was the longest road march by the United States Army in Europe since the end of WWII. On April 1, 2015, the soldiers of the "Dragoon Ride" were ceremoniously welcomed on Rose Barracks.

In March 2015, 2nd Squadron, 2CR deployed to Romania as part of Operation Atlantic Resolve South to strengthen relationships with the Romanian land forces through bilateral and multilateral training. The road march of 4th Squadron "Sabers", 2CR, through the Czech Republic and the Slovak Republic ended in Hungary with a tactical bridge crossing using Hungarian bridging assets.

Die Soldaten des „Dragoon Ritt" wurden am 1. April 2015 in den Rose Barracks feierlich empfangen.

On April 1, 2015, the soldiers of the "Dragoon Ride" were ceremoniously welcomed on Rose Barracks.

Im Reed Museum in den Rose-Barracks wird die Geschichte des traditionsreichen 2. Kavallerieregiments lebendig dargestellt.

The history of 2d Cavalry Regiment is rich in tradition and vividly displayed in the Reed Museum on Rose Barracks.

Der Achtradpanzer wurde in zehn verschiedenen Varianten in die **US-Army** eingeführt.
Ten models of the U.S. Army's eight-wheel Stryker tank were introduced into the force.

Der Stryker mit dem Mobile Gun System, einer 105-Millimeter-Kanone
A Stryker with the Mobile Gun System, a 105 millimeter cannon

Kavallerie mit Stryker-Radpanzern

Mittlerweile sind die Dragoons des 2. Kavallerieregiments nicht mehr mit Pferden, sondern mit modernen Stryker-Radpanzern ausgestattet.

Der Stryker-Achtradpanzer der US-Armee wurde in 10 Varianten in die Truppe eingeführt. Die Varianten des gepanzerten Radfahrzeuges reichen vom Führungsfahrzeug, Infanterietransporter, Mörserträger, Spürfahrzeug, Sanitätstransporter, Panzerjäger und Unterstützungsfahrzeug bis zum MGS-Stryker. Der Stryker mit dem Mobile Gun System (MGS) hat eine 105 Millimeter-Kanone. Das Fahrzeug hat somit die Feuerkraft eines herkömmlichen Panzerfahrzeugs. Durch sein geringes Gewicht sind alle Varianten des Strykers luftverladbar und auf dem Gefechtsfeld äußerst wendig

Cavalry equipped with Stryker light wheeled tanks

Today, the Dragoons of the 2nd Cavalry Regiment are no longer equipped with horses but with modern Stryker light wheeled fighting vehicles.

Ten models of the U.S. Army's eight-wheel Stryker fighting vehicle were introduced into the force. The models of these Stryker vehicles ranges from command vehicles, transport vehicles, mortar carriers, reconnaissance vehicles, MEDEVAC vehicles, anti-tank vehicles, support vehicles and MGS Stryker vehicles. The Stryker vehicles with the Mobile Gun System (MGS) are equipped with a 105 millimeter cannon. As a result, the vehicle has the fire power of a regular tank. Due to its light weight, all Stryker vehicles can be transported by air and are very easy to maneuver on the battlefield.

Apache Stryker

Militärpolizei
Military Police

18. Militärpolizeibrigade

Die 18. Militärpolizeibrigade nimmt eine Vielzahl von polizeilichen Aufgaben in den US-Garnisonen in Europa und an Einsatzorten in der ganzen Welt wahr.

Zu den Hauptaufgaben gehören der Schutz der Soldaten und ihrer Familien, Ermittlungsarbeit, Strafverfolgung, Sicherung militärischer Anlagen, Verkehrsregelung sowie militärische Operationen während Konflikten.

In Friedenszeiten nimmt die Militärpolizei polizeiliche Aufgaben wahr, die mit denen der zivilen Polizei vergleichbar sind.

Die Brigade wurde im Mai 1966 in Fort Meade, Md. aktiviert. Die Republik Vietnam war der erste Einsatzort für viele Missionen der neu aufgestellten Brigade. Nach Abschluss der tapferen Dienste in Vietnam erfolgte die Deaktivierung im März 1973.

Zur Neuaufstellung kam es im August 1985 in Deutschland in Frankfurt/Main. Danach unterstützten die Einheiten der 18. MP-Brigade die Einsätze Desert Shield und Desert Storm. 1994 zog das Hauptquartier der Brigade nach Mannheim. Weitere Einsätze folgten in Bosnien und Herzegowina. 1999 gewährleisteten Soldaten der Brigade die Sicherheit beim Gipfeltreffen in Sarajevo, Bosnien. Von 2003 bis 2008 wurde die Brigade zur Unterstützung der Operation Iraqi Freedom abberufen. Teile der Brigade waren dort auch verantwortlich für die Ausbildung der irakischen Polizei.

Im Juli 2011 wurde das Hauptquartier der Brigade von Mannheim nach Sembach verlegt. Von 2013 bis Februar 2014 war die Hauptquartierskompanie der Brigade im Rahmen der Operation Enduring Freedom in Afghanistan im Einsatz. Im März 2014 fand die Verlegung der Brigade an ihren derzeitigen Standort Grafenwöhr statt.

Die folgenden Einheiten der 18. MP-Brigade sind in Grafenwöhr stationiert: Das 709. MP-Bataillon, die 527. MP-Kompanie und die 615. MP-Kompanie in Vilseck. Weitere Kompanien der 18. MP-Brigade befinden sich in Sembach, Hohenfels, Ansbach, Wiesbaden und Stuttgart. Auch das 15. Pionierbataillon in Grafenwöhr ist nun Teil der 18. MP-Brigade.

18th Military Police Brigade

The 18th Military Police Brigade pro , ; throughout the European Theater in garrison and locations throughout the world during times of deployment. Key services include protection of soldiers and their families, investigation, law enforcement, protection of military installations, traffic control, and military operations during conflicts. During times of peace the military police provides professional law enforcement comparable to that of their civilian counterparts.

Currently the 18th MP Brigade Headquarters is located in Grafenwoehr, Germany, following a diverse, rich history.

The brigade was activated in May 1966 at Ft. Meade, Md. From there the brigade deployed to the Republic of Vietnam. Following its valorous deployment to Vietnam, the brigade deactivated in March 1973.

It reactivated in Frankfurt/Main, Germany, in August 1985. Units of the 18th MP Brigade supported missions during Operations Desert Shield and Desert Storm. In 1994, brigade headquarters moved to Mannheim, followed by deployments to Bosnia and Herzegovina. In 1999, brigade soldiers were responsible for security operations at the Sarajevo Summit in Bosnia. From 2003 to 2008, the brigade deployed in support of Operation Iraqi Freedom where parts of the brigade were responsible for the training of Iraqi police forces.

In July 2011, the brigade headquarters moved from Mannheim to Sembach. From 2013 to February 2014, the brigade's headquarters company was deployed to Afghanistan in support of Operation Enduring Freedom. In March 2014, the brigade moved to its present location in Grafenwoehr, Germany.

The following units of the 18th MP Brigade are stationed in Grafenwoehr: 709th MP Battalion, 527th MP Company and the 615th MP Company in Vilseck. Other 18th MP Brigade companies are stationed in Sembach, Hohenfels, Ansbach, Wiesbaden and Stuttgart. Additionally, the 15th Engineer Battalion is now a part of 18th MP Bde. family and also stationed in Grafenwoehr.

Freiwillige der Feuerwehr Grafenwöhr unterstützten die Soldaten der 18. MP Brigade beim Aufstellen des Baumes
Members of the city of Grafenwoehr's Volunteer Fire Department assisted soldiers of the 18th MP Brigade with putting up the tree

Der Partnerschaftsbaum: Symbol für Freundschaft und Partnerschaft

Anknüpfend an die Tradition der Maibäume wurde im Mai 2015 vor dem Hauptquartier der 18. Militärpolizeibrigade im 600er Bereich der „Partnerschaftsbaum" errichtet. Der Bundesforst, die Bauabteilung der Garnison und Soldaten deer MP-Brigade bereiteten den Baum vor und zierten ihn traditionsgemäß mit den bayerischen Farben. Freiwillige der Feuerwehr Grafenwöhr unterstützten die Soldaten der 18. MP Brigade beim Aufstellen des Baumes. Der 20 Meter hohe Stamm trägt alle Wappen der Einheiten, Dienststellen und Partnergemeinden. Der Baum ist Symbol für Freundschaft und Partnerschaft.

Die deutschen Gastgeber geben den amerikanischen Soldaten, Zivilisten und Familienangehörigen eine Heimat auf Zeit und lassen sie am kulturellen Leben in der Oberpfalz teilnehmen. Der Baum ersetzt den von der inzwischen aufgelösten 172. Infanteriebrigade errichteten Partnerschaftsbaum.

The partnership tree: A symbol of friendship and partnership

Based on the tradition of the maypole, a "partnership tree" was raised in front of the 18th MP Brigade headquarters building in the 600-area in May 2015. The Federal Forest Office, garrison DPW and soldiers of the 18th MP Brigade prepared the tree and painted it in the traditional Bavarian colors. Members of the city of Grafenwoehr's Volunteer Fire Department assisted soldiers of the 18th MP Brigade with raising the tree. It is 20 meters tall and carries crests of units and government agencies and their partner cities. The tree is a symbol of friendship and partnership.

The German hosts provide the American soldiers, civilians and family members with a home away from home and provide them with the opportunity to take part in the cultural life of the Oberpfalz. The tree replaces the partnership tree put up by the inactivated 172nd Infantry Brigade.

Soldaten und Gäste beim Aufstellen des Partnerschaftsbaumes.
Soldiers and guests when the tree was raised.

Partnerschaften und die Wappen am Baum / Partnerships and crests on the tree

JMTC / **18th MP BDE** 	 **Bundesforst** / **DMV**
USAG BAVARIA / **Grafenwöhr** 	**Ahorntal** / **Weiden**
2CR / **Vilseck** 	**Eschenbach** / **1-91 CAV**
1-2CR / **Hirschau** 	**Pressath** / **44th ESB**
2-2CR / **Sorghof** 	**Kirchenthumbach** / **4-319 AFAR**
3-2CR / **Amberg**	**Freihung** / **18th CSSB**
4-2CR / **Sulzbach-Rosenberg** 	**Kemnath** / **709th MP BN**
Fires-2CR / **Königstein**	**Erbendorf** / **15th ENG BN**
RSS-2CR / **Hahnbach**	**Edelsfeld** / **BMEDAC**
NCO Academy / **USH Delitzsch** 	**Weiherhammer** / **BDENTAC**

15th Engineer Battalion
15. Pionierbataillon

Im Juli 2013 entrollte das 15. US-Pionierbataillon in Grafenwöhr seine Truppenfahne. Es wurde von Schweinfurt nach Grafenwöhr verlegt und kompensierte die Auflösung der 172. Infanteriebrigade. „Swords up, Drive on/Schwerter hoch und voran" ist der Schlachtruf der Pioniere. Das Bataillon befehligt, kontrolliert und führt Pionieraufgaben im Garnisons- und Einsatzgebiet durch. Der Bereich erstreckt sich auf Grafenwöhr, Hohenfels, Standorte in Deutschland, Europa und auch Afrika sowie in den Einsatzländern. Bereits in den 1980er Jahren waren die US-Pioniere in Grafenwöhr maßgeblich am Ausbau der Schießbahnen des Truppenübungsplatzes beteiligt.

The 15th Engineer Battalion uncased its colors in Grafenwoehr in July 2013 when it was relocated from Schweinfurt to Grafenwoehr following the withdrawal of the 172nd Infantry Brigade. "Swords up, drive on," is the battle call of the engineers. The battalion is responsible for controlling and completing engineering projects in garrisons and at forward deployed locations. Its area of operations includes Grafenwoehr, Hohenfels, other garrisons in Germany, Europe and Africa as well as countries where the U.S. Army is deployed. In the 1980s, the engineers were already significantly involved in the expansion of ranges at Grafenwoehr Training Area.

Pioniere im Einsatz
Engineers at work

Die Einheiten des Bataillons

The units of the battalion

Das „15th Engineer Battalion" besteht aus vier Einheiten und einer Abteilung, die sich mit den verschiedensten Pionieraufgaben beschäftigen. Aufgeteilt ist dies in „Vertikale Kapazitäten", die sich mit Gebäudebau, (Stein/Holz), Betonarbeiten, Schreinerarbeiten, Wasser/Abwasser, Elektrische Verkabelung, HVAC (Heizung, Ventilation und Air-Conditioning beschäftigen.

Zu den „Horizontalen Kapazitäten" zählen: Straßenbau, Standortsicherung, Ausheben von Gräben, Kanälen, Abwasserrinnen, Abriss von Gebäuden und Strukturen, sowie der Transport.

Dazu steht den Pionieren eine beeindruckende technische Ausstattung und ein Maschinen- und Fahrzeugpark mit rund 500 Maschinen bereit. Dazu zählen Kleinfahrzeuge, Lastwagen, Tankfahrzeuge, Tieflader, Bagger, Raupen, Hebekräne, Gabelstapler, Walzen, Gräter und weitere Fahrzeuge.

Das Bataillon hat eine Stärke von 500 Soldaten und brachte rund 1500 Familienmitglieder mit nach Grafenwöhr.

The 15th Engineer Battalion consists of four units and one detachment responsible for different kinds of engineering projects. Its vertical capacities include construction of buildings made of stone and wood, concrete work, carpentry, plumbing, electrical work, heating, ventilation and air-conditioning. Horizontal capacities include road construction, camp construction, digging, demolition of buildings and other structures, as well as transportation.

The engineers have an impressive array of vehicles and equipment available to them to accomplish their mission. The motor pool includes 500 rolling pieces of equipment, to include small vehicles, trucks, tank trucks, flat bed trailers, excavators, Caterpillars, hoisting cranes, fork lifts, roller compactors and much more.

The battalion has a troop strength of 500 soldiers and about 1,500 family members.

Rund 500 Fahrzeuge und Maschinen stehen den Pionieren für ihre Arbeiten zur Verfügung
The engineers have approximately 500 vehicles and other equipment to accomplish their mission.

1st Squadron, 91st Cavalry Regiment (Airborne)
1. Luftlande-Schwadron 91. Kavallerieregiment

I-91 CAV

1-91 CAV

„Sky Soldiers" nennen sich die Soldaten der 173. Luftlandebrigade. Zu den Fallschirmspringern in Vicenza, Italien, gehört das 1. Luftlande-Schwadron des 91. Kavallerieregiments (1-91 CAV), das seit Sommer 2013 in Grafenwöhr in den Tower Barracks stationiert ist.

Die 91. US-Kavallerie wurde ursprünglich 1928 als Aufklärungstruppe gegründet und ist die älteste, erfahrenste Aufklärungstruppe der US-Armee. Die Einheit war im 2. Weltkrieg an mehreren Einsätzen in Nordafrika, Sizilien und Italien beteiligt. Das Motto der Aufklärer ist „Wachsam" (Alert). 1953 wurde die 91. deaktiviert.

Im Juni 2006 wurde das 1.Schwadron der 91. Kavallerie in den Con Barraks in Schweinfurt reaktiviert und umorganisiert. Es erhielt den Zusatz „Airborne". Nach intensiver Ausbildung folgten drei Einsätze im Rahmen der Operation Enduring Freedom in Afghanistan.

Durch ihre große Mobilität wurde die 1-91 CAV im Rahmen der NATO-Unterstützung bei verschiedenen Stabilisierungsmaßnahmen in Polen, der Tschechischen Republik, Italien, Frankreich, Litauen, Lettland, Estland, Rumänien und Israel eingesetzt. Auf den Heimatübungsplätzen Grafenwöhr und Hohenfels nimmt die Einheit an regelmäßigen Ausbildungen und internationalen Übungen teil.

Das 1. Luftlande-Schwadron des 91. Kavallerieregiments unterhält eine Partnerschaft mit der Stadt Eschenbach.

1-91 CAV

The soldiers of the 173rd Airborne Brigade call themselves "Sky Soldiers." The 1st Squadron, 91st Cavalry Regiment belongs to the paratroopers in Vicenza, Italy and has been stationed at Tower Barracks, Grafenwoehr since the summer of 2013.

The 91st U.S. Cavalry was originally activated in 1928 as a reconnaissance squadron and is the oldest and most experienced reconnaissance unit in the U.S. Army. During WWII, the unit participated in several campaigns in North Africa, Sicily and Italy. The motto of the reconnaissance troops is "Alert." The 91st was deactivated in 1953.

In June 2006 it was reactivated and redesignated as the 1st Squadron (Airborne), 91st Cavalry Regiment at Conn Barracks, Schweinfurt, Germany. After intensive training, the unit deployed three times to Afghanistan in support of Operation Enduring Freedom.

Because of its great mobility, 1-91 CAV has participated in NATO missions in Poland, the Czech Republic, Italy, France, Lithuania, Latvia, Estonia, Romania and Israel. The unit regularly trains and participates in international exercises on the local training areas in Grafenwoehr and Hohenfels.

The 1st Squadron, 91st Cavalry Regiment has a partnership with the city of Eschenbach.

Einrücken in die Chinook CH-47 auf dem Airfield
Boarding a Chinook CH-47 on the airfield

1-91 CAV in den baltische Staaten
1-91 CAV in the Baltic states

4-319th AFAR
4th Battalion 319th Airborne Field Artillery Regiment
4. Bataillon, 319. Luftlande Feld-Artillerie-Regiment"

„König der Herde" ist der Beinahme der „4-319th". Auftrag der Luftlandesoldaten ist es, die kämpfende Truppe mit Artilleriefeuer zu unterstützen.

Das Bataillon wurde ursprünglich als 319. Feldartillerie-Regiment 1917 im Lager Gordon in Georgia gegründet und im gleichen Jahr im 1. Weltkrieg in Frankreich eingesetzt. 1919 wurde das Bataillon wieder demobilisiert. Zur Teilnahme am 2. Weltkrieg folgte 1942 die Aktivierung und Neuorganisation als 319. Glider Field Artillery Batallion. Die 319te nahm an Kampangen der 82. Airborne Division unter anderem bei der Landung in der Normandie und in Holland teil.

Nach einer aktiven und inaktiven Zeit kam es 1988 in Italien zur Neuaufstellung und schließlich zur Eingliederung in die 173. Luftlandebrigade, die ihren Hauptsitz in Vicenza, Italien, hat. Das Bataillon unterstützte mit zahlreichen Einsätzen den Globalen Krieg gegen den Terrorismus und war beteiligt an der Operation Iraqi Freedom und an mehreren Einsätzen der Operation Enduring Freedom in Afghanistan.

Seit 2006 hatte die 4-319. ihren Hauptsitz in den Warner-Barraks in Bamberg. Im Herbst 2013 zog das Bataillon nach Grafenwöhr um. Die Fallschirm-Artilleristen haben eine Partnerschaft mit der Marktgemeinde Kirchenthumbach.

„King of the Herd" is the nickname of the „4-319th." The mission of the airborne soldiers is to provide direct supporting fires to the troops on the battlefield.

The battalion was originally constituted in 1917 at Camp Gordon, Ga. as the 319th Field Artillery Regiment and deployed that same year to France during WWI. It was demobilized again in 1919.

In 1942, it was reorganized and redesignated as the 319th Glider Field Artillery Battalion to participate in WWII. The 319th took part in campaigns of the 82nd Airborne Division, including assault landings in Normandy and Holland.

Following several activations and deactivations, it was reactivated again in Italy in 1988 and became a part of the 173rd Airborne Brigade which is headquartered in Vicenza, Italy. The battalion participated in numerous deployments in support of the Global War on Terrorism to include Operation Iraqi Freedom and Operation Enduring in Afghanistan.

Since 2006, the 4-319th AFAR was headquartered at Warner Barracks, Bamberg, Germany. During the fall of 2013, the battalion relocated to Grafenwoehr. The airborne artillerymen have a partnership with the market town of Kirchenthumbach.

„Heavy Equipment Drop und Live-Fire"

Luftlandeübungen auf dem Truppenübungsplatz gehören mittlerweile zum laufenden Übungsbetrieb. Mit entsprechender Ausbildung stellen die Luftlandesoldaten ihre ständige Einsatzbereitschaft sicher.

Die Fallschirmspringer der 4-319. üben auch das Absetzen von „Heavy Equipment" mit anschließendem Live Fire. Aus den C-130 Hercules-Transportflugzeugen der Luftwaffe wird neben Kleinmaterial eine Plattform mit einem Hummer-Leicht-LKW und der montierten Haubitze abgeworfen. An den riesigen Transportfallschirmen schwebt die tonnenschwere Last, die mit Dämmmaterial auf der Plattform verstaut ist, sicher zu Boden. In weiteren Überflügen folgt das Absetzen der Luftlande-Artilleristen. Nach dem Entpacken des Materials werden an der 105-Millimeter-Haubitze vom Typ M 119 die Sicherheitsprüfungen durchgeführt und die Waffe in Stellung gebracht. Geführt durch die Feuerleitung wird in die rund acht Kilometer entfernte Impact Area des Truppenübungsplatzes geschossen.

„Heavy Equipment Drop and Live Fire

Airborne operations at Grafenwoehr Training Area have become a regular part of the training missions here. The exercises ensure the readiness of the airborne artillerymen.

The paratroopers of the „4-319th" also practice the drop of heavy equipment with subsequent live fire. Together with other, smaller equipment, a platform with a HUMVEE that is equipped with a howitzer is dropped from an Air Force C-130 Hercules transport aircraft. Attached to huge transport parachutes, the load that weighs several tons and is attached to the platform with insulating material, safely floats to the ground. Several overflights follow, dropping the airborne artillerymen. After unpacking the equipment, safety tests are conducted on the 105mm-M 119 howitzer and the weapons system is put in position. Guided by fire control, the soldiers shoot into the impact area of the training area that is eight kilometers away.

Die tonnenschwere Last mit einem Hummer-Leicht-LKW und der auf einer Plattform verzurrten Artillerie-Haubitze schwebt an riesigen Transportfallschirmen sicher zu Boden.
Attached to huge transport parachutes, the load that weighs several tons and is attached to the platform with insulating material, safely floats to the ground.

Nach dem Entpacken und der Sicherheitsüberprüfung an der Feldhaubitze wird das Geschoss mit dem Kaliber 105 Millimeter in die rund acht Kilometer entfernte Impact Area abgefeuert.
After unpacking the equipment and performing safety tests on the howitzer, the 105mm-gun is fired into the impact area that is about eight kilometers away.

18th CSSB
18th Combat Sustainment Support Battalion
18. Kampfunterstützungsbataillon

Das 18. Kampfunterstützungsbataillon stellt weltweit die Logistik und den Erhalt der Einsatzbereitschaft kämpfender Truppenteile sicher. Dies betrifft die Bereiche Versorgung, Munition, Wartung, Instandhaltung und Transport. Das Bataillon unterstützt die US-Armee in Europa zur Verlegung und Rückverlegung von Truppen in die Einsatz- und Krisengebiete.

Als 3. Ordnance Bataillon wurde die Einheit im Juli 1940 in Aberdeen Proving Grounds in Maryland gegründet, anschließend umorganisiert und umbenannt. Das Bataillon verlegte im Frühjahr 1944 nach Europa und unterstützte im Rahmen der 51. Ordnance Group unter anderem die 1. US-Armee. Für seine hervorragenden Dienste im Zweiten Weltkrieg wurde das Bataillon ausgezeichnet. Die Demobilisierung erfolgte im Dezember 1946 in Paris in Frankreich.

Im August 1951 wurde die Einheit in Deutschland wieder aktiviert. Das Bataillon verlegte 1955 nach Hanau, wo es mehrere Umbenennungen und Umstrukturierungen erfuhr. Nach 47 Jahren Dienst in Hanau folgte im Juni 2002 die Verlegung nach Grafenwöhr und die Neuausrichtung mit den Aufgaben Wartung bis Transport und Munitionsverwaltung.

In den letzten Jahren hat das 18. Kampfunterstützungsbataillon mit seinen unterstellten Einheiten folgende Einsätze unterstützt: Operation Iraqi Freedom, Operation Joint Endeavor/Joint Guard in Ungarn, NATO-Einsätze im Rahmen der Operationen Allied Force und Leuchtende Hoffnung in Tirana, Albanien. Weiterhin wurden drei Kosovo Force Rotationen im Camp Able Sentry in Mazedonien durchgeführt. Das 18. CSSB unterhält eine Patenschaft mit der Marktgemeinde Freihung.

The 18th Combat Sustainment Support Battalion (18th CSSB) provides expeditionary logistics worldwide to support and sustain deployed troops with supplies, ammunition, maintenance, repair and transport. The battalion supports U.S. Army Europe troop deployment and redeployment to forward deployed locations and contingencies.

Originally constituted in July 1940 as the 3rd Ordnance Battalion at Aberdeen Proving Grounds, Md., it was subsequently reorganized and redesignated as 8th Ordnance Battalion. In the spring of 1944, the battalion deployed to Europe as part of the 51st Ordnance Group, providing support to the 1st Army. The battalion received awards for its distinguished service during World War II and was demobilized in Paris, France, in December 1946.

In August 1951, the battalion was reactivated in Germany and moved to Hanau in 1955 where it was redesignated and restructured several times. In June 2002, after 47 years of service in Hanau, it was transferred to Grafenwoehr and shifted its focus from maintenance to transportation and ammunition management.

In the past years, the 18th Combat Sustainment Support Battalion and its subordinate units have supported the following operations: Operation Iraqi Freedom, Operation Joint Endeavor/Joint Guard in Hungary, and NATO operations as part of Operations Allied Force and Shining Hope in Tirana, Albania. Additionally, it conducted three Kosovo Force rotations at Camp Able Sentry in Macedonia. 18th CSSB has a partnership with the community of Freihung.

Die Einheiten des 18. CSSB
Units of the 18th CSSB

Marktgemeinde und Reservistenkameradschaft Freihung mit der 18. CSSB und 2. EOD
The community and the German Army Reserves Association of Freihung with the 18th CSSB and 2nd EOD

Umschlags- und Versorgungsarbeit bei der 18. CSSB
Movement of goods and supplies at the 18th CSSB

Ausbildung im schweren Bombenschutzanzug mit dem ferngesteuerten Teleroboter
Training with a remotely controlled robot, wearing a heavy protective suit.

EOD-Soldaten bergen die entschärfte 1000-Pfund-Bombe, die im April 2015 auf dem Baugelände der neuen Grundschule gefunden wurde.

EOD soldiers recover a defused 1,000-pound bomb found in April 2015 on the construction site of the new elementary school.

702nd EOD
702nd Ordnance Company (Explosive Ordnance Disposal)
702. Kampfmittelbeseitigungskompanie

702. Kampfmittelbeseitigungskompanie

Das Erkennen, Identifizieren und Beseitigen von Kampfmitteln und improvisierten Sprengmitteln ist der gefährliche Job der Soldaten der 702. EOD-Kompanie.
Als 2. Artillerie-Munitionsräumdienst wurde die Einheit im Januar 1943 in Aberdeen Proving Ground, Maryland aufgestellt. Die Kampfmittelbeseitiger waren im Zweiten Weltkrieg in Tunesien, der Normandie, in Nordfrankreich, im Rheinland und in den Ardennen eingesetzt. Es folgten mehrere Deaktivierungen und Wiederaufstellungen sowie ein Einsatz auf den Philippinen. Nach ihrer Verlegung nach Deutschland und der Stationierung in Grafenwöhr als 2nd EOD-Kompanie erfolgte im Juni 1998 die Umbenennung in 702. Kampfmittelbeseitigungskompanie. Abstellungen von Soldaten und Kommandos zur Munitionsbeseitigung in den verschiedensten Krisen- und Einsatzgebieten hatte die 702. EOD zur bewältigen. Im April 2013 kehrte die Einheit von einer längeren Verwendung in Afghanistan zurück.
Kampfmittelbeseitiger sind ausgebildete Spezialisten die eine umfangreiche Schulung und Einweisung in alle Arten von Munition, Sprengmittel und Abwurfmunition vergangener Kriege erhalten. Sie erlernen verschiedene Methoden und Verfahren, um nicht explodierte Munition oder auch Minen unschädlich zu machen. Die Soldaten sind auch für den Einsatz auf dem chemisch, biologischen und atomaren Sektor ausgebildet.
Für ihre Arbeit stehen den Spezialisten Identifizierungsunterlagen und -anweisungen sowie eine umfangreiche Ausstattung mit Fahrzeugen, ferngesteuerten Manipulatoren (Telerobotern), Bombenschutzanzügen, Zünderausdrehgeräten, Röntgen- und Messgeräten, spezielle technische Werkzeuge, Sprengmittel und vieles mehr zur Verfügung.
Eine Partnerschaft und Zusammenarbeit betreibt die 702. EOD mit den Feuerwerkern der Bundeswehr-Truppenübungsplatzkommandantur und mit der Reservistenkameradschaft Freihung.

702nd Ordnance Company

The dangerous job of soldiers of the 702nd Ordnance Company (702nd EOD) is to recognize, identify and remove explosive ordnance and improvised explosive devices.
The unit was originally activated as the 2nd Ordnance Bomb Disposal Squad in January 1943 at Aberdeen Proving Ground, Md. In World War II, the unit was deployed to Tunisia, Normandy, Northern France, Rhineland and Ardennes-Alsace. Several de- and reactivations followed to include a deployment to the Philippines. Since its relocation to Germany and stationing in Grafenwoehr as 2nd Ordnance Detachment, the unit was officially designated as the 702nd Ordnance Co. (EOD) on June 16, 1998. Soldiers and commands of the 702nd EOD deployed to various crises and forward deployed locations to remove explosive ordnance. In April 2013, the unit returned from a long deployment to Afghanistan.
EOD soldiers are trained specialists in all types of ammunition and explosives to include those of past wars. They are trained to defuse unexploded ammunition and mines, using a variety of methods and techniques. They are also trained to deal with chemical, biological, radiological, nuclear (CBRN) incidents. To accomplish their mission, the soldiers refer to special ordnance identification manuals and have a variety of special equipment at their disposal, including vehicles, remotely controlled robots, protective suits, fuse removal devices, X-ray and measuring devices, explosives and other equipment.
The 702nd EOD cooperates and has a military partnership with EOD soldiers of the Germany Army Command on Grafenwoehr Training Area and the Freihung German Army Reserves Comradeship.

Die Soldaten der 702. Kampfmittelbeseitigungskompanie im August 2015
The soldiers of 702nd EOD in August 2015

44th ESB
44th Expeditionary Signal Battalion
44. Expediertes Fernmeldebataillon

Das 44. Expedierte Fernmeldebataillon (ESB) wurde im Februar 1944 aktiviert und war während des Zweiten Weltkriegs auf dem europäischen Kontinent im Einsatz. Nach dem Zweiten Weltkrieg wurden mehrere Teile der Einheit aktiviert und deaktiviert. Die Fernmelder nahmen dann an den Kriegen in Vietnam, im Irak und in Afghanistan teil und unterstützten Einsätze in Ruanda und auf dem Balkan in den 1990gern. Nach jahrzehntelanger Stationierung in Deutschland, begann das Bataillon im April 2012 mit der Verlegung von Schweinfurt nach Grafenwöhr, die mit dem Ausrollen der Truppenfahne im August 2012 in den Tower Barracks abgeschlossen wurde. Zeitgleich kam die Charlie-Kompanie erfolgreich aus dem Kampfeinsatz in Afghanistan zurück, und damit das gesamte Bataillon wieder zusammengeführt. Heute umfasst das Bataillon 501 Soldaten und ihre Familien.

Das 44. ESB spielte eine entscheidende Rolle bei der Unterstützung von Einsätzen und Übungen in ganz Europa. Dazu gehören die Operationen Atlantic Resolve im Baltikum, Fearless Guardian in der Ukraine und Active Fence in der Türkei sowie viele weitere zur Unterstützung des US-Heeres in Europa, der NATO und der alliierten Partner von Grossbritannien bis in die Türkei und von Spanien bis Estland. Zusätzlich unterstützt das Bataillon auch weiterhin die laufenden Einsätze in Afghanistan und in Teilen Afrikas.

Der Auftrag des 44. ESB ist der Aufbau, Betrieb und die Verteidigung von Datennetzwerken des US-Heeres und seiner Koalitionspartner über Satelliten- und Mikrowellenverbindungen. Seine Soldaten sind dafür ausgebildet, rasch an Einsatzorte zu verlegen und dort diese Systeme einzurichten - jederzeit und überall. Das Motto der Einheit ist „Team-44, HERAUSRAGEND!"

The 44th Expeditionary Signal Battalion (ESB) activated in February 1944 and deployed to the European continent during WWII. Since WWII, the battalion activated and deactivated several parts of the unit. The signal soldiers then deployed to the wars in Vietnam, Iraq, and Afghanistan and supported operations in Rwanda and the Balkans during the 1990s. Stationed in Germany for several decades, the battalion began relocating from Schweinfurt to Grafenwoehr in April 2012 and finished the move in August 2012 with the official uncasing of its colors at Tower Barracks. During this time, Charlie Company successfully returned from combat operations in Afghanistan thus reuniting the entire battalion. Today, the battalion is comprised of 501 soldiers and their families

The 44th ESB played a critical role in supporting operations and exercises throughout Europe. These include Operation Atlantic Resolve in the Baltics, Operation Fearless Guardian in Ukraine, Operation Active Fence in Turkey, and numerous others in support of U.S. Army Europe, NATO, and allied partners from the United Kingdom to Turkey and from Spain to Estonia. Additionally, the battalion continues to support ongoing operations in Afghanistan and parts of Africa.

The 44th ESB mission is to build, operate, and defend Army and coalition data networks via satellite and microwave communication links. Its soldiers are proficient in rapid deployment and establishment of these systems anytime, anywhere. The unit motto is "Team-44, OUTSTANDING!"

Moderne Kommunikationsausstattung heute
Modern communication equipment today

Fernmeldesoldaten 1927. Telefon und Strippenziehen war damals angesagt
Signal soldiers 1927. Those were the days of landlines and installing wires.

Die Ansicht vom Fesselballon auf das Truppenlager nach Osten um 1912
View from the tethered balloon on the military camp to the east circa 1912

Blick vom Hubschrauber auf den westlichen Lagerteil mit den neuen EBG-Bauten im Jahr 2006
View from a helicopter on the western part of the military camp with the new EB-G buildings in 2006

US-Armee Garnison Bavaria
U.S. Army Garrison Bavaria

Das Herz der Militärgemeinde

Die Aufgabe der US-Armee Garnison Bavaria (USAG Bavaria) kann im Großen und Ganzen mit dem Service verglichen werden, den eine zivile Stadtverwaltung ihren Bürgerinnen und Bürgern bietet und dennoch ist der militärische Auftrag weit umfangreicher. Serviceleistungen auf vielen Gebieten sowie das Sicherstellen bester Lebensqualität für die Soldaten und ihre Familien stehen an oberster Stelle.

Zur US-Armee Garnison Bavaria gehören die Militärstandorte Grafenwöhr, Vilseck und Hohenfels mit den beiden Übungsplätzen sowie die US-Einrichtungen in Garmisch. Die Garnison arbeitet eng mit dem 7th Army Joint Multinational Training Command (JMTC) zusammen und gewährleistet jeglichen Service zur Erfüllung der Aufgaben des JMTC.

Ein großes Team von Fachkräften, bestehend aus Soldaten und Zivilangestellten steht dem Garnisonskommandeur zur Bewältigung der Standortaufgaben zur Verfügung. Das Spektrum reicht von der Familienbetreuung über Freizeit, Erholung, Kinderbetreuungseinrichtungen, Wohnungsbüro, Service- und Wartungsarbeiten bis hin zur Öffentlichkeitsarbeit.

Vormals wurden diese Standortaufgaben vom 409. Base Support Bataillon wahrgenommen, das der 100. Gebietsunterstützungsgruppe (100th Area Support Group) unterstellt war. Die Umgliederung und Umbenennung zur „US-Armee Garnison Grafenwöhr" fand im Oktober 2005 statt. Seit September 2013 heißt die Garnison „US-Armee Garnison Bavaria".

The heart of the military community

By and large, the mission of the U.S. Army Garrison Bavaria (USAG Bavaria) can be compared to the service that a civilian city administration provides to its citizens and yet, the military tasks are considerably broader. Providing services in many areas and guaranteeing the best quality of life for soldiers and their families are the first priorities.

U.S. Army Garrison Bavaria is comprised of the military installations in Grafenwoehr, Vilseck and Hohenfels with the two training areas and the U.S. facilities in Garmisch. The garrison works closely with the 7th Army Joint Multinational Training Command (JMTC) and provides every service needed to JMTC so it can fulfill its mission.

A large team of subject matter experts consisting of soldiers and civilian employees is available to the garrison commander to complete the garrison mission. It ranges from family support, morale, welfare and recreation, child care, housing, service and maintenance to public affairs.

The garrison mission was formerly supported by the 409th Base Support Battalion which belonged to the 100th Area Support Group. The restructuring and renaming to U.S. Army Garrison Grafenwoehr took place in October 2005. Since September 2013, the garrison is called "U.S. Army Garrison Bavaria."

**Kommandeure der US-Armee Garnison Bavaria
(vormals 100. ASG und USAG Grafenwoehr)**

*Commanders of the U.S. Army Garrison Bavaria
(formerly 100th ASG and USAG Grafenwoehr)*

Oberst
Washington J. Sanchez, Jr.
1987 – 1989

*Colonel
Washington J. Sanchez, Jr.
1987 – 1989*

Oberst
Nick C. Harris
1989 – 1991

*Colonel
Nick C. Harris
1989 – 1991*

Oberst
James G. Snodgrass
1991 – 1993

*Colonel
James G. Snodgrass
1991 – 1993*

Oberst
Gary M. Tobin
1993 – 1995

*Colonel
Gary M. Tobin
1993 – 1995*

Oberst
Frank J. Gehrki III
1995 – 1997

*Colonel
Frank J. Gehrki III
1995 – 1997*

Oberst
Philip D. Coker
1997 – 2000

*Colonel
Philip D. Coker
1997 – 2000*

Oberst
Gregory J. Dyson
2000 – 2002

*Colonel Gregory
J. Dyson
2000 – 2002*

Oberst
Richard G. Jung, Sr.
2002 – 2005

*Colonel
Richard G. Jung, Sr.
2002 – 2005*

Oberst
Brian T. Boyle
2005 – 2008

*Colonel
Brian T. Boyle
2005 – 2008*

Oberst
Nils C. Sorenson
2008 – Juli 2010

*Colonel
Nils C. Sorenson
2008 – July 2010*

Oberst
Avanulas R. Smiley
Juli 2010 - Nov. 2011

*Colonel
Avanulas R. Smiley
July 2010 - Nov. 2011*

Oberst
James E. Saenz
Jan. 2012 - Juli 2014

*Colonel
James E. Saenz
Jan. 2012 - July 2014*

Der Truppenübungsplatz Grafenwöhr ist ein wahrer Schatz, sowohl für die Bürger der Oberpfalz, als auch für die Soldaten, Familien und Zivilangestellten, die hier leben, arbeiten und trainieren. Generationen von US-Militärfamilien hatten das Privileg diese Region als ihre „Heimat" bezeichnen zu dürfen, wenn auch nur für kurze Zeit. Ihre Erfahrungen hier, werden sie dagegen ein ganzes Leben bei sich tragen.

Von der großzügigen und einladenden lokalen Bevölkerung bis hin zu der unglaublich reichhaltigen Flora und Fauna – die Oberpfalz hat etwas ganz Spezielles. Gerald Morgensterns Buch fängt das ein und hilft uns allen, die Geschichte dieser großartigen Region und ihrer unglaublichen Naturressourcen zu schätzen.

Oberst Mark A. Colbrook, Kommandeur, US-Armee Garnison Bavaria, seit Juli 2014

Die oben geäußerte Meinung ist meine eigene und stellt nicht die offizielle Politik oder Auffassung der US-Armee, des US-Verteidigungsministeriums oder der US-Regierung dar.

Oberst Mark A. Colbrook

Colonel Mark A. Colbrook

Grafenwoehr Training Area is a true treasure to both, the citizens of the Oberpfalz and the soldiers, families, and civilians that live, work, and train here. Generations of U.S. military families have had the privilege to call this area "home," even if for only a short while, but carry with them those experiences for a lifetime. From the generous and welcoming local population to the incredibly diverse plant and wildlife, there is something special about living in the Oberpfalz. Gerald Morgenstern's book captures that and helps us all appreciate the history of this great area and the incredible natural resources contained within it.

Colonel Mark A. Colbrook, Commander, U.S. Army Garrison Bavaria, since July 2014

The views expressed above are my own and do not reflect the official position of the U.S. Army, Department of Defense, or the U.S. Government.

Der bayerische Innenminister Joachim Herrmann vertrat im September 2013 bei einer feierlichen Zeremonie vor dem Hauptquartier den bayerischen Ministerpräsidenten Horst Seehofer. Die Garnison wurde in „US-Armee Garnison Bavaria" umbenannt. Zu ihr gehören die Standorte Grafenwöhr, Vilseck, Hohenfels und Garmisch

In September 2013, Bavarian Interior Minister Joachim Herrmann represented Bavarian Minister President Horst Seehofer at a festive ceremony in front of the headquarters building when the garrison was renamed as „U.S. Army Garrison Bavaria." It is comprised of the military installations in Grafenwoehr, Vilseck, Hohenfels and Garmisch

Wirtschaftliche Bedeutung
Economic Impact

Die US-Armee und der Truppenübungsplatz sind einer der bedeutendsten Wirtschaftsfaktoren in der Region. Auf 665,1 Millionen Euro beziffert die US-Armee den jährlichen „Economic-Impact", der in die Region fließt. Alle Zahlen entsprechen dem Stand des US-Haushaltsjahres 2013.

Arbeitsplätze
Über 2200 deutsche Arbeitnehmer sind in Grafenwöhr und Vilseck angestellt. Neben den festangestellten Mitarbeitern beim US-Militär gibt es zusätzlich noch hunderte deutsche und amerikanische Arbeitsstellen bei zivilen Vertragsfirmen auf dem Truppenübungsplatz.

Lehrlingsprogramm
Erst 2015 legte die US-Armee ein neues Ausbildungsprogramm auf. Von 1998 bis 2011 lief das alte Programm bei dem 79 Lehrlinge die Ausbildung abgeschlossen haben, davon wurden 73 von der US-Armee weiterbeschäftigt. Sie sind in vielen Abteilungen der Handwerks- und Servicebereiche eingesetzt.

Löhne und Gehälter
Die Lohn- und Gehaltszahlungen für die deutschen Arbeitnehmer belaufen sich nach den Zahlen vom Oktober 2013 auf jährlich 172 Millionen Euro. Die Zahlungen erfolgen vollständig aus Mitteln des US-Verteidigungshaushalts.

Wohnungen - Mieten
111 Millionen Euro sind Miet- und andere Aufwendungen für den Unterhalt von angemieteten Häusern und Wohnungen. Derzeit leben zirka 18.500 amerikanische Soldaten und Zivilisten „off-post," das heißt außerhalb des Kasernengeländes in US-Wohnsiedlungen. Zusätzlich werden etwa 2.000 Wohnungen auf dem privaten Markt kurzfristig angemietet.

The U.S. Army and the training area contribute significantly to the regional economy. The annual economic impact amounts to 665,1 million Euro. All numbers pertain to U.S. fiscal year 2013 and cover several areas, ranging from jobs to housing.

Jobs
Currently, more than 2,200 German employees work for the Army in Grafenwoehr and Vilseck. Besides the jobs provided directly by the U.S. military, there are hundreds of German and American positions offered by civilian contract firms on the training area.

Apprentice Program
In 2015, the U.S. Army started a new apprentice program. The previous program ran from 1998 to 2011. Seventy-nine apprentices completed their training, 73 of them permanently employed with the U.S. Army. They hold blue and white collar jobs in various departments.

Salaries and wages
Based on numbers from October 2013, annual salaries and wages for German employees amounted to 172 million Euro. They are paid from U.S. defense budget funds.

Housing - Rental costs
One-hundred-eleven million Euro were spent for housing maintenance and rental costs. About 18,500 American soldiers and civilians live off post in U.S. housing areas. Additionally, 2,000 apartments are privately leased.

Baumaßnahme „Townhouses in Grafenwöhr" - 20 Millionen Euro gehen an Generalunternehmer aus der Region
Townhouse construction in Grafenwoehr: 20 million Euro are paid to regional general contractors

Die US-Armee ist ein zertifizierter Ausbildungsbetrieb
The U.S. Army is a certified vocational training provider

Scheibenfertigung im US-Scheibenhof
Target production at the U.S. target machine shop

Private Ausgaben

Die privaten Ausgaben der US-Soldaten und ihrer Familien in der US-Armee Garnison Bavaria, dazu zählen die Standorte Grafenwöhr, Vilseck, Hohenfels und Garmisch, können nur geschätzt werden. 54,6 Millionen Euro werden auf den US-Banken in den Kasernen von US-Dollars in Euro umgewechselt. Die Ausgaben über Kreditkarten sind nicht mit einberechnet.

Trotz einer eigenen Versorgung in der Kaserne, profitieren Souvenir-, Lebensmittel-, und Bekleidungsgeschäfte, Friseure, Taxiunternehmer und andere Dienstleister. Die Gastronomie und das Hotelgewerbe florieren. Zahlreiche Autoverkäufer bieten vor den Kasernentoren US-Versionen der verschiedensten Marken an. Die Ausgaben der täglich mehreren hundert Besucher, die dienstlich auf den Truppenübungsplätzen zu tun haben und dann oft die deutsche Infrastruktur mitnutzen, sind in den genannten Zahlen nicht eingeschlossen.

Baumaßnahmen - Aufträge - Versorgung

2013 wurden 327,6 Millionen Euro für Bauaufträge, Instandhaltungsmaßnahmen, Serviceleistungen und die medizinische Versorgung in der Garnison ausgegeben. Dies sind in erster Linie Ausgaben für laufende Verträge und besondere Baumaßnahmen, wie beispielsweise der 2014/15 in Grafenwöhr ausgeführte Bau von 25 Doppelhäusern zwischen Tor 1 und Tor 3 für rund 20 Millionen Euro.

Soldaten

Der Schwerpunkt der Stationierung des US-Heeres liegt in Bayern mit rund 9.600 US-Soldaten. Am Standort Grafenwöhr leben etwa 12.000 US-Amerikaner - Soldaten und Zivilangestellte - mit ihren Familien.

Eine Vielzahl von Fahrzeugen stehen im Bauhof der US-Armee Garnison bereit.

The garrison's DPW motor pool features a variety of vehicles.

Private spending

Private spending of U.S. soldiers and their families from U.S. Army Garrison Bavaria, which includes the installations in Grafenwoehr, Vilseck, Hohenfels and Garmisch, can only be estimated. At on-post local banks, 54.6 million Euro were exchanged from U.S. dollars into Euro. Expenditures paid for with credit cards are not included.

Souvenir shops, supermarkets, clothing stores, hairdressers and barber shops, taxi firms and other service providers profit from the military although the U.S. Army operates its own stores. The restaurant and the hotel sector flourish. Numerous car dealers offer a variety of car brands with U.S. specs outside the installations' gates. Not included in those numbers are expenditures of several hundred visitors and contractors working on the training areas on a daily basis, using the German infrastructure.

Construction - Contracts - Supplies

In 2013, 327.6 million Euro were paid for maintenance contracts, construction, services and medical support in the garrison. Most of the money was spent on running contracts and special construction projects, such as the construction of 25 townhouses between Gates 1 and 3 in Grafenwoehr at a cost of 20 million Euro in 2014/15.

Soldiers

The majority of U.S. Army soldiers in Germany are stationed in Bavaria. Twelve-thousand Americans and their families, including 9,600 soldiers, are currently stationed in Grafenwoehr and Vilseck.

Löschpanzer im Einsatz
Fire-fighting tanks on duty

Old Fire-fighting tank

Fire Department
Lagerfeuerwehr

Sicherheit rund um die Uhr

Dienst rund um die Uhr zur Sicherheit der Soldaten und ihrer Familien leisten die Männer der Fire Departments in Grafenwöhr und Vilseck. Neben Aufgaben in der Brandbekämpfung auf Schießbahnen und in Wohngebieten zählen bei den Fire-Fightern heute technische Hilfeleistungen und Erstversorgungseinsätze zum Tagesgeschäft.
Zahlreiche Alarmierungen werden durch Meldeanlagen ausgelöst, mit denen alle neuen und renovierten Gebäude in den Kasernen ausgestattet sind.

Security around the clock

The firemen of the fire departments in Grafenwoehr and Vilseck are on duty around the clock to ensure the security of the Soldiers and their families. Apart from fighting fires on the ranges and in homes, nowadays technical aid and first aid are everyday business for the fire fighters. Many alarms are caused by automatic alarm systems which are installed in all new and renovated buildings.

Die Lagerfeuerwehr mit den freiwilligen Feuerwehren der Stadt Grafenwöhr
The fire department with the Volunteer Fire Departments of the City of Grafenwoehr

September 1950: Die Feuerwehrleute und Fahrzeuge der Fire Station Grafenwöhr, die damals zu Nürnberg gehörte.
September 1950: The firemen and vehicles of the Grafenwoehr fire station which belonged to Nuremberg.

Oktober 2015: Die diensthabende Schicht des Fire Department
Ocotober 2015: The on duty firemen of the fire department.

Beste technische Ausstattung

Modernste Ausrüstung steht den hauptamtlichen Kräften zur Verfügung. Neben Tanklöschfahrzeugen, Rüstwägen, Drehleiter, Wechsellader- und Führungsfahrzeugen sind auch Löschpanzer im Dienst der Lagerfeuerwehr. Mit diesen umgebauten ehemaligen Munitionsträgern rücken die Männer häufig zu Range-Feuern und Waldbränden aus. Möglich ist hierbei auch die Unterstützung durch große Löschhubschrauber mit Außenlastbehältern. Auch am US-Airfield ist eine Wachstation ständig besetzt. Modernste Flugfeldlöschfahrzeuge stehen für alle Fälle bereit. Eine enge Zusammenarbeit findet mit den freiwilligen Feuerwehren in Grafenwöhr und den Rettungskräften in der Region statt.

The best technical equipment

The full-time fire fighters have the most modern equipment. Apart from fire trucks, rescue vehicles, an aerial ladder, swap body vehicles and command vehicles, the training area's fire department also owns fire-fighting tanks. The men use these modified former tanks to combat range and forest fires. Often, they are supported by helicopters with large outboard cargo containers. The U.S. airfield also has a fire station. There, the most modern airport fire-fighting vehicles are ready for use, if needed. There is a close cooperation with the Grafenwoehr volunteer Fire Departments and the rescue workers of the region.

Die Bundeswehr unterstützt bei der Waldbrandbekämpfung. Ein Transporthubschrauber CH-53 mit 5000 Liter Außenbehälter bekämpft die Flammen aus der Luft.
The German Armed Forces support the fighting of forest fires. A CH-53 transport helicopter with a 5,000 liter outboard cargo container fights the flames from the air.

Schulen schools

Die Geschichte der Schulen in der Militärgemeinde beginnt bereits vor 1936. Durch den Bevölkerungsanstieg in Grafenwöhr reichten die Schulräume im Rathaus nicht mehr aus und es mussten zeitweise Klassen in Kasernengebäude ins Lager verlegt werden. 1936 wurde in Grafenwöhr ein neues Schulhaus eröffnet.

Die erste amerikanische Schule wurde 1946 in der Nähe des alten Lazaretts, heute JMTC-Hauptquartier, gebaut. Der Komplex der „Elementary School Grafenwoehr" ist auch heute noch auf diesem Platz. Mehrmals wurde die Schule erweitert, die Unterlagen von 1949 und 1953 liegen in der Plankammer der US-Bauverwaltung. 2016 feiert die Grundschule somit ihr 70-jähriges Jubiläum. Wegen der Raumnot in der Elementary School existieren bereits Pläne für einen Neubau. Der Baugrund gegenüber dem Bundeswehrgebäude wurde 2015 vorbereitet.

Durch den ständigen Ausbau in Vilseck und Grafenwöhr, das EB-G (Effiziente Basing-Grafenwöhr) Ausbauprogramm und den damit verbundenen Zuzug von amerikanischen Soldaten und ihren Familien, gibt es im Schuldirektorat heute folgende Schulen: Grafenwoehr Elementary School, Netzaberg Elementary School, Netzaberg Middle School, Vilseck Elementary School und Vilseck High School. Amerikanische Lehrer unterrichten die Kinder im Alter von 5 bis 17 Jahren in den verschiedenen Schulstufen. Alleine die Schulen auf dem Netzaberg bieten über 1400 Schülern Platz. Rund 60 Schulbusse bringen täglich die amerikanischen Kinder zu ihren Schulen in Grafenwöhr, auf dem Netzaberg und nach Vilseck.

The history of schools in the military community started before 1936 when classrooms in the town hall did not suffice due to the population increase in Grafenwoehr. As a result, classrooms had to be established in barracks buildings on post. In 1936, a new school building was opened in Grafenwoehr.
The first American school was built in 1946 near the old military hospital, today JMTC headquarters. The buildings of Grafenwoehr Elementary School are still located there. The school was expanded several times. The respective construction plans from 1949 and 1953 can be found in the archives of the department of public works. In 2016, the elementary school will celebrate its 70th anniversary. Due to the shortage of space at the elementary school, plans for the construction of a new school have been made. The building grounds across from the German Army building were prepared in 2015.

Due to the constant expansion of Vilseck and Grafenwoehr, the EB-G (Efficient Basing - Grafenwoehr) construction program and the subsequent influx of American soldiers and their families, the school directorate now operates the following schools: Grafenwoehr Elementary School, Netzaberg Elementary School, Netzaberg Middle School, Vilseck Elementary School and Vilseck High School. American teachers teach the students aged between 5 and 17 in the various schools. The schools on Netzaberg alone offer space for more than 1,400 students. About 60 school busses transport the American kids to their schools in Grafenwoehr, on Netzaberg and in Vilseck every day.

Netzaberg Elementary School

Das Schulhaus mit der Sonnenuhr ist noch immer Teil der derzeitigen Grafenwoehr Elementary School.
The school house with the sun dial is still part of Grafenwoehr Elementary School.

Das Gebäude der ersten amerikanischen Schule von 1946 wurde schon 1949 erweitert.
The first American school established in 1946 was expanded in 1949.

Tower Barracks Libary

Rund 60.000 Medien davon 45.000 Bücher und ein umfangreiches Programm bietet die Bücherei den Amerikanern in der Garnison. 1950 begann im Fachwerkbau direkt unter dem Wasserturm die Geschichte der Bücherei. Das Fachwerkhaus wurde vorher als MP-Station genutzt und ist heute ein Bürogebäude. 1995 zog die Bücherei an ihren jetzigen Standort neben der Dental Clinic. Die Libary gehört zur Abteilung FMWR (Freizeit- und Familienbetreuung) der US-Armee Garnison Bavaria.

The library offers Americans in the garrison about 60,000 media, including 45,000 books, and a large program. The history of the library began 1950 in a half-timbered building near the Water Tower. The building was formerly used as MP-station and is now an office building. In 1995, the library moved to its current location next to the Dental Clinic. The library is part of the FMWR (Family, Morale, Welfare and Recreation) department of the U.S. Army Garrison Bavaria.

Die Bücherei heute
The current library

Die alte Bücherei unter dem Wasserturm
The old library building near the Water Tower

Wild B.O.A.R.

Eingebettet in die Natur: das Freizeit- und Erholungszentrum Wild B.O.A.R.
Embedded in nature: The outdoor recreation center "Wild B.O.A.R."

Freizeit, Erholung und die Wiedereingliederung nach Einsätzen bietet den Amerikanern das „Wild B.O.A.R." - Bavaria Outdoor Adventure Recreation Center.
Der Keilerkopf eines Wildschweins (Engl. *boar*) begrüßt am Eingang die Gäste. Schwarzkittel und Rotwild sind auch die nächsten Nachbarn des Freizeitzentrums, das idyllisch in die Natur eingebettet, direkt am Dickhäuter-Weiher liegt. Der bayerische Innenminister Joachim Herrmann war im September 2013 Gast bei der Eröffnung. Geplant wurde das Center von einer Weidener Architektengruppe und einem Amberger Landschaftsplaner. Die Bausumme betrug 8,5 Millionen Euro.
Die Anlage besteht aus dem Hauptgebäude mit Verwaltung, Restaurant mit Biergarten und einem Verkaufs- und Multifunktionsraum. Beeindruckend ist die Indoor-Kletterhalle, deren Boulder-Wand eine Höhe von 15 Metern hat. Einmieten können sich Soldaten und ihre Familien in sechs Cabins. Ein Lagergebäude bietet Platz für Räder, Sport- und Skiausrüstungen und Material, das im Outdoor-Recreation-Center ausgeliehen werden kann. Alle Gebäude sind mit Lärchenholz und Holzschindeln verkleidet.

The **"Wild B.O.A.R."** - *Bavaria Outdoor Adventure Recreation center offers leisure time activities, recreation and reintegration to the Americans. The head of a wild boar greets guests at the entrance. Boars and red deer are also the closest neighbors of the recreation center that is idyllically embedded into the surrounding nature and directly located at Dickhäuter Lake. Bavaria's Interior Minister Joachim Herrmann was among the guests when the center was opened in September 2013. The center was planned by a group of architects from Weiden and landscape architects from Amberg. The construction cost was 8.5 million Euro.*
The center consists of the main building that has administration offices, a restaurant with a beer garden, and a sales and multi-purpose room. The indoor rock climbing center features a 15-meter-high boulder wall. Six cabins are available for rent for soldiers and their families. A storage building offers room for bicycles, sports and skiing equipment and material that can be rented at the outdoor recreation center. All buildings are encased with larch wood and wood shingles.

Der Hochseilgarten mit der Indoor-Kletterhalle im Hintergrund.
The high ropes course with the indoor rock climbing center in the background.

Ein Paintballfeld, Campingplatz mit Pavillon, Spielgeräte, Bootssteg, Sitzecken und Grillplätze sowie ein Sensoric Park mit verschiedenen Stationen runden die Anlage ab. Trainiert werden kann auch in einem riesigen Hochseilgarten, der mit seinem Hauptturm und 62 Stationen, Höhen bis zu 15 Metern aufweist. Ein Naturlehrpfad mit grünem Klassenzimmer schließt sich direkt an das neue Center an.
Das „Wild B.O.A.R." wird von der Abteilung FMWR (Freizeit- und Familienbetreuung) der US-Armee Garnison Bavaria geführt. Angeboten werden auch Jagdkurse und Hobbyangeln sowie ein umfassendes Freizeitprogramm mit Ski-, Kletter- und Städtereisen.

The center also features a paintball field, a camp ground with pavilion, a playground, boat landing, lounge areas, BBQ areas and a sensoric park with various stations. Guests can also train on the large high ropes course which features a main tower and 62 stations with heights of up to 15 meters. A nature trail with a green classroom is located next to the center.
The "Wild B.O.A.R." is managed by the FMWR department of the US Army Garrison Bavaria. The center also offers hunting and fishing classes and a large leisure time program with ski, climbing and city trips.

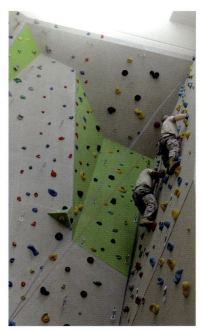

15 Meter Höhe hat die Indoor-Kletterhalle.
The indoor rock climbing center is 15 meters high.

KONTAKT-Club

Während des Krieges war der achteckige Bau in der Nähe des Wasserturms als der Zeitungskiosk Kaupert bekannt. Später war er Clubhaus des Deutsch-Amerikanischen Golfclubs. Heute hat im Building 108 der German-American KONTAKT-Club Grafenwöhr sein Domizil.
Unter der Schirmherrschaft des Bundesverbandes der Deutsch-Amerikanischen Freundschaft (BDAF) wurden in vielen Standorten KONTAKT-Clubs gegründet. Mit KONTAKT soll die Deutsch-Amerikanische Freundschaft gefördert und gestärkt werden.
Gemeinsame Stammtische im Clubhaus, Bowling-, Kegelabende und Turniere, Beteiligung am Deutsch-Amerikanischen Volksfest, Kinoabende, Weinfahrten, Ausflüge, Ausbuttern mit Volksmusik, Besuche im Altenheim, Grillnachmittage und vieles mehr sind Aktivitäten des Grafenwöhrer KONTAKT-Clubs. Vorsitzender Walter Brunner und seine Frau Anni bieten den deutschen und amerikanischen Clubmitgliedern dieses Angebot im KONTAKT-Newsletter und auf der Facebook-Seite Grafenwoehr/kontaktclub an.

During WWII, the octagonal building near the Water Tower was known as the Kaupert newsstand. Later, it was the club house of the German-American golf club. Today, building 108 is the home of the German-American KONTAKT Club Grafenwoehr.
KONTAKT clubs, organized under the federal association of German-American Friendship (BDAF), were established on several installations. The mission of KONTAKT is to promote and strengthen German-American friendship.
Joint meetings in the club house, bowling and Kegel (German type of bowling) evenings and tournaments, participating in the German-American Volksfest, movie evenings, wine trips, excursions, butter churning with traditional Bavarian music, visits to the senior citizens home, BBQs in the afternoon and much more are the activities offered by the Grafenwoehr KONTAKT-Club. Chairman Walter Brunner and his wife Anni offer German and American club members these events in the KONTAKT newsletter and on the Facebook page Grafenwoehr/kontaktclub.

Heimat des KONTAKT-Clubs ist der achteckige Kiosk in der Nähe des Wasserturms um 1970 und heute.
The octagonal building near the Water Tower is the home of the KONTAKT Club shown here 1970 and today.

Events

Neujahrsempfang und Unabhängigkeitstag

Eine Reihe von gesellschaftlichen Veranstaltungen bringen Deutsche und Amerikaner näher, dienen zur Pflege der Freundschaft und sollen zum beiderseitigen Verständnis beitragen. Die Veranstaltungen beginnen mit dem Neujahrsempfang. Militärs und zivile Gäste aus Kirche, Politik, von der Betriebsvertretung, Wirtschaft und dem öffentlichen Leben werden alljährlich vom Kommandeur des JMTC und dem Garnisonskommandeur dazu eingeladen. Mit vierteljährlichen Auszeichnungen werden deutsche Angestellte für langjährige Betriebszugehörigkeit geehrt. Der größte amerikanische Feiertag ist der Independance-Day. Am 4. Juli wird der Unabhängigkeitstag immer mit einem großen Brillantfeuerwerk beendet.

New Year's reception and Independence Day

A number of social events bring Germans and Americans together, foster their friendship, and are intended to increase mutual understanding. Events start with the New Year's reception. Every year, the commanding general of JMTC and the garrison commander invite military personnel and civilian guests representing the church, politics, the works council, the economy and public life to this event. Every quarter a longevity awards ceremony is held for civilian employees. The most important American holiday is Independence Day. Every Independence Day on the 4th of July ends with a large firework display.

Unabhängigkeitstag
Independence Day

Neujahrsempfang mit Abgeordneten, Behördenvertretern und Ehrengästen, links der Präsident des **KONTAKT** Clubs, Walter Brunner und seine Frau Anni.

New Year's Reception with politicians, officials and guests of honor; on the left, KONTAKT Club president Walter Brunner with his wife Anni.

Neujahrsempfang 2015
New Year's reception 2015

Feier des amerikanischen Unabhängigkeitstages - *Celebration of Independence Day*

Weihnachtskonzert der **USAREUR** Band
USAREUR Band christmas concert

Konzert des Bundeswehr Gebirgsmusikkorps Garmisch-Partenkirchen in der Stadthalle im Jubiläumsjahr
Concert of the German Army Mountain Music Corps Garmisch-Partenkirchen in the Stadthalle in the anniversary year

Konzert im Stadtpark mit der **USAREUR**-Dixieland Band
Concert of the USAREUR Dixieland Band in the city park

So wie damals die Regimentskapelle der königlich bayerischen Armee durch die Straßen marschierte, gehören Konzerte von Militärkapellen auch heute noch zum kulturellen Programm in Grafenwöhr.

Just like in the days when the Royal Bavarian Army marched through the streets, concerts by military bands are still a part of Grafenwoehr´s culctural program.

Tree-Lighting Ceremony

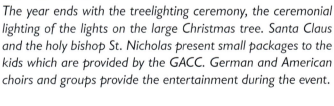

Mit der Treelighting-Ceremony, der feierlichen Entzündung der Lichter am großen Weihnachtsbaum schließt sich dann der Jahreskreis. Santa Claus und der heilige Bischof Nikolaus beschenken die Kinder mit Päckchen, die der DAGA zur Verfügung stellt. Deutsche und amerikanische Chöre und Gruppen gestalten die Feier.

The year ends with the treelighting ceremony, the ceremonial lighting of the lights on the large Christmas tree. Santa Claus and the holy bishop St. Nicholas present small packages to the kids which are provided by the GACC. German and American choirs and groups provide the entertainment during the event.

Die DAGA-Präsidenten: James Federline als Santa Claus, Helmuth Wächter und sein Vizepräsident Anton Dürr

The GACC presidents: James Federline as Santa Claus, Helmuth Wächter and his vice president Anton Dürr

Bischof Nikolaus und Santa Claus beschenken die kleinen und großen Kinder.

Bishop St. Nicholas and Santa Claus present gifts to the little and grown children.

"Sautrogrennen" mit prominenten Startern beim Fischerfest
"Pig Trough-Race" with VIP competitors at the Fishermen´s festival

Gemeinsamer Jubel bei der Fußball-Weltmeisterschaft
Celebrating together during the Soccer World Championship

Gemeinsam arbeiten und feiern

Immer mehr beteiligen sich die amerikanischen Mitbürger auch an vielen Veranstaltungen und Festen, Sportwettkämpfen oder sind gar Mitglieder in örtlichen Vereinen. Besucht werden dann unter anderem das Fischerfest oder das Maibaumfest. Viele Begegnungen, Freundschaften und Kontakte zwischen Deutschen und Amerikanern am Arbeitsplatz in der Nachbarschaft oder bei anderen Gelegenheiten tragen weiterhin zum gegenseitigen Verstehen und zu einem guten Miteinander bei.

Working and celebrating together

More and more American residents take part in local events, festivities, and sports competitions, or are members of local clubs. Some of the events they participate in are the Fischerfest and the Maypole ceremony. Many encounters, friendships and contacts between German and Americans are established at work, in neighborhoods, or on other occasions and continue to foster mutual understanding and cooperation.

Maibaumaufstellen 2015 - Maypole ceremony 2015

Volksfest

Eine große Waffenschau mit deutschen und amerikanischen Fahrzeugen ist die Hauptattrakrion beim Deutsch Amerikanischen Volksfest
The main attraction is the large weapons display with german and american tanks and military vehicles.

Volksfesteröffnung - *Volksfest opening*

Deutsch-Amerikanisches Volksfest

Am ersten Augustwochenende zieht es regelmäßig über 100.000 Menschen nach Grafenwöhr auf den Platz des Camp Kasserine. Die US-Army-Garnison und der Deutsch Amerikanische Gemeinsame Ausschuss (DAGA) laden seit über 50 Jahren zum Deutsch Amerikanischen Volksfest ein. Viele Fahrgeschäfte und Vergnügungsstände, ein großes Bierzelt, eine Zeltstadt mit Verkaufsständen und ein reichhaltiges Angebot von internationalen kulinarischen Genüssen, Bands, Musikgruppen und Vorführungen werden geboten. Hauptattraktion ist eine große Waffenschau mit deutschen und amerikanischen Panzern und Militärfahrzeugen.

German-American Volksfest

Every first weekend in August more than 100,000 people come to Camp Kasserine on the Grafenwoehr Training Area. For more than fifty years, the U.S. Army Garrison Grafenwoehr and the German American Community Council (GACC) invite guests to celebrate the German-American Volksfest. Many rides and booths, a large beer tent and a tent city with sales booths offering a large variety of international, culinary delicacies, bands, music groups and performances entertain the guests. The main attraction is the large weapons display with german and american tanks and military vehicles.

Festeröffnung und Bieranstich - *Fest opening and keg tapping*

Über 100.000 Besucher zieht es jährlich auf den Platz des Camp Kasserine. In ausgelassener Stimmung wird miteinander gefeiert und die deutsch-amerikanische Freundschaft gepflegt.

Every year, it attracts more than 100,000 visitors come to the fest at Camp Kasserine to celebrate together in a relaxed atmosphere and foster German-American friendship.

German-American Volksfest

Blick vom Wasserturm über die Militärgemeinde - *View from the Water Tower onto the military community*

Durchfahrt durch das Lager mit der **NEW-Radltour 2003**: Ein besonderes Kettenfahrzeug auf der Panzerstraße unterwegs
The 2003 NEW-Bike Tour passed through the training area: A special track vehicle on the tank trail.

USO - United Service Organizations

„Jeder Augenblick zählt" ist das Motto von USO - United Service Organisation. Die gemeinnützige Einrichtung hat es sich zur Aufgabe gemacht das Wohlbefinden der amerikanischen Truppen und ihrer Familien zu steigern. Hauptamtliche und ehrenamtliche Kräfte bieten eine Vielzahl von kostenlosen Aktivitäten und Dienstleistungen. USO ist in den Tower-Barracks im Gebäude 150 gegenüber der Main Post Chapel zu finden. Im Oktober 2015 wurde eine USO-Einrichtung im Gebäude 1164 im Camp Aachen eröffnet. Infos und Angebote auf facebook und Webpages.

USO - United Service Organizations

„*Every moment counts,*" *is the motto of the United Service Organizations (USO). The The USO is a private, nonprofit, non-partisan organization whose mission is to support the troops by providing morale, welfare and recreation-type services to American soldiers and their families. Full-time and volunteer workers provide a variety of free activities and services. The USO facility in building 150 on Tower Barracks across from the post chapel. A new USO facility opend in October 2015 in Camp Aachen, Building 1164. For more information and activities, go to facebook and Internet.*

EB-G
(Efficient Basing-Grafenwoehr)

Prägender Wirtschaftsfaktor seit 100 Jahren

Das Militär ist in der Region seit 100 Jahren Garant für Beschäftigung und lukrative Aufträge für die heimische Wirtschaft. Für 8,9 Millionen Mark wurden in den Jahren 1909 bis 1915 rund 250 Gebäude im Truppenlager Grafenwöhr errichtet. Spektakulär waren damals die Kasernenbauten für das III. Bayerische Armeekorps im Fachwerkstil. Um die zahlreichen Bauprojekte, Rodungen und Entwässerungen zu bewältigen, wurden in den Jahren 1909 bis 1912 jährlich rund 1000 Arbeiter aus verschiedenen Nationen beschäftigt. Nicht weniger eindrucksvoll ist das Projekt, das den 100. Geburtstag des Platzes begleitet.

Standortoptimierung

Dem Wasserturm wuchsen in den vergangenen Jahren die Baukräne über den Kopf. Das Synonym für die gigantische Maßnahme, die über fast ein Jahrzehnt hinweg die Bauwirtschaft boomen ließ, heißt EB-G: Efficient Basing-Grafenwoehr. Die Standortoptimierung umfasste ein Gesamtvolumen von 700 Millionen Euro. Es entstanden innerhalb des Lagers 50 Neubauten und 100 bestehende Gebäude wurden umgebaut und saniert. Das in seiner Größe bisher einmalige Projekt dient der Neustationierung einer kompletten Brigade in Grafenwöhr mit rund 4000 Soldaten, ihren Familienangehörigen und zivilen Bediensteten. Ergänzt wird das EB-G Programm von einem privaten Mietwohnungsprojekt. 1600 Wohneinheiten sind für die Soldaten und ihre Familien notwendig. 830 davon sind auf dem Netzaberg entstanden und weitere sollen noch in der Region gebaut werden. Insgesamt spricht man bei den Kasernenbauten und dem Wohnungsprojekt von einer Investition mit einem Volumen von einer Milliarde Euro.

Important economic factor for 100 years

The military has been a consistent source for employment and profitable contracts for the local employment for 100 years. 250 buildings were built on main post Grafenwoehr for 8.9 million Marks between 1909 and 1915. The barracks buildings for the 3rd Bavarian Army Corps in their Franconian half-timbered style were considered spectacular buildings at the time. About 1,000 workers from various nations were employed every year between 1909 – 1912 to complete the many construction projects, forest clearances and drainage projects. The project accompanying the 100th anniversary of the training area is just as impressive.

Efficient Basing - Grafenwoehr

During the few past years, large construction cranes towered over the Water Tower. The acronym for the gigantic construction measure that allowed the construction industry to grow for more than a decade is EB-G, or Efficient Basing - Grafenwoehr. It had a total economic value of 700 million Euro. On main post, 50 new buildings were built and 100 existing buildings were remodeled and renovated. This project, which is unique in its size, supports the stationing of an entire brigade with about 4,000 soldiers, their family members, and civilian employees in Grafenwoehr. The EB-G program is augmented by a privately financed housing project. Of the 1,600 housing units needed to accommodate the soldiers and their families, 830 of them were built on Netzaberg, the others are to be built in the region. A total of one billion Euro were invested into the military construction project and into the construction of the housing units.

September 2005: Baukräne wachsen gen Himmel und dem Wasserturm über den Kopf.

September 2005: Construction cranes rise into the sky and tower over the Water Tower.

Platz für Fahrzeuge und Panzer. Die technischen Bereiche der Bataillone mit Werkstätten und Motorpools
Room for vehicles and tanks. The technical areas of the battalions with maintenance buildings and motor pools

1910 – 2010

Parallelen weist die Gründung des Lagers auch mit dem heutigen EB-G Projekt auf. 1907 richtete das bayerische Kriegsministerium eine Heeresbauleitung unter der Führung des königlichen Baurates Wilhelm Kemmler in Grafenwöhr ein. Mit der Planung und Bauausführung wurden der in Nürnberg lebende Architekt Jürgen Sievers und ein großer Mitarbeiterstab beauftragt.

Zur Umsetzung des Mammutprojekts unserer Tage nahm im Februar 2002 die Baudienststelle Grafenwöhr mit dem Leitenden Baudirektor Klaus Gerstendorff, einem Nürnberger, als neue Abteilung der Regierung der Oberpfalz ihre Arbeit auf. Tür an Tür wurden im Camp Aachen mit den Fachkollegen der US-Bauverwaltung der Garnison und dem U.S. Army Corps of Engineers die einzelnen Projekte abgewickelt. Planung und Bauausführung übernahmen zivile Architekturbüros und Baufirmen.

1910 – 2010

There are parallels between the establishment of the main camp and today's EB-G project. In 1907, the Bavarian War Ministry established a construction office, headed by Royal Engineer Wilhelm Kemmler, in Grafenwoehr. The planning efforts and the construction were led by Nuremberg architect Jürgen Sievers and his large staff. To realize the huge EB-G project, the government of the Upper Palatinate established a construction office in Grafenwoehr in February 2002. All projects were planned in Camp Aachen next door to and with the colleagues of the EB-G section of the Garrison's Department of Public Works and the US Army Corps of Engineers – Europe Division. Civilian architects, planners and construction companies were hired to complete the construction projects.

Um 1910: Für die damalige Zeit waren moderne Maschinen im Einsatz. Die Bauleute und Handwerker sind stolz auf ihr Werk.
Around 1910: The most modern machines of the time were used. The construction workers and craftsmen are proud of their work.

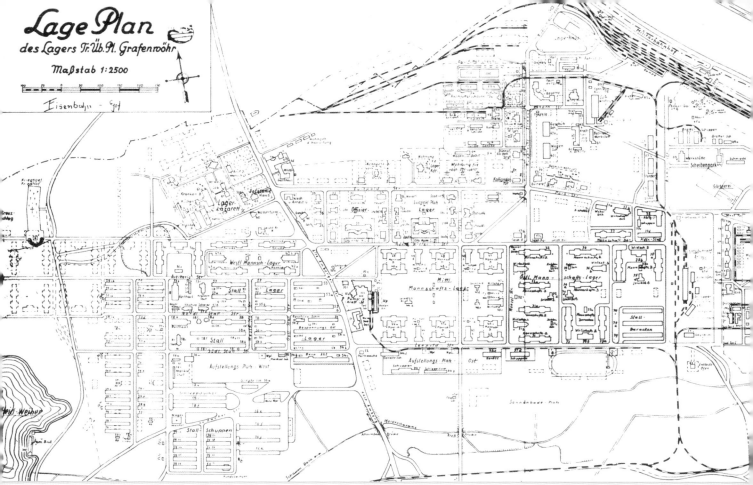

Der Plan des Lagers von 1940 lässt die Perioden der Erweiterung erkennen. Unten links der Heidweiher
A plan of the camp from 1940 shows the periods of expansion. The Heidweiher pond is seen on the bottom left.

50 Neubauten

Kernstück der EB-G Baumaßnahmen ist der sogenannte BCT-Bereich (Brigade Combat Team) am Heidweiher. Um das ehemalige Soldatenschwimmbad, das nun als riesiges Regenrückhaltebecken genutzt wird, entstanden zwölf neue Unterkunftsgebäude für unverheiratete Soldaten sowie die Bataillons-Komplexe. Zu diesen Bereichen gehören die Gebäude für den Brigadestab und die Bataillonsstäbe, die Verwaltungsgebäude für 28 Kompanien, die Wartungshallen, Werkstätten, Schleppdächer und Motorpools. Die technischen Bereiche sind alle direkt an die Panzerstraße angebunden, um eine schnelle Verlegung auf die Schießbahnen zu ermöglichen. Notwendig war die Errichtung einer umfangreichen Infrastruktur mit Straßen, Parkplätzen, Kreisverkehr sowie Wasserversorgung und -entsorgung.

Im Zuge des Baus der Straße zum Netzaberg mit zusätzlicher Anbindung an die Staatsstraße Grafenwöhr-Eschenbach waren zwei Brückenbauwerke notwendig. Im Village Center am Netzaberg entstanden Grund- und Mittelschule, Kindergarten, Jugendzentrum sowie eine Tankstelle mit kleinem Einkaufsmarkt.

Auf dem Gelände des ehemaligen Camps Tunisia steht heute ein riesiges Sportzentrum. Gebaut wurden außerdem die neue Zufahrt über das Tor 6, der Kontrollbereich am Tor 3, der neue US-Scheibenhof, Fernmeldegebäude, Heizzentrale, das gigantische Einkaufszentrum mit Großparkplatz sowie die Tankstelle mit kleinem Supermarkt, um nur die wichtigsten und größten Projekte zu nennen.

50 new buildings

The centerpiece of all EB-G construction is the so-called BCT (Brigade Combat Team) area at Heidweiher pond. Twelve new barracks buildings for single soldiers and the brigade buildings were built around the former soldier's swimming pool that is now being used as a water retention basin. The BCT area includes buildings for the brigade and battalion headquarters staff, administration buildings (Company Orderly Rooms) for 28 companies, maintenance buildings, repair shops and motor pools. The technical areas are directly connected to the tank trail to guarantee a fast deployment to the ranges. A large infrastructure of roads, parking lots, traffic circle, water and waste water connections had to be built a well.

Two bridges had to be built as part of the construction of the road to Netzaberg and its connection to the state street between Grafenwoehr and Eschenbach. An elementary and middle school, a child development center, a youth services center along with a gas station and small shoppette were built at Netzaberg Village Center.

Today, a large physical fitness center is located on the area that used to be Camp Tunisia. Other construction projects include the new Gates 3 and 6, the target machine shop, a new communications building, a new central heat building, a gigantic shopping center with parking lot, and the gas station with a shoppette to name just a few.

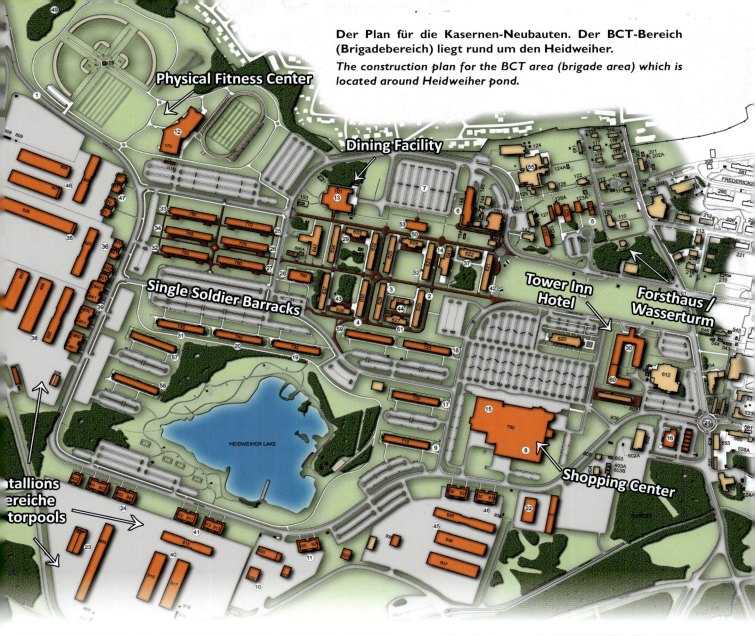

Der Plan für die Kasernen-Neubauten. Der BCT-Bereich (Brigadebereich) liegt rund um den Heidweiher.

The construction plan for the BCT area (brigade area) which is located around Heidweiher pond.

50 Neubauten und 100 Umbauten beinhaltet das EBG-Programm. Hier der Neubau eines Mannschaftsblocks, dahinter werden Gebäude aus den Jahren 1937/38 renoviert und teilweise neu aufgebaut.

The EB-G program includes the construction of 50 new buildings and the renovation of 100 buildings. Shown here is a new barracks building. The buildings from 1937/38 in the background are either being renovated or newly reconstructed.

Der Heidweiher: Damals Soldatenschwimmbad, heute Rückhaltebecken für das Oberflächenwasser

Heidweiher pond: Today, the former soldiers' swimming pool is a water retention basin for surface water

100 Umbauten

Ein Schwerpunkt der Umbauten lag im Camp Normandie. Aus den alten Baracken entstand der Campus der NCO-Academy, der einzigen Unteroffiziersschule der US-Armee außerhalb der Vereinigten Staaten. Dafür wurde auch eine eigene Truppenküche gebaut. Neun kleinere Gebäude, einschließlich des alten Lazaretts wurden zusammengefasst und modernisiert und dienen nun als Hauptquartier des Joint Multinational Training Commands (JMTC). Zu den Umbauten zählen auch das US-Rathaus, die Zahnarztklinik mit Ambulanz sowie die neue Truppenküche. Die Kasernen aus den Jahren 1937/38 und der 600er-Bereich wurden modernisiert oder komplett erneuert zur Schaffung von acht Hauptquartiers- und drei Unterkunftsgebäuden. Auch das Hauptquartier der US-Garnison (Gebäude 500) ist eine umgebaute Kaserne aus der Zeit um 1910.

100 reconstructions and renovations

One focus of the reconstruction measures was at Camp Normandy. The old barracks were turned into the campus of the NCO Academy, the only non-commissioned officers academy outside the United States of America. The academy also received a separate dining facility. Back on Main Post, nine smaller buildings, including the old hospital, were combined and modernized to become the new JMTC headquarters building. Also remodeled were Building 244, the medical and dental clinic, and the new dining facility. The barracks that were built in 1937/38, forming the so-called 600 area, were modernized and completely renovated to be turned into eight headquarters and three barracks buildings. The garrison headquarters' building (Building 500) is also a remodeled barracks building built around 1910.

Spektakulär für die damalige Zeit: Vom Reißbrett weg wurde das Lager gebaut.

Unusual for the time (1910): This camp was completely planned on the drawing board prior to construction.

Offizielle Feier des Bauabschlusses im April 2010, doch es soll noch weitergehen. Bürgermeister Helmuth Wächter, Landrat Simon Wittmann, Regierungspräsidentin Brigitta Brunner, Innenminister Joachim Herrmann, Staatssekretär Dr. Andreas Scheuer, Oberst Nils C. Sorenson, Oberst Brian T. Boyle, Brigadegeneral Steven L. Salazar und Oberst John Kem stellten sich zum Erinnerungsbild.
EB-G transition ceremony in April 2010. Mayor Helmuth Wächter, County Commissioner Simon Wittmann, Government President Brigitta Brunner, Minister of the Interior Joachim Herrmann, State Secretary Dr. Andreas Scheuer, Colonel Nils C. Sorenson, Colonel Brian T. Boyle, Brigadier General Steven L. Salazar and Colonel John Kem pose for a photo.

Noch kein Ende

Die offizielle Bauabschlussfeier des EB-G Programms fand am 28. April 2010 statt. Der Staatssekretär im Bundesbauministerium, Dr. Andreas Scheuer, der bayerische Innenminister Joachim Hermann, Landrat Simon Wittmann, Brigadegeneral Steven L. Salazar und Oberst John Kem, vom U.S. Army Corps of Engineers zeigten sich in ihren Ansprachen glücklich über das herausragende Werk. Salazar machte aber auch deutlich, dass das Bauen in Grafenwöhr noch nicht zu Ende ist. Es sollen Mittel für weitere sechs große Unterkunftsgebäude beantragt werden. Die Vision der Standortoptimierung werde erst dann Realität, „wenn genügend Wohnraum für die amerikanischen Familien vorhanden ist", so Salazar.

No end in sight

The official EB-G transition ceremony was held on April 28, 2010. In their speeches, Dr. Andreas Scheuer, Parliamentary State Secretary in the German Federal Department of Construction, Bavarian Minister of the Interior Joachim Herrmann, County Commissioner Simon Wittmann, Brigadier General Steven L. Salazar, and Colonel John Kem of the U.S. Army Corps of Engineers – Europe Division expressed their happiness about the outstanding project. But Salazar clearly pointed out that construction at Grafenwoehr has not come to an end yet. Funds will be requested for six additional large barracks. The vision of Efficient Basing – Grafenwoehr will only be realized when "there is sufficient housing for the American families," said Salazar.

Beeindruckend in den Dimensionen: Bauten für insgesamt 700 Millionen Euro entstehen.
The dimensions are impressive. Buildings at a total cost of 700 million Euro are constructed.

Single Soldier Barracks

Beeindruckende Größen. Drei der bislang gebauten Blöcke für alleinstehende Soldaten. Am oberen linken Bildrand sind im Vergleich dazu die Wohnblöcke in der Eichendorffstraße zu erkennen.

Three of the already completed barracks for single soldiers. Impressive in size compared to the apartment buildings on Eichendorffstraße seen in the upper left corner.

Zwölf neue Unterkunftsgebäude für alleinstehende Soldaten wurden bislang am Heidweiher gebaut. Die Wohnblöcke unterscheiden sich in ihrer Ausstattung erheblich von den bisherigen Kasernenbauten mit großen Mannschaftsstuben. Nach dem „1+1-Unterbringungs-Standard" der US-Armee verfügt jeder Soldat bzw. Soldatin über ein eigenes Zimmer. Je zwei dieser Zimmer sind zu einem Apartment zusammengefasst. Die Räume haben einen großen begehbaren Kleiderschrank. Das Badezimmer teilen sich die beiden Soldaten, ebenso den Vorraum, in dem eine kleine Küche mit Kühlschrank, Mikrowellenherd und zwei Herdplatten eingebaut ist. Die dreigeschossigen Gebäude mit einer Gesamtfläche von je 8100 Quadratmetern haben 22 Apartments pro Etage. Im Dachgeschoss gibt es elf größere Apartments für Unteroffiziere. Jeder Block bietet Platz für 143 Soldaten. Die durchgängig betonierten Unterkünfte sind sehr stabil und widerstandsfähig und erfüllen den aktuellen Sicherheitsstandard der US-Armee. Die Gesamtkosten pro Gebäude belaufen sich auf zirka elf Millionen Euro. Weitere Unterkunftsblöcke sind in Planung.

Twelve new barracks for single soldiers have so far been built around Heidweiher pond. The interior of the barracks differs greatly from the former barracks buildings with large rooms. Following the U.S. Army's 1+1 standard, each soldier has his or her own room. Two of these rooms make up an apartment. The rooms have a large walk-in closet. The two soldiers share the bathroom, and the foyer with a small kitchenette equipped with a refrigerator, a microwave oven and two hot plates. The three-story buildings with a total floor space of 8,100 square meters, feature 22 apartments on each floor. Eleven larger apartments for non-commissioned officers are located in the attic. Each building has room for 143 soldiers. The concrete buildings are very stable and robust and fulfill the force protection security standards. The total cost for each building amount to about eleven million Euro. Additional barracks are in the planning stage.

Community Service Center

US-Rathaus

Von der Heeresbäckerei zum hochmodernen US-Rathaus: Dort, wo einst Kommissbrot gebacken wurde, residieren nun Service- und Verwaltungsdienststellen der US-Armee Garnison Grafenwöhr. Um 1937 errichtete die Wehrmacht an der Wache 3 das dominierende Gebäude als Großbäckerei. Nach 1945 nutzten es die Amerikaner weiter. Für rund 6,5 Millionen Euro wurde das geschichtsträchtige Gemäuer zu einem repräsentativen Rathaus der US-Militärgemeinde, dem Community Service Center umgebaut und erweitert.

Kommissbäckerei

Zur Versorgung der Wehrmacht auf dem Übungsplatz und im süddeutschen Raum wurde die Kommissbäckerei im Zuge der Erweiterung des Übungsplatzes im Dritten Reich gebaut. Silos, die rund um die Bäckerei standen, dienten zur Bevorratung eines Teils der Reichsreserve an Getreide. In ihrer großzügig dimensionierten Bauweise war die Heeresbäckerei damals einer der rationellsten und fortschrittlichsten Großbetriebe. Produkt der Heeresbäckerei war das kastenförmige Kommissbrot. Das Mehl wurde in Säcken über das direkt am Gebäude verlaufende Gleis angeliefert und im Obergeschoss gelagert. Soldaten und zivile Angestellte waren bis Kriegsende hier im Einsatz. Zwölf doppelstöckige Ausziehbacköfen der Firma Pfleiderer waren die Herzstücke in der riesigen Backstube. Aus Koksbunkern wurden die Öfen von der Rückseite her beheizt.
Bei der schweren Bombardierung 1945 entging die Heeresbäckerei, obwohl sie direkt im Zentrum des Angriffs lag, der Zerstörung.

Community Service Center

An Army bakery is turned into a modern U.S. town hall. Service and administration offices of the U.S. Army Garrison Grafenwoehr are now located in a building where once bread was baked for the German Army. Around 1937, the Wehrmacht built the building that towers over Gate 3 to house an industrial bakery. After 1945, the Americans continued using it. For more than 6.5 million Euro the historic building was remodeled and expanded to become a representative town hall known as Community Service Center for the U.S. military community.

Industrial bakery

The bakery was built to provide bread to the soldiers stationed in Grafenwoehr and Southern Germany when the training area was expanded during the Third Reich. Silos, located around the bakery, were used to store a part of the Reich's grain reserve. With its spacious floor plan, the bakery was one of the most efficient and modern industrial bakeries of the time. A rectangular shaped, coarse grain bread was produced at the bakery. Flour was delivered in sacks via the railroad tracks adjacent to the building and stored upstairs. Soldiers and civilians worked there until the end of World War II. Twelve two-story rack ovens produced by the Pfleiderer Corporation were the heart of the large bakery. The ovens were heated from the rear with coal out of bunkers. The bakery, although located in the center of the 1945 air raids, was not destroyed during the attacks.

Mit 112 Metern Länge und einer Gesamtnutzfläche von 8500 Quadratmetern ist das Community Service Center das größte Rathaus in der Region.

The Community Service Center is the largest town hall in the region with a length of 112 meters and a total floor space of 8,500 square meters.

Die alte Heeresbäckerei stand zwischen dem Getreidesilo und dem Magazin an der Wache 3.
The old Army bakery was located between the grain silo and a warehouse at Gate 3.

Donuts und Rosinenbrot

Noch 1945 wurde hier unter der Regie der US-Armee mit deutschen Angestellten und auch Kriegsgefangenen weiterhin Brot gebacken. Wie Zeitgenossen erzählten, lief der Betrieb rund um die Uhr in drei Schichten mit jeweils 60 Mann. Viele Grafenwöhrer fanden in der Not der Nachkriegszeit hier Arbeit und konnten in den Pausen mit Kaffee, Brot und Salzbutter auch ihren Hunger stillen. Die Vorliebe der Amerikaner für süßes Gebäck war der Grund dafür, dass bald auch eine Konditorei entstand. Neben Kuchen und Torten waren vor allem Donuts gefragt, ein typisch amerikanisches Schmalzgebäck. Verwendet wurde amerikanisches Weizenmehl, das per Bahn von Bremerhaven nach Grafenwöhr transportiert wurde. Im Obergeschoss waren die Mehlsäcke gestapelt. Über große Trichter und Rutschen wurde Mehl in die Rühr- und Knetwerke der darunter liegenden Backstube gekippt. Bäcker bereiteten den Teig zu. An großen Tischen waren sechs bis acht Mann mit dem Wiegen und Portionieren beschäftigt. In Kastenformen ging es dann in die Öfen. So entstanden täglich über 20 000 der schmackhaften Weiß- und Rosinenbrote.

Das Brot diente zur Versorgung im Lager. Sattelschlepper lieferten es auch an weitere US-Standorte.

Vermutlich bis Anfang der 1960er Jahre lief der Betrieb in der Großbäckerei. Danach wurde das Gebäude 244 für Büros und als riesiger Lagerraum genutzt. Zeitweise war es auch Ausweichquartier für die US-Telefonvermittlung. Die Öfen und die Bäckerei hatten endgültig ausgedient. Anstatt kleiner Brötchen werden im neuen Community Service Center große und kleine Entscheidungen für den Standort „gebacken". Die alte Heeresbäckerei kommt so zu neuen Ehren.

Donuts and raisin bread

After 1945, the bakery continued to bake bread with German employees and prisoners of war under the control of the U.S. Army. Eye witnesses said that baking operations were conducted 24/7 with three shifts of 60 workers each. Many Grafenwoehr residents found work here during those trying times after the war and were also able to satisfy their hunger with coffee, bread and salted butter during the breaks.

The Americans' preference for sweet cakes was the reason why a pastry shop was soon added. Apart from cakes and tarts, mainly donuts, a traditional American lard pastry, were produced. The flour used was American wheat flour that was transported from Bremerhaven to Grafenwoehr by train. The flour sacks were stored upstairs. Through large funnels and slides, the flour reached the stirring and kneading machines in the bakery below. Bakers prepared the dough. Six to eight workers weighed and portioned the dough on large tables. It was then put in the oven in rectangular baking pans. More than 20,000 of the tasty loafs of white bread and raisin bread were produced that way every day. The bread was produced for the Grafenwoehr garrison and delivered by truck to other U.S. military installations.

The bakery was presumably operated until the beginning of the 1960s. Afterwards Building 244 was used as office and storage space. For a while, the U.S. switchboard was located there as well.

The ovens and the bakery had become a remnant of the past. Today, small and big decisions are made in the Community Service Center where once small breads were baked. The old Army bakery has been put to new use.

Heute ist das Community Service Center das dominierende Gebäude an der Lagerwache.
Today, the Community Service Center towers over Gate 3.

Die Backöfen wurden von der Rückseite her mit Koks befeuert.
The ovens were heated from the rear with coal.

So sah die alte Kommissbäckerei aus. Bis Anfang der 1960er Jahre wurde hier fleißig gebacken. Danach war das Gebäude 244 nur mehr Lagerraum.
A photo of the old bakery. Bread was baked until the beginning of the 1960s. After that, Building 244 was used as a storage facility.

Herzstücke der Backstube waren die zwölf großen doppelstöckigen Ausziehbacköfen.
Über 20 000 Brote konnten täglich gebacken werden.
Twelve two-story rack ovens produced by the Pfleiderer Corporation were the heart of the large bakery. More than 20,000 breads could be baked daily.

Ein Gleisanschluss führte direkt zur Heeresbäckerei. Mehl und auch die Kohlen für die Feuerungen wurden per Bahntransport angeliefert.
The Army bakery was directly connected to the railroad system. Flour and coal for the ovens were delivered by train.

Die Abrissbagger leisteten ganze Arbeit. Das Getreidesilo musste der Wache 3 weichen und machte den Blick auf die frühere Heeresbäckerei frei.
The dredgers did a great job. The grain silo was demolished to make room for Gate 3 and made room for an unobstructed view of the former Army bakery.

Das Community Service Center war die erste Großbaustelle des EB-G Programms.
The Community Service Center was the first large construction project of the EB-G program.

Auftakt zum EB-G Programm

Als eines der ersten Projekte des EB-G Programms („Efficient Basing Grafenwöhr" – Standortoptimierung Grafenwöhr) fiel im Oktober 2003 der Startschuss für den Bau des neuen US-Rathauses. Zuvor musste das Getreidesilo am Lagereingang abgebrochen werden.

Die alte Bäckerei wurde völlig entkernt. Wenige Veränderungen gab es im Kellergeschoss. Neben den notwendigen Technikräumen entstanden Lagerflächen. Im Erdgeschoss sowie im ersten Obergeschoss wurden insgesamt 48 Büroräume, vier Konferenzsäle sowie Sozialräume, Nebenräume und Toilettenanlagen eingebaut.

Im Zentrum des 112 Meter langen Rathauses verschafft ein neuer Eingangsbereich mit kreisrundem Treppenhaus und Wartezonen den Überblick. Zwei weitere Treppenhäuser mit Ein- und Ausgängen liegen im östlichen und westlichen Gebäudeteil. Neu aufgesetzt auf den Baukörper wurde als Reserve ein zweites Obergeschoss; der Innenausbau soll bei Bedarf zu einem späteren Zeitpunkt folgen. Das Dachgeschoss nimmt die Technikzentralen für Lüftung und Kühlung auf. 300 Pkw-Stellplätze sind südlich des Community Service Centers angeordnet; auch dafür musste ein altes Magazin weichen.

Das größte Rathaus der Region

Das Community Service Center in der früheren Heeresbäckerei ist mit einer möglichen Gesamtnutzfläche von 8500 Quadratmetern (einschließlich der Lagerflächen) in seinen Ausmaßen das größte Rathaus der Region.

In diesen Büros sind die verschiedensten Dienststellen untergebracht, darunter das Wohnungsbüro (Housing Office), die Finanzverwaltung, die zentrale Auftragsvergabestelle, die Personalbüros für deutsche und amerikanische Mitarbeiter und das Passbüro.

Die Bauarbeiten dauerten nur 14 Monate. Der obere Stock wurde nur im Rohbau erstellt und bietet jederzeit Erweiterungsmöglichkeit.
Construction lasted 14 months. The interior of the upper floor was left unfinished and provides space for a future expansion of office space.

Start of the EB-G program

Construction of the new town hall started in October 2003 and was one of the first projects of the Efficient Basing – Grafenwoehr (EB-G) program. Before construction could start, the large grain silo at the entrance to the training area had to be demolished. The old bakery was completely cored. Only a few things were changed in the basement where engineering and storage rooms were built. A total of 48 offices, four conference rooms, break rooms, storage room and rest rooms were built on the first and second floors.

A new lobby with a round stairwell and waiting areas is the center of the 112 meter-long town hall. Two other stairwells with entrance and exit doors are located in the eastern and western part of the building. A third, additional floor was put on top of the building to allow for extra office space in the future. The completion of its interior will be done as required. The exhaust and cooling system are located in the attic. Another old warehouse was demolished to make room for 300 parking spaces south of the Community Service Center.

The largest town hall in the region

With a floor space of 8,500 square meters (including storage space), the Community Service Center in the former bakery is the largest town hall in the region. The following offices are located in the building: housing office, finance office, regional contracting office, civilian personnel center, human resources office, Army community services, installation access and pass office.

Dining Facility

Die neue Dining Facility, dahinter die alte hölzerne Turnhalle
The new dining facility; seen behind it is the old wooden gym

Auch hier sind die Zahlen beeindruckend: 600 Sitzplätze und eine Kapazität von 1800 Mahlzeiten pro Frühstück, Lunch oder Dinner. Die neue Truppenküche im Hauptlager ist nach modernsten Gesichtspunkten eingerichtet. Für 7,8 Millionen Euro wurden der alte Küchenbau und der Speisesaal zu einer modernen Großküche umgebaut. Die Planung begann im Mai 2002, im Juli 2004 war der Baubeginn, im August 2007 wurde die Dining Facility eröffnet. Das Gebäude hat eine Fläche von 3200 Quadratmetern. Schon mehrmals wurden die Armee-Köche bei Wettbewerben mit Preisen bedacht.

Here, the numbers are impressive as well: 600 seats and a capacity of 1,800 meals per breakfast, lunch or dinner. The new dining facility on main post is equipped with state-of-the-art technology. The old kitchen and dining area were turned into a modern facility for about 7.8 million Euro. Planning started in May 2002, construction in July 2004. The new facility was opened in August 2007. The building has a floor space of 3,200 square meters. Its Army chefs have won several awards during cooking competitions.

Modernste Ausstattung steht für die Armee-Köche zur Verfügung. Die Küche hat eine Kapazität von 1800 Mahlzeiten.
State-of-the-art equipment is at the Army chef's disposal. The kitchen has a capacity of 1,800 meals.

Architektur am Speisesaal
Architecture of the dining hall

Physical Fitness Center

Das Physical Fitness Center auf dem Platz des ehemaligen Camps Tunisia gehört zu den größten und modernsten Sportanlagen in ganz Bayern. Zirka zwölf Millionen Euro ließ sich die US-Armee die Anlage kosten. Sie bietet nicht nur eine willkommene Freizeitbeschäftigung, sondern fördert die Fitness der Soldaten. Die große Zweifachhalle ist in erster Linie für Ballsportarten konzipiert. Sie hat zwei Galerien mit einer integrierten Inndoor-Lauf- und Aufwärmbahn. 1000 Tribünenplätze sind in den Seitenwänden versenkt.

Hinter der riesigen Glasfassade erstreckt sich der Fitnessbereich, in dem rund 200 elektronisch gesteuerte Trainingsgeräte, Spinning-Räder, Hantelbänke und Kraftmaschinen stehen. Allein die Kosten dafür beliefen sich auf zirka zwei Millionen US-Dollar. Drei separate Übungsräume stehen für Spinning, Aerobic, Judo und andere Sportarten zur Verfügung. Im Foyer ist ein künstlicher Kletterfelsen für Bouldering die Attraktion. Anmeldung, Technikraum, Wäscherei, Verwaltung sowie der Umkleide- und Duschbereich mit zwei Saunen bilden den Funktionstrakt der Halle. Das gesamte Gebäude hat eine Grundfläche von 6060 Quadratmetern.

Im Außenbereich bietet die Anlage den Sportlern drei Softball-Felder (Baseball), ein Fußballfeld (Soccer) sowie ein Leichtathletikstadion. Ausgestattet ist der Freibereich mit großen Flutlichtmasten. Das gesamte Areal kann auf einer Laufbahn umrundet werden, die genau eine Länge von einer Meile hat.

Der Bau des Physical Fitness Centers begann im April 2005, Eröffnung war im März 2006.

The physical fitness center was built on the grounds of the former Camp Tunisia and is one of the largest and most modern sports facilities in Bavaria. The U.S. Army invested about twelve million Euro into the facility. It not only offers a much appreciated past time but also fosters the fitness of the soldiers. The large duplex gymnasium was mainly built for basketball games. It has two galleries with an integrated indoor running track. Seats for 1,000 spectators are hidden in the side walls.

The fitness area, with more than 200 electronically powered fitness devices, spinning bikes, weight-lifting benches and cardiovascular training equipment, is located behind a large glass facade. The cost for the equipment alone amounted to about two million U.S. dollars. Three separate exercise rooms for spinning, aerobics, judo and other sports are available. An artificial boulder for rock climbing practice is the attraction in the foyer. Reception desk, engineering room, laundry room and administration offices and the locker rooms and showers with two saunas make up the functional wing of the facility. The entire building has a floor space of 6,060 square meters.

The outdoor area offers athletes three softball fields, a soccer field and a track and field arena, and is equipped with large floodlight towers. A running track, with a length of exactly one mile, runs around the entire outdoor area. Construction of the physical fitness center started in April 2005 and it was opened in March 2006.

Das Physical Fitness Center setzt neue Maßstäbe. Es kostete 12 Millionen Euro, hier die Außenfassade der großen Halle, des Fitnessbereichs und des Funktionstrakts.

The physical fitness center sets new standards. It cost 12 million Euro. Pictured here is the exterior of the gym, the fitness area and the functional wing.

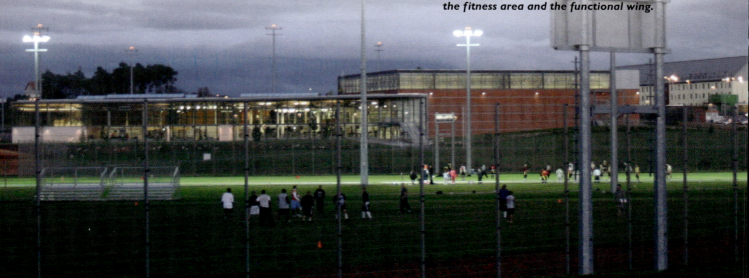

Der Fitnessbereich: Planung, Bau und Nutzung

The fitness area: Planning, construction, use

Die große Sporthalle mit den Tribünenplätzen. Oben ist die Galerie mit der Lauf- und Aufwärmbahn.

The large gym with the bleachers. On top is the gallery with the running track.

Eines der größten Einkaufszentren der US-Armee in Europa mit 1000 Parkplätzen vor der Türe
One of the largest shopping centers of the U.S. Army in Europe with about 1,000 parking spaces out front

Shopping Center

Mit Gesamtkosten von zirka 28 Millionen Euro ist das Shopping Center eines der teuersten Einzelprojekte im EB-G Programm und eines der größten Einkaufszentren der US-Armee in Europa. Im sogenannten Food Court gibt es verschiedene Fast Food-Essensangebote. Im Post Exchange (PX/14100 Quadratmeter) werden Kleidung, Elektrogeräte, Sportartikel, Spielwaren und alle Dinge des täglichen Bedarfs angeboten. In einer Ladenstraße sind zehn Geschäfte zu finden, darunter ein Herren- und ein Damenfriseur, ein Optiker, ein Blumenladen und ein Kosmetikstudio. Der Supermarkt (Commissary) bietet auf einer Fläche von 5500 Quadratmetern ein reichhaltiges Angebot an Lebensmitteln.

Der Parkplatz ist für ca. 1000 Fahrzeuge ausgelegt. Der Bau des Shopping Centers startete im Oktober 2005 und wurde im Juli 2007 vollendet. Die offizielle Eröffnung war am 26. September 2007. Die Gesamtverkaufsfläche des Komplexes beträgt 19600 Quadratmeter.

With a total cost of about 28 million Euro, the shopping center is one of the most expensive projects of the EB-G program. One of the largest shopping centers of the U.S. Army in Europe consists of a food court with various fast food restaurants, a post exchange (PX/14,100 square meters), where clothes, electronics, sports articles, toys and other articles for everyday use are sold, a mall with ten stores, among them a barber shop, a beauty shop, an optometrist, a flower shop and a day spa, and a commissary which offers a large variety of food products on a floor space of 5,500 square meters.

The parking lot has room for about 1,000 vehicles. Construction of the shopping center started in October 2005 and was completed in July 2007. It was officially opened on September 26, 2007. The sales floor of the shopping center has a size of 19,600 square meters.

Baubeginn für das Einkaufszentrum war im Oktober 2005, vorher musste das Baugelände geräumt und nach Blindgängern abgesucht werden.
Construction of the shopping center started in October 2005. Before construction could be started, the area had to be cleared and swept for unexploded ordnance.

Der Rohbau des Einkaufszentrums im Mai 2006. Das Tower Theater, rechts oberhalb der Baustelle, wirkt gegen den 20 000 Quadratmeter-Bau winzig.
The shell of the shopping center in May 2006. The Tower Theater, to the top right of the construction area looks tiny compared to the 20,000 square meter-building.

Das Warensortiment lässt keine Wünsche offen.
The assortment of goods leaves nothing to be desired.

Im Food Court
Inside the food court

HOTEL

Vom „Tower Inn Hotel" zum „Grafenwöhr Army Lodging"
From the „Tower Inn Hotel" to the "Grafenwoehr Army Lodging" Facility

18,5 Millionen für neues Hotel

Das „Tower Inn Hotel" im alten Militärgasthaus hat ausgedient. Direkt gegenüber dem Wasserturm entstand an der Lexington Avenue in unmittelbarer Nähe von Burger King, Bowling Center, Java Cafe´, Kino und US-Shopping Center das neue „Grafenwoehr Army Lodging". Der Grundstein für das riesige Gebäude wurde im März 2009 gelegt, im April 2010 konnte Richtfest gefeiert werden. Die offizielle Eröffnung fand im September 2011 statt. Die Baukosten für das neue Haus betrugen zirka 18,5 Millionen Euro. Generalunternehmer für den Hotelbau war die Firma Mickan aus Amberg, geplant wurde es vom Amberger Architekturbüro Harth + Flierl.

18.5 million Euro for a new hotel

The times of the "Tower Inn Hotel" are over. The new Grafenwoehr Army Lodging facility is located on Lexington Avenue, across from the Water Tower and the parade field. It is within walking distance of Burger King, the bowling center, Java Café, theater and shopping center. The groundbreaking ceremony for the new hotel took place in March 2009, the topping-out ceremony was held in April 2010, and it was officially opened in September 2011. The construction cost for the new building was approximately 18.5 million Euro. General contractor for the new hotel was Mickan Construction Co. from Amberg, the architects were Harth + Flierl, also from Amberg.

„Tower Inn Hotel" im Offizierslager

Die neue Anlage ersetzt das „Tower Inn" Hotel. Die Rezeption und einige Räume waren im alten Militärgasthaus untergebracht. Die insgesamt 72 Zimmer waren verteilt auf sieben Gebäude, die als Offizierswohnungen in der Gründerzeit um 1910 errichtet wurden. Das „Tower Inn Hotel" entsprach nicht mehr den Infrastrukturstandards. Mit dem Bau des modernen, zeitgerechten Hotels wurde auch dem Bedarf an mehr Hotelraum entsprochen, der mit der Erweiterung der Garnison entstanden ist.

"Tower Inn" hotel in the officers' quarters

The new facility replaced the "Tower Inn" hotel. The reception and some rooms were located in the old military guest house. Its 72 rooms were located in seven buildings who were built in 1910 as officers' barracks. The "Tower Inn" no longer met current infrastructure standards. The construction of the modern, up-to-date lodging facility also met the increased need for more hotel rooms, a result of the garrison's expansion.

Auf sieben Häuser des ehemaligen Offizierslagers waren die 72 Zimmer des alten „Tower Inn" Hotels verteilt.
The 72 rooms of the old "Tower Inn" hotel were located in seven different buildings of the former officers' barracks.

„Grafenwoehr Army Lodging" mit 136 Zimmern

Das dreistöckige U-förmige Gebäude hat eine Grundfläche von 8605 Quadratmetern und verfügt über 136 Zimmer. Davon sind 72 Standardzimmer, 18 Zimmer mit kleiner Kitchenette für einen längeren Aufenthalt und 46 Familiensuiten mit Wohn- und Schlafzimmer und kleiner Küchenzeile. Ein Teil der Räume ist behindertengerecht ausgestattet, ein weiterer Teil erlaubt den Aufenthalt mit Haustieren. „Es wird dem Standard eines Marriott oder Ramada Inn Hotels gleich kommen. Wir bieten ein Daheim-Zuhause-Gefühl und wollen, dass sich unsere amerikanischen Gäste wohlfühlen", blickte Managerin Waltraud Schill-Rückert beim Richtfest schon auf die Eröffnung im September 2011 voraus.

"Grafenwoehr Army Lodging" facility features 136 rooms

The three-story, U-shaped building features a floor space of 8.605 square meters and 136 rooms. 72 are standard rooms, 18 rooms have a small kitchenette for a longer stay, and 46 are family suites with a living room and a bedroom and a small kitchenette. Some of the rooms are equipped for the handicapped while other rooms allow their occupants to bring pets. "It will offer the standard of a Marriott or Ramada Inn hotel. We offer an "at home feeling" and want our American guests to feel comfortable", said hotel manager Waltraud Schill-Rückert at the topping-out ceremony with regard to the hotel opening in September 2011.

„Grand Opening" im September 2011. Kinder streuten Rosenblätter für die ersten Gäste.
Grand Opening in September 2011. Children spread rose leaves for the first guests.

Die große Lobby mit offenem Feuerplatz
The large lobby features a fire place

Neben Burger King und Bowlingbahn entstand der riesige Hotelkomplex, dessen Dachstuhl ganz aus Stahl gefertigt ist.
The large lodging facility is located adjacent to Burger King and the bowling center. Its roof structure is completely made of steel.

Umweltschutz
Environmental Protection

Schutz von Boden, Luft und Wasser

"... Wir müssen die Wälder, die Landschaft, die Fische, das Wild und die uns anvertrauten Ressourcen schützen. Zwar liegt unsere Priorität eindeutig in der Erfüllung der militärischen Mission; trotzdem ist es unsere Pflicht, das der Armee zur Verfügung gestellte Land und die natürlichen Ressourcen so zu nutzen und zu erhalten, dass sie auch künftigen Generationen zur Verfügung stehen."
Dieses Zitat aus einem Brief, den General John A. Wickham, ehemals Stabschef der US-Armee, 1986 verfasste, hat sich die Umweltschutzabteilung der US-Armee-Garnison Grafenwöhr zur Philosophie gemacht.

Umweltschutzabteilung

Die Abteilung fand ihre Anfänge im Jahr 1979 mit einem Umweltingenieur und ist seitdem zu einer Personalstärke von 22 Mitarbeitern mit Fachkräften für den technischen Umweltschutz und den klassischen Naturschutz gewachsen. Bei allen Fragen des Umweltschutzes ist sie Ansprechpartner für das Militär, deutsche Behörden, US-Zivilbevölkerung und die Öffentlichkeit. Die Abteilung arbeitet eng mit dem Bundesforst zusammen.

Protection of soil, air and water

*"... We must protect the forests, range lands, fish, wildlife, and other natural resources entrusted to our care. Though priority must be given to military missions, we must use and maintain army land and natural resources in a manner that assures its preservation and availability for future generations."
This quote, taken from a letter that General Wickham, former Chief of Staff of the Army, wrote in 1986 has become the philosophy of the environmental office of the U.S. Army Garrison Grafenwoehr.*

Environmental Office

The department was established in 1979 and manned with one environmental engineer. Today, it has 22 employees covering technical as well as traditional areas of environmental protection. The office is the point of contact for the military, German authorities, U.S. civilians and the public. The office works closely with the Federal Forest Office.

Erfolge beim Nist-Programm: Ein Fischadler im künstlichen Horst.

Successful nesting programs: An osprey in an artificial nest.

Ausgleichsmaßnahmen

Bei der Planung von neuen Bauprojekten auf dem Übungsplatz – insbesondere beim EB-G-Programm – werden die deutschen Behörden unterstützt. Die Umweltabteilung ermittelt Daten über bedrohte Arten, Geologie, Bodenbeschaffenheit, Grundwasser, mögliche Altlasten und stellt diese den Planern und Behörden zur Beurteilung der Umweltauswirkungen zur Verfügung. Ausgleichsmaßnahmen werden koordiniert und auch selbst durchgeführt. Sie umfassen die Entwicklung von offenen Heideflächen und Trockenrasen, die Anpflanzung von Sträuchern und Bäumen, das Konvertieren von Nadelwäldern in Mischwälder und das Renaturieren von Bächen und Weihern.

Mitigation projects

The environmental office supports German authorities regarding the planning of new construction projects on the training area, especially those of the EB-G program. It collects data about endangered species, geology and soil conditions, ground water, possible contamination and provides them to the planners and to the German authorities so they can determine the possible environmental impact. Mitigation projects are coordinated and executed. They include the development of open heath land, dry grassland, the planting of bushes and trees, the conversion of coniferous forests into mixed forests and the renaturation of creeks and ponds.

Lernen von der Natur: Spaß bei der Umwelterziehung und bei Aktionswochen
Learning from nature: Having fun while learning about the environment and during Earth Week

Schwäne auf der Panzerstraße - im Gänsemarsch zum Wasserturm
Swans on the tank trail - walking in single file to the Water Tower

Recycling-Waschanlagen *All wash racks recycle water*

Der Natur angepasst: Einzelkämpfer beim getarnten Vorgehen im Wasser

Adapted to nature: Lone soldiers training undercover in the water

Grünes Grafenwöhr

Bis Mitte der 90er Jahre kam es durch den Übungsbetrieb teilweise zu starker Bodenerosion. Gezielte Maßnahmen führten dazu, dass der Übungsplatz Grafenwöhr jetzt wieder grün ist. Es wurden Rückhaltebecken gebaut, Bodenauflockerung und Wiederbegrünung durchgeführt. Zum Erhalt eines realistischen Übungsumfeldes wird ein „Integriertes Übungsplatzmanagement" angewandt. Ausbildungsflächen werden rotierend zugewiesen, durch spezielle Kennzeichnung („Seibert-Stakes") sind erosionsgefährdete Flächen gesperrt.

Gefahrstoff- und Sondermüllmanagement

Vor allem bei der Wartung von Fahrzeugen werden Gefahrstoffe wie Schmiermittel, Kühlmittel, Reiniger etc. benötigt. Diese müssen ordnungsgemäß gelagert, Sondermüll vorschriftsmäßig entsorgt werden. Betankungs- und Wartungsvorgänge finden auf insgesamt 60 dafür eingerichteten Flächen statt. Diese sind mit Ölabscheidern versehen. Ein dichtes Netz von mehr als 150 Sondermüllsammelstellen auf dem gesamten Übungsplatz macht es den Soldaten leicht, Umweltschutz zu betreiben. Auf den großen Mehrzweck-Waschanlagen für die Panzer und Radfahrzeuge wird das Wasser in einem Recyclingkreislauf verwendet, ölverschmutzter Schlamm wird nachbehandelt.

Green Grafenwoehr

Training caused a large amount of erosion until the mid-Nineties. Special renaturation measures were taken and now Grafenwoehr Training Area is green again. Water retention basins were built, the ground was de-compacted and reseeded. Integrated training area management is used to preserve a realistic training environment. Training areas are rotated and areas prone to erosion are specially marked ("Seibert stakes").

Management of hazardous material and hazardous waste

Hazardous materials such as lubricants, cooling liquids, cleaning solutions etc. are mainly needed for vehicle maintenance. They have to be correctly stored and hazardous waste has to be disposed of orderly. Refueling and maintenance takes place on a total of 60 areas that were specially constructed for that purpose. All have oil-water separators. A dense net of more than 150 hazard waste collection points distributed around the entire training area make it easy for the soldiers to practice environmental protection. Water is recycled on the large multi-purpose wash racks for tanks and wheeled vehicles and the oil-contaminated mud is treated.

Renaturierung ehemaliger Klärteiche als Ausgleichsmaßnahme für Bauprojekte

Renaturation of former sedimentation ponds, a mitigation measure for construction projects

Fischaufstieg am Stauwerk der Frankenohe
Fish ladder at the Frankenohe barrage

Grund- und Oberflächenwasser

Zur optimalen Überwachung des Grundwassers besteht ein Monitoring-System mit über 200 Grundwasserbrunnen auf dem Übungsplatz und an der ehemaligen Mülldeponie Haderbühl. Oberflächenwasserproben werden regelmäßig an Fließgewässern und einigen Weihern genommen. In mehrjährigem Abstand werden auch Fischproben auf Schwermetalle untersucht. So soll eine optimale Wasserqualität auf dem Übungsplatz gewährleistet werden.

Groundwater and surface water

A monitoring system on the training area and former Haderbühl landfill with more than 200 groundwater wells has been installed to optimally monitor the groundwater. Surface water samples are regularly taken in rivers and some lakes. Fish are perennially tested for heavy metals. The goal is to guarantee an optimal water quality on the training area.

„Seibert Stakes" und Erosionsverbauten
"Seibert stakes" and erosion control measures

Soldaten beim Einsatz für die Umwelt: Handarbeit beim Dammbau
Soldiers at work to protect the environment: Building a dam by hand

Geschützte Spezies im Militärareal: Grünspecht, Sonnentau, Gelbbauchunke, Fledermaus und Schwalbenschwanz
Protected species on the training area: Green woodpecker, sundew, yellow-bellied toad, bat and dove tail

800 bedrohte und gefährdete Arten

Jüngste wissenschaftliche Forschungen haben bewiesen, dass militärische Übungsareale Rückzugsgebiete bedrohter und gefährdeter Tier- und Pflanzenarten sind. Der militärische Übungsbetrieb schafft abwechslungsreiche und offene Landschaften und damit optimale Lebensbedingungen. Das strikte Betretungsverbot des Übungsplatzes für die Allgemeinheit trägt zur Artenvielfalt bei. In den vergangenen Jahren ließ die Umweltabteilung verschiedene Studien und Erhebungen durchführen. Die sensationelle Anzahl von rund 3000 verschiedenen Arten von Pflanzen, Insekten, Amphibien, Säugetieren und Vögeln wurde dabei innerhalb des Übungsgeländes registriert. Zirka 800 davon sind als bedroht oder gefährdet auf der sogenannten „Roten Liste" klassifiziert.

800 threatened and endangered species

Recent scientific studies have proven that military training areas are refuges for threatened and endangered animal and plant species. The military training provides for diversified and open landscapes with optimal living conditions. The fact that the training area is closed to the public has a positive impact on the variety of species. During the past years, the environmental office contracted out several studies and surveys. The sensational number of 3,000 species of plants, insects, amphibians, mammals and birds were registered on the training area. Approximately 800 of them are classified as threatened or endangered and listed on the so-called "Red List".

Hopfenohe an der Europäischen Wasserscheide
Hopfenohe at the European water divide

Bewahrung alter Obstbaumsorten bei Pappenberg
Preservation of old fruit tree varieties near Pappenberg

Wollgras-Wiese
Cotton grass

Vom Schwarzstorch bis zur Fledermaus

Gelder in Millionenhöhe wurden von der US-Armee in den vergangenen Jahren für den Erhalt der Natur und den Umweltschutz ausgegeben. Die Umweltabteilung hat neben den technischen Maßnahmen zahlreiche Projekte im Zuge des NATURA 2000-Programms umgesetzt. Unter anderem wurden Bruthöhlen für den Eisvogel angelegt und Fischaufstiege an Wehranlagen geschaffen. Nisthilfen wurden für Fischadler und Schwarzstorch gebaut. Keller in den verlassenen Ortschaften und alte Bunker dienen Fledermäusen als Schlaf- und Schutzplätze. Alte Obstbaumsorten in den ehemaligen Dörfern wurden vor dem Aussterben bewahrt.

Black storks and bats

Over the past years, the U.S. Army spent millions for the preservation of nature and the protection of the environment. Apart from technical measures, the environmental office has also implemented numerous NATURA 2000-program projects. Nests for kingfishers and fish passes were built. Nesting platforms for ospreys and black storks were installed. Basements in the abandoned villages and old bunkers are used by bats as shelters and roosting places. Old fruit tree varieties in the former villages were saved from extinction.

Sumpf- und Torflandschaft der Schießbahn 132 im Röthelweiher-Gebiet
Marsh and peat lands of Range 132 near Röthelweiher Lake

Die Umweltschutzabteilung der US-Armee Garnison Grafenwöhr wurde in den Jahren 2000, 2006 und 2010 für das beste Umweltprogramm eines US-Armee-Standortes außerhalb der USA ausgezeichnet.

The environmental office of the US Army Garrison Grafenwoehr won the award for the best environmental program of a US Army installation outside the continental United States in 2000, 2006 and 2010.

Pause in grüner Natur

Taking a break in nature

Umweltbewusstsein und Auszeichnung

Weltweit hat die US-Armee begonnen ein Umweltmanagementsystem nach den gültigen Standards einzuführen. Umweltschulungen, spezielle Anweisungen, Broschüren, Internetseiten, Informationssysteme und die Erziehung der Kinder zu mehr Umwelt- und Naturschutz sind Projekte und Massnahmen der Umweltabteilung. Mit Führungen durch den Übungsplatz, Ausstellungen, Lehrpfaden, Info-Tafeln oder der jährlichen Aktionswoche „Earth Week" wird das Umweltbewusstsein der Soldaten und ihrer Familien geweckt und geschult. Für all ihre Bemühungen und Erfolge hat die Umweltabteilung schon mehrere Preise erhalten. 2000, 2006 und 2010 wurde an die Grafenwöhrer Abteilung die Auszeichnung für das beste Umweltprogramm auf US-Heeresebene verliehen. Auch der Umweltschutzpreis 2010 des US-Verteidigungsministeriums für das beste Umweltprogramm eines US-Militärstandortes außerhalb der USA ging an die US-Armee-Garnison Grafenwöhr, die sich als Heeresabteilung gegen die Vertreter der weiteren Waffengattungen (Air Force, Navy und Marine Corps) durchsetzte.

Environmental awareness and awards

World-wide, the U.S. Army has begun to implement an environmental management system according to current standards. Environmental training, special directives, brochures, web pages, information systems and the education of children to practice environmental and natural protection are projects and measures of the environmental office. The environmental awareness of soldiers and families is raised and trained with tours through the training area, exhibitions, nature trails, information boards or the annual awareness week "Earth Week." The garrison environmental office has received various awards for all its efforts and successes. In 2000, 2006 and 2010 the Grafenwoehr office won the award for the best environmental program of a U.S. Army installation outside the United States of America. In 2010, the U.S. Army Garrison Grafenwoehr also won the U.S. Department of Defense award for the best environmental program of a U.S. Army installation outside the United States of America, after successfully competing against the other services (Air Force, Navy and Marine Corps).

Im Juni 2011 wurde von hohen Repräsentanten des Ministeriums bei einer Feier im Pentagon in Washington der Umweltschutzpreis 2010 des US-Verteidigungsministeriums an die Vertreter der US-Armee-Garnison Grafenwöhr verliehen.

During a ceremony at the Pentagon in June 2011, the 2010 Environmental Award of the U.S. Department of Defense was awarded to representatives of the U.S. Army Garrison Grafenwoehr by high-ranking representatives of the defense department.

Kraniche und Schwarzstörche zählen zu den Brutvögeln im Übungsplatzgelände
Cranes and black storks are breeding birds in the training area

Durch konsequente Arbeit von Forst, Umweltabteilung und Militär ist aus dem Truppenübungsplatz inzwischen ein Schatzkästchen geworden, das eine einzigartige Vielfalt an Arten beherbergt: Seeadler, Wildkatze, Schwarzstorch, Fischadler, Luchs, Rohrweihe, Kranich und Rohrdommel zählen zu den geschützten Arten auf dem Übungsplatz

Because of the consistent work of forest office, environmental office and the military, the training area has become a treasure chest that accommodates a unique variety of species: White-tailed eagle, wild cat, black stork, osprey, lynx, marsh harrier, crane and bittern are among the endangered species living on the training area.

Ruinen bei Hermannshof am Schlatterweiher
Ruins near Hermannshof at Schlatterweiher Lake

Forst   Forest

Militärische Nutzung und Naturschutz in Einklang zu bringen, ist der Auftrag der Forstverwaltung seit 100 Jahren. Durch allerhöchstes Dekret des Prinzregenten Luitpold von Bayern wurde am 1. April 1910 ein Militärforstamt in Grafenwöhr geschaffen. Bis zur Errichtung des Heeresforstamtes Zossen-Döberitz bei Berlin im Jahre 1932, war es das einzige Forstamt seiner Art im damaligen Deutschen Reich. Gleich neben dem Wasserturm wurde im alpenländischen Stil ein Landhaus für die Dienst- und Wohnräume des Forstvorstehers gebaut. Wechselvoll ist die Geschichte der Grafenwöhrer Forstverwaltung. Am Ende des Buches ist die Geschichte in der Zeittafel dargestellt

Zum 100jährigen Bestehen wurde dem Bundesforstbetrieb der „Kreativpreis des Bundes der Steuerzahler in Bayern e. V." verliehen. Gewürdigt werden damit die zweckoptimierte Verwendung von Steuergeldern und die eigenen betriebswirtschaftlichen Ergebnisse, aber auch die Erfolge im Ausgleich zwischen militärischer Nutzung, Natur, Artenschutz, Waldbau und Jagd.

Consolidating military use and environmental protection has been the task of the forest administration for 100 years. On April 1, 1910, Prince Regent Luitpold of Bavaria directed the establishment of a military forest office in Grafenwoehr. It was the only forest office of its kind in the former German Reich until the establishment of the Army forest office in Zossen-Döberitz near Berlin in 1932. A country house was built in an Alpine architectural style directly next to the Water Tower to house the office and living quarters of the forest officer. A chronology of the history can be found at the end of the book

The Federal Forest has been awarded the "Creativity Award of the Bavarian Taxpayers' Association" to celebrate its 100th anniversary. The award honors the cause-optimized use of taxes and the income it generates as well as the successes made regarding the balance between military training, the preservation of nature, the protection of species, forestry and hunting.

Die ersten Förster des königlich bayerischen Forstamtes um 1910
The first forest rangers of the Royal-Bavarian Forest Office circa 1910

Revierförster und Forstverwaltung 2006
District forest rangers and forestry administration in 2006

Die Mannschaft des Bundesforstbetriebs Grafenwöhr im Juli 2013
The team of the Federal Forest Office Grafenwoehr in July 2013

Die Holzwirtschaft ist eine beachtliche Einnahmequelle des Bundesforstbetriebs.
The timber industry is a considerable source of income for the Federal Forest Office.

Waldarbeiter des Reviers Schwarzen Berg in den 30er Jahren
Forest workers of the Schwarzer Berg district in the 1930s

„Im Zuge einer ausgezeichneten und vertrauensvollen Zusammenarbeit mit den US-Streitkräften sowie den deutschen Behörden gelingt es, die Nachhaltigkeit der natürlichen Ressourcen und die Nutzungsmöglichkeiten der Landschaft umfassend zu sichern. Diese Gemeinschaftsleistung dient allen, den US-Streitkräften aber auch der deutschen Bevölkerung."
Ulrich Maushake, Forstdirektor, Leiter Bundesforstbetrieb Grafenwöhr

"We are able to comprehensively secure the sustainability of the natural resources and the use of the landscape because of the excellent and trusting cooperation with the U.S. Forces and the German authorities. This common effort benefits all, the U.S. Forces as well as the German population."
Ulrich Maushake, Forest Director, Chief, Federal Forest Office Grafenwoehr

„Aufräumen" mit Vollerntern nach einem starken Windbruch im Juli 2013
"Clean-up" with harvesters after the wind breakage in July 2013

Himmel der Hirsche
Deer Haven

Kanonendonner und Rotwild

„Deer haven – Hirschhimmel" nennen die amerikanischen Soldaten oft den Truppenübungsplatz Grafenwöhr. Gewehrsalven und Kanonendonner stehen nicht im Widerspruch zum Rotwild, im Gegenteil: Der Übungsplatz ist das wildreichste Gebiet Deutschlands – auf seine Größe gesehen, vermutlich europaweit das Areal mit der größten Rotwild-Dichte. Riesige Rudel durchstreifen die Wälder und sind beim Äsen auf den großen Freiflächen zu sehen, völlig unbeeindruckt vom militärischen Betrieb. Seit den 1970er Jahren hat der Bestand nach unkontrolliertem Abschuss während des Krieges und in der Nachkriegszeit wieder erheblich zugenommen. Das Betretungsverbot des Übungsplatzes und die Tatsache, dass die weiträumigen Gefahrenbereiche der Zielgebiete menschenleer sind, wirken sich positiv auf den Wildbestand aus.

The roar of cannons and red deer

The training area is often called a "deer haven" by the American soldiers in Grafenwoehr. Gun fire and the roar of cannons do not conflict with red deer – on the contrary: The training area is the area with the largest amount of red deer in Germany – and based on its size, probably the area with the largest density of red deer in Europe. Large packs roam through the forests and can be seen grazing in the large open areas, completely unimpressed by the military training. The stock of animals has significantly increased since the 1970s because of uncontrolled shooting during the war and the years after war. The fact that the training area is not open to the public and that the large surface danger zones of the impact area are free of people also have a positive impact on the animal stock.

Feisthirsche vor der Brunft in der Impact Area. -Deer during rutting season in the impact area

Kämpfe und Hirschröhren zur Brunftzeit
Deer fights and call during rutting season

Wild zwischen Panzerwracks in der Impact Area
Deer between tank wrecks in the impact area

Ein „ungerader" 18-Ender bekommt Besuch - An "uneven" 18 point antler welcomes his visitors

Schwarzkittel mit Frischlingen
Wild boars with young boars

Junger Fuchs
Young Fox

Für ein Forschungsprojekt wurden Hirsche mit Funksender bebändert.
Deer were ribboned with radios for a research project.

Der gelenkte Hirsch

Für die Hege und Pflege von Wild und Wald ist der Bundesforst zuständig. Forstbeamte betreuen in neun Revieren das Areal. 2008 wurden für ein Forschungsprojekt 20 Hirsche und Hirschkühe mit Funksendern bebändert. Via Satellit werden die Wanderung und das Raumverhalten der Hirsche nachvollzogen. Erste Ergebnisse beweisen, dass die Nutzung von Freiflächen durch das Wild in der oft steppenartigen und hügeligen Landschaft den Wald schonen und dadurch Verbissschäden reduziert werden können. Es ist eine Art Lenkung des Hirsches zu erkennen.

The controlled deer

The Federal Forest Office is responsible for game keeping and for the preservation of the forest. Forest officers in nine forest districts take care of the training area. In 2008, twenty stags and does were tagged with radios in support of a research project. The deer's movement and use of space is tracked via satellite. First results show that the movement of the deer in the often dry and hilly open areas preserve the forest and reduce the damage caused by deer bites. A control of the deer movement is noticeable.

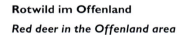

Rotwild im Offenland
Red deer in the Offenland area

Neben alten Bunkeranlagen - ein Rotwildrudel im offenen Grasland
A pack of red deer in the open grass land next to the old bunkers

Jagdglück und Transport eines erlegten Hirsches anno dazumal und heute
Hunter's luck and transport of a shot deer in the past and today

Beachtliche Strecken werden nach den Jagden gelegt. Zur Erfüllung der Abschusszahlen wird mit Drückjagden in den Bestand eingegriffen.
A significant amount of deer was killed during a hunt. Driven hunts are held to fulfill the necessary amount of shootings and to control the deer population.

Jagdhornbläser geben an der aufgelegten Strecke das Signal „Jagd vorbei – Halali"
Hunting horn players give the signal "Hunt over – mort" next to the shot deer

Bei den Trophäen sind vereinzelt Besonderheiten festzustellen – rechts eine Trophäe mit drei Stangen.

Occasionally, special trophies are detected: A trophy with three antlers on the right.

Die Jagd

Die Gesamtzahl des Rotwilds lässt sich nur schätzen und kann aus den Abschusszahlen, die jährlich bei rund 1500 Stück liegen, erahnt werden.

Die Jagd wird zur schießfreien Zeit in Einzeljagden durchgeführt. Passionierte Jäger zahlen für Trophäen prächtiger Althirsche stolze Preise von mehreren tausend Euro. Weiterhin wird in großen Drückjagden gegen Ende des Jahres kurz und energisch in den Wildbestand eingegriffen, um die Abschusszahlen zu erfüllen. Prinzip der Drückjagd ist es, das Wild langsam und ohne Panik vor die Ansitze zu bewegen. Erlegt werden im „Deer haven" auch eine große Zahl von Schwarzwild, Rehen und weiterem jagdbaren Wild. Trophäen, Wildbrett und die Holzwirtschaft sind für den Bundesforstbetrieb Grafenwöhr eine willkommene und beachtliche Einnahmequelle.

Hunting

The total amount of game can only be estimated by the annual amount of shot deer which totals approximately 1,500 animals. Individual hunting takes place during range down times. Passionate hunters pay several thousand Euro for the trophies of grand old stags. To quickly and effectively control the stock of wild game and to fulfill the necessary amount of shootings, large driven hunts are held towards the end of the year. The concept of the driven hunt is to move the deer slowly and without creating a panic in front of the raised hides. A large number of wild boars, roe deer and other wild game are shot in "deer heaven." Trophies, meat and timber are a welcome and significant source of income for the Federal Forest Office Grafenwoehr.

Rotwildschau im Gut Heringnohe
Red deer show at Gut Heringnohe

Hirsche im Bastgeweih
Young stags with velvet on their antlers

Nicht Fuchs und Hase sondern Adler und Hirsch sagen sich auf dem Truppenübungsplatz gute Nacht. Von einem Hochsitz aus beobachtet ein Seeadler vorbeiziehendes Wild. Der enorme Rotwildbestand ist auch ein Grund für das große Seeadler-Aufkommen in Grafenwöhr.

Sitting on a raised blind, a white-tailed eagle is observing deer that passes by. The enormous deer population is one reason why there are so many white-tailed eagles in Grafenwoehr.

Menschenleeres Gebiet. Die offene Oberpfälzer Hügellandschaft im Truppenübungsplatz ist ein ideales Terrain für das Rotwild.

Deserted land. The open area of the Upper Palatine hills is an ideal territory for red deer.

Adler   Eagle

Militär und Natur sind kein Widerspruch

Der Übungsplatz wird immer mehr zum „Adler-Paradies". Fischadler und der größte mitteleuropäische Greifvogel, der Seeadler, ziehen über dem Sperrgebiet ihre Kreise. Neben dem ungeheuren Rotwildbestand zeigen die Adler, dass Natur und Militär kein Widerspruch sind.

Seit Ende der 1980er Jahre entwickelte sich im Übungsplatz eine eigenständige Adlerpopulation. Im April 2010 gab der Bundesforst in der Pressemitteilung: „Bundesadler im Aufwind" bekannt, dass der Truppenübungsplatz Grafenwöhr Keimzelle für die Ausbreitung des Seeadlers in Süddeutschland ist. Dies bestätigte auch die staatliche Vogelschutzwarte in Garmisch-Partenkirchen.

Military and nature do not contradict each other

The training area is turning more and more into a paradise for eagles. Ospreys and the largest bird of prey in Central Europe, the white-tailed eagle, circle above the training area. Like the huge population of red deer, they are proof that military and nature do not contradict each other.

An independent eagle population has developed in the training area since the end of the 1980s. In an April 2010 news release entitled "Federal Eagle on the Upswing," the Federal Forest Office announced that Grafenwoehr Training Area has become the nucleus of the spread of the white-tailed eagle in southern Germany. That was confirmed by the State Bird Observatory in Garmisch-Partenkirchen.

Der Adler im Wappen des Bundesforstes
The eagle is part of the crest of the Federal Forest Office

Der Adler ist im Sperrgebiet gelandet. Das Betretungsverbot für den Truppenübungsplatz wirkt sich positiv auf den Lebensraum des Seeadlers aus.
The eagle has landed. The restricted access to the training area has a positive impact on the habitat of the white-tailed eagle.

Adler über Grafenwöhr zeigt dieser Schnappschuss. Zwei Seeadler kreisen über den Weiten des Übungsplatzes. Die Teleaufnahme lässt den Wasserturm und den Parkstein zum Greifen nahe erscheinen.
This snapshot shows two white-tailed eagles circling above the wide open spaces of Grafenwoehr Training Area. The telephoto makes the Water Tower and the Parkstein Mountain seem to be within grasp.

Noch satt braun ist das Gefieder des jungen S adlers, der sich auf einer Föhre im Übungspl niedergelassen hat. Mit zunehmenden Alter w den die Kopffedern des Adlers grau. Weiß gefä sind die Unterseite und die hinteren Federn Schwanzes. Der amerikanische Name für den S adler lautet daher auch „White-tailed Eagle".
The feathers of the young white-tailed eagle that is r ting on a pine in the training area are still dark bro As the eagle gets older, its head feathers turn grey. underside and back feathers of the tail are white, ving the eagle its name.

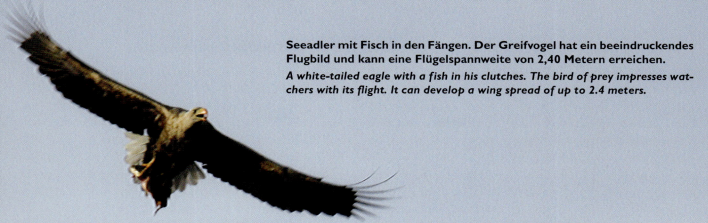

Seeadler mit Fisch in den Fängen. Der Greifvogel hat ein beeindruckendes Flugbild und kann eine Flügelspannweite von 2,40 Metern erreichen.
A white-tailed eagle with a fish in his clutches. The bird of prey impresses watchers with its flight. It can develop a wing spread of up to 2.4 meters.

Im Schutz militärischer Sicherheitsbereiche

Im Revier Tanzfleck wurde Mitte der 1980er Jahre der erste Fischadlerhorst in der nördlichen Oberpfalz ausgemacht. Die Wälder sowie große Weiherflächen im Südosten des Übungsplatzes und das Sumpf- und Torfgebiet des Röthelweihers begünstigen dort den Adlerstandort. Auf seinen Streifenfahrten kann Revierförster Frank Gerstenmeier täglich die Fisch- und Seeadler beobachten. Für den Forstmann erfüllen die Seeadler die Funktion einer Art Gesundheitspolizei. Die Adler sind Aasfresser und leben von Fallwild und den Fischen in den Seen. Den Wildreichtum nennt der Bundesforst auch als Grund für den enormen Adlerbestand. Militär und Natur sind für die Förster kein Widerspruch, im Gegenteil: Das militärische Sperrgebiet sorgt für ein Betretungsverbot. Dass die Tiere durch den Schießbetrieb zu Schaden kommen ist eher unwahrscheinlich, denn unmittelbare Schussbereiche werden von Wild und Adlern gemieden. Holzscheiben sind auf den Ranges die Ziele der Soldaten. Es besteht ein absolutes Schießverbot auf alle Lebewesen. Zuwiderhandlungen werden drastisch bestraft.

Protected by military security zones

In the mid 1980s, the first osprey aerie in the northern Oberpfalz region was discovered in the Tanzfleck district. The forests and large lakes in the southeast of the training area and the swamp and peat area of the Röthelweiher Lake promote eagle habitats. District forest ranger Frank Gerstenmeier observes ospreys and white-tailed eagles on his daily patrols. According to the forest ranger, the white-tailed eagles serve as a kind of medical police. Eagles are scavengers and feed off dead animals and fish in lakes. The dense game population, says the Federal Forest Office, is one reason for the large amount of eagles. For the forest rangers, military and nature do not contradict each other. On the contrary: The military training area is off limits and it is unlikely that the animals are injured by live-fire exercises. Game and eagles avoid active live-fire areas. The soldiers' targets on the ranges are wooden disks. It is absolutely forbidden to fire on any living creature. Violations lead to drastic punishments.

Schwere Flügelschläge sind notwendig bis der Seeadler in die Höhe kommt.
Heavy wing beats are necessary to lift a white-tailed eagle up into the air.

Seeadler als Gesundheitspolizei: Die Seeadler ernähren sich von Fischen in den Weihern und von verendetem Wild. Das Bild wurde von einer automatischen Wildkamera aufgenommen.
White-tailed eagles serve as medical police: They feed off dead animals and fish in lakes. This photo was taken by a photo trap.

Pflege und Beringung der Adler

Die Revierförster des Bundesforstes und die Umweltabteilung der US-Armee-Garnison Bavaria kümmern sich um den Adlerbestand. Stefan Härtl, er ist in der US-Umweltabteilung mit für den Naturschutz zuständig, führt regelmäßig die Adlerbeobachtung und Kontrolle der Horststellen durch. Zehn junge Seeadler und 14 Fischadler hat er seit 2010 im Truppenübungsplatz heranwachsen sehen. Dies sind in erster Linie Tiere, die auch durch Diplom-Biologen Dr. Daniel Schmidt-Rothmund vom Vogelschutzzentrum Mössingen beringt werden. Die Kosten für die Beringung, Anschaffung von künstlichen Nisthilfen und die Horstpflege teilen sich die US-Umweltschützer und der Bundesforst. Während die Fischadler den Winter in wärmeren Gefilden in Afrika oder Spanien verbringen sind die Seeadler das ganze Jahr in der Region. Besonders im Herbst und im Winter sind den Schätzungen zufolge 15 bis 20 Seeadler auf dem Platz.

Care and banding of the eagles

The forest rangers of the Federal Forest Office and the environmental office of the US Army Garrison Bavaria look after the eagle population. Stefan Härtl from the environmental office is responsible for nature protection and regularly observes eagles and controls their aeries. Since 2010, he saw 10 young white-tailed eagles and 14 ospreys grow up on the training area. Most of them are birds that were banded by certified biologist Dr. Daniel Schmidt-Rothmund from the Bird Protection Center Mössingen. The cost for banding, purchase of artificial nesting aids and care of the aeries is split between the U.S. environmental office and the Federal Forest Office. While the ospreys spend the winter in warmer areas in Africa or Spain, the white-tailed eagles remain in the region all year long. It is estimated that 15 to 20 white-tailed eagles are on the training area in fall and winter.

Seeadlerküken bei der Beringung
White-tailed eagle fledglings are banded.

Revierförster Frank Gerstenmeier (links) und Stefan Härtl von der US-Umweltabteilung bei der Beringungsaktion eines jungen Fischadlers.
District forest officer Frank Gerstenmeier (left) and Stefan Härtl from the US environmental office during the banding of a young osprey.

Dr. Daniel Schmidt-Rothmund nimmt zur Beringung die Adler aus ihrem Horst.
Dr. Daniel Schmidt-Rothmund takes eagles out of their aerie to band them.

Fischadler in ihrem Horst hoch über dem Röthelweihergebiet
Ospreys in their aerie high above the Röthelweiher Lake district

Altenweiher Ursprung

Impressionen

95 Jahre Truppenübungsplatz   60 Jahre U.S. Armee in Grafenwöhr, Hohenfels & Vilseck   50 Jahre Bundeswe

95 - 60 - 50

2005 feierten Deutsche und Amerikaner gemeinsam das Jubiläum 95 – 60 – 50. Begangen wurde der 95. Geburtstag des Übungsplatzes, 60 Jahre US-Armee in Grafenwöhr und das 50-jährige Bestehen der Deutschen Bundeswehr. Mit einem Militärkonzert am Wasserturm, dem amerikanischen Unabhängigkeitstag und dem Bürgerfest wurden die Feierlichkeiten begangen. Die Festmeile zog sich vom Rathaus über das Museumsgelände und die Alte Amberger Straße bis zum Wasserturm und sollte so auch symbolisch die guten Verbindungen zwischen der Stadt und den Militärs auf dem Übungsplatz aufzeigen. Präsentiert wurde auch eine große Ausstellung mit Militärfahrzeugen der verschiedensten Perioden. Bei kurzen Lagerrundfahrten wurde ein Blick in das neue Baugebiet und das militärische Übungsareal ermöglicht. Das Fest war quasi die Generalprobe für das 100-jährige Jubiläum des Truppenübungsplatzes.

Germans and Americans jointly celebrated the 95 – 60 – 50 anniversary in 2005. The event marked the 95th anniversary of the training area, the 60th anniversary of the U.S. Army in Grafenwoehr and the 50th anniversary of the German Armed Forces. The anniversary was celebrated with a military concert at the Water Tower, the American's Independence Day and a citizens' fest. Fest activities extended from the town hall, past the museum, along Alte Amberger Straße and all the way to the Water Tower and symbolized the good relations between the city and the military at the training area. A large exhibition of military vehicles from various time periods was also conducted. Short tours of the training area offered a glimpse of the new construction site and the military training facilities. The fest could have been considered a dress rehearsal for the 100th anniversary.

Kinderparade mit bunten Luftballons
Children's parade with colorful balloons

Feiern vom Rathaus bis zum Wasserturm
Celebration from the town hall to the Water Tower

Standkonzert des Heeresmusikkorps 4 mit anschließendem Marsch zum Wasserturm
Concert of German Army Music Corps 4 followed by a parade to the Water Tower

Festeröffnung und Bieranstich
Fest opening and tapping of the keg

Ausstellung von historischen Militärfahrzeugen im Stadtpark
Exhibition of historic military vehicles in the city park

100 Jahre Truppenübungsplatz Grafenwöhr
100 Years Grafenwoehr Training Area

Soldaten der Bundeswehr in historischen Uniformen brachten am Jubiläumstag die Krupp-Kanone aus dem Jahr 1910 in Stellung. Brigadegeneral Johann Berger feuerte als Symbol für die ersten 100 Jahre Truppenübungsplatz den „historischen Schuss" ab. Das neue Jahrhundert eröffnete ein Schuss aus einer amerikanischen Panzerhaubitze M 109 „Paladin".

On the day of the anniversary, German Army soldiers in historic uniforms put a Krupp canon from 1910 in position. Symbolizing the first 100 years of the training area, Brigadier General Johann Berger fired the "historic shot." The new century was opened by a shot from an American M 109 „Paladin" howitzer.

Großer Zapfenstreich - Historisches und Modernes zum Jubiläum

Mit einer Festwoche vom 27. Juni bis zum 4. Juli 2010 wurde der 100. Geburtstag des Truppenübungsplatzes groß gefeiert. Auftakt war die Eröffnung der beiden Sonderausstellungen im 1.Oberpfälzer Kultur- und Militärmuseum „100 Jahre Truppenübungsplatz" und „100 Jahre Bundesforst". Südstaatenfeeling herrschte anschließend im Stadtpark mit der USAREUR-Dixieland-Band, die so für einen gelungenen Start in die Jubiläumswoche sorgte.

„Doppelschlag" zum Geburtstag

Am Jubiläumstag selbst wurde pünktlich um 8 Uhr mit einem „Doppelschlag" auf der Grünhundhöhe an die Gründung erinnert. Dort, wo am 30. Juni 1910 das 2. königlich-bayerische Fußartillerieregiment den ersten offiziellen Artillerieschuss abgefeuert hatte, wurde auch das nächste Jahrhundert militärischen Trainings eingeläutet. Soldaten des Deutschen Militärischen Vertreters (DMV) hatten in Uniformen der königlich-bayerischen Artillerie ein historisches Geschütz in Stellung gebracht und geladen. Brigadegeneral Johann Berger vom Wehrbereichskommando IV betätigte bei der morgendlichen Zeremonie die Abzugsleine der Krupp-Kanone aus dem Jahr 1910 und erinnerte so an das geschichtliche Geschehen. Den symbolischen Wechsel ins zweite Jahrhundert vollzog anschließend Brigadegeneral Steven L. Salazar. Der Kommandeur des Joint Multinational Training Command (JMTC) der 7. US-Armee feuerte mit einer 155-mm-US-Panzerhaubitze „Paladin". Die beiden Generäle enthüllten im Beisein ehemaliger Kommandeure und Ehrengäste ein neues Marterl mit einer Gedenktafel, die in Deutsch und Englisch an die beiden markanten Ereignisse von 1910 und 2010 erinnert.

Grand Tattoo – Historic and Modern Events featured during the anniversary

The 100th anniversary of Grafenwoehr Training Area was celebrated with a week of festivities from June 27 to July 4, 2010. It started with the opening of two special exhibitions at the Grafenwoehr Museum entitled "100 Years Grafenwoehr Training Area" and "100 Years Federal Forest." Following the opening, the USAREUR-Dixieland Band brought the feeling of the American South to the city park and ensured a perfect start into the fest week.

"Double Shot" on the Birthday

On the day of the anniversary, the establishment of the training area was remembered with a double shot of artillery at exactly 8 a.m. on Grünhund Hill. There, where the 2nd Royal-Bavarian Foot Artillery Regiment fired the first official artillery shot on June 30, 1910, the next century of military training was ushered in. Dressed in uniforms of the Royal-Bavarian artillery, soldiers of the Office of the German Military Representative had positioned and loaded a historic canon. During the early morning ceremony, Brigadier General Johann Berger, the Deputy Commanding General of Defense District Command IV pulled the lanyard on the Krupp canon from 1910 to commemorate the historic event. The symbolic change into the training area's second century was then made by Brigadier General Steven L. Salazar. The commanding general of the 7th U.S. Army's Joint Multinational Training Command (JMTC) fired a 155-mm U.S. „Paladin" howitzer. Accompanied by former commanders and distinguished guests, both generals then unveiled a new monument with a commemorative plaque written in German and English, commemorating those two significant events in 1910 and 2010.

Ein neues Marterl mit Gedenktafel erinnert in deutscher und englischer Sprache an die Ereignisse am 30. Juni 1910 und 2010.

A new monument with a commemorative plaque written in German and English, commemorates the events on June 30, 1910 and 2010.

Brigadegeneral Steven L. Salazar (links) und Brigadegeneral Johann Berger enthüllen gemeinsam mit Ehrengästen und ehemaligen Kommandeuren, darunter auch Generalleutnant Mark P. Hertling, das neue Monument auf der Grünhundhöhe.

Accompanied by distinguished guests and former commanders, among them Lieutenant General Mark P. Hertling, Brigadier General Steven L. Salazar (left) and Brigadier General Johann Berger unveiled the new monument on Grünhund Hill.

Feuerzauber zum Jubiläum. Soldaten des DMV stellen in historischen Uniformen mit einer Krupp-Kanone aus dem Jahr 1910 vor dem Großen Zapfenstreich den ersten Schuss nach.

Magic fire for the anniversary. Before the Grand Tattoo, soldiers of the Office of the German Military Representative dressed in historic uniforms re-enact the first shot with a Krupp canon from 1910.

Mit einer feierlichen Flaggenparade begann auf dem Paradeplatz der Festakt zum 100. Jubiläum.
The ceremonial act celebrating the 100th anniversary started with a ceremonial flag parade on the parade field.

Flaggenparade und Großer Zapfenstreich

Mit rund 4000 Besuchern fand am Abend des 30. Juni der Höhepunkt der Jubiläumswoche auf dem Paradefeld vor dem Wasserturm statt. Mit einer feierlichen Flaggenparade wurden durch die Paradeformationen die Farben der beiden Nationen geehrt sowie die deutsche und amerikanische Fahne feierlich eingeholt. Der stellvertretende US-Botschafter Greg Delawie, Regierungspräsidentin Brigitta Brunner und Generalmajor Gert Wessels, der kommandierende General im Wehrbereich IV, bekräftigten in ihren Ansprachen die Freundschaft und außergewöhnliche Partnerschaft zwischen den beiden Nationen. Herausgestellt wurden die geschichtliche Entwicklung und die Bedeutung des Truppenübungsplatzes Grafenwöhr, der für viele mehr als nur ein militärisches Trainingsgelände ist.

Nachgestellt wurde vor großem Publikum nochmals die Abgabe des ersten Schusses aus der historischen Feldhaubitze. Vor der malerischen Kulisse des stimmungsvoll beleuchteten Wasserturms inszinierte die Bundeswehr mit dem Gebirgsmusikkorps Garmisch-Partenkirchen und dem Logistikbataillon 472 aus Kümmersbruck den Großen Zapfenstreich.

Flag Parade and Grand Tattoo

The highlight of the anniversary week, visited by about 4,000 guests, was held on the evening of June 30 on the parade field in front of the Water Tower. With a ceremonial flag parade the colors of both nations were honored and the German and American flag ceremonially lowered. Deputy U.S. Ambassador Greg Delawie, Government President Brigitta Brunner and Major General Gert Wessels, the commanding general of Defense District Command IV, endorsed the friendship and extraordinary partnership between both nations in their speeches. They focused on the historic development and the importance of Grafenwoehr Training Area which for many is more than just a military training area.

The first shot was also re-enacted with a historic canon in front of the large audience. The German Army with its Mountain Music Corps Garmisch-Partenkirchen and soldiers from Logistic Battalion 472 stationed in Kümmersbruck presented the Grand Tattoo in front of the picturesque backdrop of the atmospherically lit Water Tower.

Großer Zapfenstreich vor der illuminierten Kulisse des Wasserturms. Das Gebirgsmusikkorps und das Logistikbataillon 472 würdigten mit der Zeremonie das 100-jährige Bestehen des Truppenübungsplatzes.

Grand Tattoo in front of the illuminated backdrop of the Water Tower. The German Army's Mountain Music Corps and Logistic Battalion 472 honored the 100th anniversary of the training area with that ceremony.

Rund 4000 Zuschauer verfolgten den Jubiläumsfestakt und den Großen Zapfenstreich.

About 4,000 visitors attended the ceremonial act and the Grand Tattoo.

Die Schießvorführungen des Panzerbataillons 104 und des Panzergrenadierbataillons 122 waren die Höhepunkte bei den Lagerrundfahrten.
The highlight of the tours was the live fire by the German Army's Armor Battalion 104 and Armored Infantry Battalion 122.

Lagerrundfahrten, Schießen und militärisches Gerät

Vom Rathaus bis zum Wasserturm erstreckte sich die Festmeile beim Bürgerfest. Im Stadtpark und in der Unteren Torstraße präsentierten deutsche und tschechische Sammler eine Ausstellung historischer Militärfahrzeuge und Ausrüstungsgegenstände. Vom wassergekühlten MG 08 aus dem Ersten Weltkrieg über Kettenkräder, Wehrmachtsfahrzeuge, sämtliche amerikanische Jeeps bis hin zur Artillerie-Haubitze M1 „Long Tom" reichte die Palette der Raritäten. Geöffnet war für die Besucher das Museum mit seinen Sonderausstellungen zum Jubiläum. Der Heimatverein und die Soldaten des DMV boten während des gesamten Wochenendes Rundfahrten in den Lagerbereich und das Übungsgelände an. Attraktion war dabei die Schießvorführung des Panzerbataillons 104 aus Pfreimd und des Panzergrenadierbataillons 122 aus Oberviechtach auf der Schießbahn 117.

Training Area Tours, Live Fire and Military Equipment

During the citizens' fest, the party mile reached from the town hall to the Water Tower. German and Czech collectors presented an exhibition of historic military vehicles and equipment in the city park and on Untere Torstraße. The spectrum of rarities covered everything from the water-cooled MG 08 dating back to World War I, chain wheels, Wehrmacht vehicles, all types of American jeeps to the artillery's howitzer M1 „Long Tom." The museum with its special anniversary exhibitions was open for visitors. The Grafenwoehr Historic Society and the soldiers of the Office of the Military Representative offered tours of Grafenwoehr main post and the training area throughout the entire fest weekend. The highlight of the tours was the live fire on Range 117 by the German Army's Armor Battalion 104 stationed in Pfreimd and Armored Infantry Battalion 122 stationed in Oberviechtach.

Ein komplettes Camp mit GI und Army-Girl versetzte die Besucher in Staunen.
A complete camp with GI and Army girl amazed the visitors.

Soldaten aus Kaisers Zeiten am wassergekühlten MG 08
Soldiers from the times of the German Empire at the water-cooled MG 08

Militärisches Gerät aus 100 Jahren wurde im Stadtpark gezeigt.
Military equipment from 100 years was shown in the city park.

Bürgerfest mit Unabhängigkeitstag

Kinderumzug mit dem Spielmannszug der Freiwilligen Feuerwehr, Bieranstich, Livemusik mit verschiedenen Bands und Gruppierungen, Frühschoppen, Auftritte von verschiedenen Vereinen, Tanzvorführungen der Flying Boots sowie Spielstationen für Kinder gehörten zum weiteren Programm des Bürgerfestes. Wirte und Vereine boten den Gästen eine große Auswahl an kulinarischen Köstlichkeiten und Getränken. Am Sonntag, 4. Juli, dem Amerikanischen Unabhängigkeitstag, wurde die Festmeile um den Paradeplatz vor dem Wasserturm erweitert, der Turm selbst wurde für Besichtigungen geöffnet. Der Hollywoodstar Gary Sinise mit seiner „Lieutenant Dan Band" begeisterte im Festzelt die amerikanischen und deutschen Fans. Ein großes Brillantfeuerwerk beendete den Unabhängigkeitstag und zugleich die Feierlichkeiten zum 100-jährigen Bestehen des Truppenübungsplatzes.

Citizens' Fest and Independence Day

A children's parade with the band of the Volunteer Fire Department band, the tapping of the keg, live music by various bands and music groups, the traditional "Frühschoppen," performances by various clubs, country line dance performances by the Flying Boots as well as various activities for kids were part of the extended program of the citizens' fest. Restaurant owners and clubs offered guests a large variety of culinary specialties and beverages. On Sunday, July 4, the American Independence Day, the fest area was extended to the parade field in front of the Water Tower, and the tower itself was opened for visitors. Hollywood star Gary Sinise excited German and American fans in the fest tent with his "Lieutenant Dan Band." A large fireworks display marked the end of Independence Day and the end of the festivities celebrating the 100th anniversary of the training area.

Line Dance boten die Flying Boots auf der Bühne an der Festmeile.
The Flying Boots presented line dance on the stage of the fest area.

Hollywoodstar Gery Sinise genoss das Bad in der Menge.
Hollywood star Gary Sinise enjoyed the splash in the crowd.

Deutsche und Amerikaner waren beim Bürgerfest in bester Feierlaune.
Germans and Americans had the best party mood at the citizens' fest.

Netzaberg

Kasernen 1937/38, gestern - heute - *Barracks 1937/38, yesterday - today*

Zitate - Remarks

„Der Truppenübungsplatz Grafenwöhr als ein „kleines Stück Amerika in der Oberpfalz" bietet seit mehr als 70 Jahren unseren amerikanischen Freunden nicht nur optimale militärische Ausbildungs- und Übungsmöglichkeiten. Vielmehr ist er für viele Soldatinnen und Soldaten inzwischen zu einem Ort geworden, der auch so etwas wie „Heimat" bedeutet. Zu verdanken ist dies dem freundschaftlichen und vertrauensvollen Miteinander zwischen Deutschen und Amerikanern, das speziell im Landkreis Neustadt seit jeher gepflegt und geschätzt wird. Gegenseitiger Respekt, ein offener und ehrlicher Umgang miteinander und auch ein „offenes Ohr" für die Belange und gegenseitigen Interessen waren und sind hierfür eine stabile und auch zukunftsfähige Basis. Deshalb bin ich mir sicher, dass diese gute Nachbarschaft auch die kommenden Jahre und Jahrzehnte Bestand haben wird!"
Andreas Meier, Landrat des Landkreises Neustadt an der Waldnaab

"Grafenwoehr Training Area is a "small piece of America in the Oberpfalz" and has not only offered our American friends optimal military training and exercise opportunities for more than 70 years but has also become a place that many Soldiers call "home." This is the result of the friendly and trustful cooperation that Germans and Americans have always cultivated and enjoyed particularly in Neustadt County. Mutual respect, open and honest contact with one another and the willingness to always lend a sympathetic ear to each other's needs and interests have been and will be its stable and sustainable basis . Therefore, I believe that this good neighborhood will continue for the coming years and decades!"
Andreas Meier, County Commissioner, Neustadt an der Waldnaab County

„Zum 100-jährigen Bestehen des Truppenübungsplatzes Grafenwöhr möchte ich der gesamten Region und den Soldaten recht herzlich gratulieren. Grafenwöhr - oder „Graf", wie es bei den US-Soldaten schlicht heißt – ist zu einem Stück Amerika mitten in der Oberpfalz in dieser Zeit geworden. Hier wird die Partnerschaft zwischen Deutschen und Amerikanern jeden Tag aufs Neue mit Erfolg gelebt."
Albert Rupprecht, Mitglied des Deutschen Bundestags, Wahlkreisabgeordneter

"I would like to congratulate the entire region and the soldiers on the 100th anniversary of the Grafenwoehr Training Area. Over time, Grafenwoehr, or "Graf," as it is simply called by U.S. soldiers, has become a piece of America in the middle of the Oberpfalz region. Here, the partnership between Germans and Americans successfully comes to life every day."
Albert Rupprecht, Member of the German Federal Parliament

„Nach wie vor ist der Truppenübungsplatz Grafenwöhr der modernste Truppenübungsplatz in Europa. Hier hat die US Army ihren Standard ständig und das, man beachte, auch im Bezug auf den Umweltschutz, weiter verbessert. Aus meiner Einschätzung kann unsere Bundeswehr nirgendwo so gut wie hier, alle Aspekte ihrer Ausbildung und Einsatzvorbereitung trainieren. Wie sie alle wissen, geraten viele Dinge in Vergessenheit in dieser schnelllebigen Zeit. Gerade deshalb, ist es aus meiner Sicht wichtig, dass sich Gerald Morgenstern dieser Geschichte Grafenwöhrs und des Truppenübungsplatzes verschrieben hat. Es benötigt Menschen wie ihn, die uns helfen die Erinnerungen an das Geschehene zu bewahren. Er ist ein Mann der sich vielerorts einbringt und engagiert, wobei die Geschichte Grafenwöhrs und die unvergleichbar schöne Natur seine große Liebe geworden sind. Ich empfehle ihnen, lassen sie sich von ihm in die Geschichte und Natur des Truppenübungsplatzes entführen. Ob sie in Erinnerungen schwelgen, hieraus ihre Lehren ziehen oder einfach nur staunen, darüber das dieser Truppenübungsplatz mit zu den schönsten Naturreservaten in Deutschland zählt und das, trotz militärischer Nutzung, sei ihnen überlassen."
Hans Joachim Gehrlein, Oberstleutnant a. D., DMV und Kommandant von Juni 2012 bis August 2015

"Grafenwoehr Training Area still is the most modern training area in Europe. Here, the U.S. Army has continuously improved its standards, to include those regarding environmental protection. In my opinion, there is no better place for the German Armed Forces to comprehensively train and prepare for deployment. As you all know, many things are forgotten in our fast-paced times. Therefore, I believe it is important that Gerald Morgenstern has dedicated himself to telling the history of Grafenwoehr and the training area. We need people like him who help us preserve the memories of the past. He is a person who is active and dedicated in many places whereupon the history of Grafenwoehr and the incommensurable beautiful nature have become his great love. Allow him to whisk you away into the history and nature of Grafenwoehr Training Area. Whether you reminisce about the past, learn a lesson from reading the book, or simply are astonished that this training area is one of Germany's most beautiful nature preserves despite its military use, remains up to you."
Hans Joachim Gehrlein, LTC (RET), German Military Representative and Commander, June 2012 to August 2015

„Wir Deutschen und Bayern haben den Amerikanern viel zu verdanken und dürfen das nie vergessen! Aus den Besatzern von damals sind längst Freunde geworden und der Truppenübungsplatz Grafenwöhr mittlerweile auch ein Ausdruck für gelebte deutsch-amerikanische Freundschaft. Mir persönlich liegt eine Kontinuität dieser intensiven Beziehung mit den Amerikanern sehr am Herzen. Darüber hinaus wissen wir im Landkreis Amberg-Sulzbach selbstverständlich auch um die wirtschaftliche Bedeutung der US-Armee mit ihren Soldaten und deren Angehörigen hier vor Ort. Auch in Zukunft hoffe ich deshalb auf eine weiterhin positiv verlaufende Entwicklung zugunsten der Region und der Menschen, die hier leben, Deutsche wie Amerikaner."
Richard Reisinger, Landrat des Landkreises Amberg-Sulzbach, Oktober 2015

"The people of Germany and Bavaria owe much to Americans, and we should never forget that! The former occupants have long become friends and Grafenwoehr Training Area has meanwhile become an example of practiced German-American friendship. Personally, the continuation of these intensive relations with Americans are very dear to me. Additionally, we who live here in Amberg-Sulzbach County also know about the economic impact of the U.S. Army with its soldiers and family members stationed here. Therefore, I hope for a continuous positive development in the future regarding the region and the people who live here, Germans and Americans."
Richard Reisinger, County Commissioner, Amberg-Sulzbach County, October 2015

„Ich hatte das Privileg und die Ehre das wohl schönste Naturschutzgebiet zu kommandieren, das zufällig auch der wichtigste Truppenübungsplatz der Welt ist.
Grafenwöhr ist ein besonderer Ort, wo Streitkräfte trainieren können, um den Frieden in der Welt zu sichern, wo Pflanzen und Tiere gedeihen und wo Naturliebhaber die Schönheit dieses magischen Orts erleben können. Grafenwöhr ist ein glänzendes Beispiel dafür, was Menschen erschaffen können, wenn sie zusammenarbeiten und die Natur respektieren."
Generalmajor Walter E. Piatt, Stellv. kommandierender General des US-Heeres in Europa, Juli 2014 - März 2015

Die oben geäusserte Meinung ist meine eigene und stellt nicht die offizielle Politik oder Auffassung der US-Armee, des US-Verteidigungsministeriums oder der US-Regierung dar.

"I had the privilege and honor to command the most beautiful nature preserve that just happens to be the world's major military training area. Grafenwoehr is a special place where militaries are able to train to secure peace in the world, where plants and animals flourish, and nature enthusiasts are able to experience the beauty of this magical place.
Grafenwoehr is a shining example of the good humans can produce when we work together and respect nature."
Major General Walter E. Piatt, Deputy Commanding General, U.S. Army in Europe, July 2014 - March 2015

The views expressed are my own and do not reflect the official policy or position of the Army, Department of Defense, or U.S. Government.

„Mehr als einhundert Jahre lang, erweckte das Wort Grafenwöhr in deutschen und amerikanischen Soldaten Visionen und Erinnerungen an einen Ort, wo die Ausbildung hart und das Umfeld rauh war. Aber heute steht das Wort für das Joint Multinational Training Command..., einen Ort wo Alliierte und Partner sich durch teilstreitkraftgemeinsame Einsatzverbände auf das gegenwärtige Operationsgebiet vorbereiten. Ich habe in vielen Orten der Welt geübt und gelebt – aber für mich sind „Graf" und JMTC die Kronjuwelen. Modernes Üben mit Alliierten und Partnern, tolle Einrichtungen für die Soldaten und ihre Familien und die großartige Lebensqualität, die sich ihnen im südlichen Deutschland, in Bayern, bietet. Meiner Ansicht nach, gibt es keinen besseren Ort, um Soldat zu sein!"
Generalleutnant Mark P. Hertling, US Armee
Kommandierender General des US-Heeres in Europa, März 2011

Die oben geäusserte Meinung ist meine eigene und stellt nicht die offizielle Politik oder Auffassung der US-Armee, des US-Verteidigungsministeriums oder der US-Regierung dar.

"For more than 100 years, the word "Grafenwoehr" generated visions and stories from German and U.S. soldiers of a place where training was tough and the environment was harsh. But today, the word Grafenwoehr is synonymous with the Joint Multinational Training Command, a place where allies and partners come together to train soldiers through joint task forces for the current operating environment. I've trained – and lived – in many places all over the world, and to me "Graf" and the JMTC are the crown jewels. State of the art training with allies, tremendous facilities for soldiers and their families, and the great quality of life that's associated with the southern German area of Bavaria. To me, there's no place better to be a soldier!"
Lt. Gen. Mark P. Hertling, U.S. Army
Commanding General, U.S. Army in Europe, March 2011

The views expressed are my own and do not reflect the official policy or position of the Army, Department of Defense, or U.S. Government.

Zeittafel 1900 - 1945 Chronology

1900
Aufstellung des III. bayerischen Armeekorps in Nürnberg
1900
Commissioning of the 3rd Bavarian Army Corps in Nuremberg

1904 - 1910
Ablösung von 10 Ortschaften, Weilern und Gehöften - zirka 250 Menschen werden umgesiedelt
1904 - 1910
Displacement of 10 villages, hamlets and farms – about 250 people are resettled

1. April 1908
Prinzregent Luitpold von Bayern erlässt die Verfügung für den „Truppenübungsplatz Grafenwöhr" und genehmigt die Errichtung der „Garnison Grafenwöhr"
April 1, 1908
Prince Regent Luitpold of Bavaria directs the establishment of the Grafenwoehr Training Area and approves the commissioning of the Grafenwoehr garrison

1913
Flugfeld bei Hammergmünd wird eröffnet
1913
Opening of the airfield near Hammergmünd

1902 - 1904
Erkundung südlich von Grafenwöhr
1902 - 1904
Survey of the area south of Grafenwoehr

1907 - 1915
Bau des Lagers; Vorstand der Bauleitung war der königliche Baurat Wilhelm Kemmler, bauleitender Architekt Jürgen Sievers (von 1913 bis 1933 Vorstand der Bauleitung)
1907 - 1915
Construction of the camp; Royal Engineer Wilhelm Kemmler headed the construction team and Jürgen Sievers was the head architect. From 1913 to 1933 he was also head of the construction team.

30. Juni 1910
Erster offizieller Artillerieschuss auf dem Übungsplatz
June 30, 1910
First official artillery shot on the training area

1914 - 1918
Erster Weltkrieg – reger Übungsbetrieb – Grafenwöhr wird größtes Kriegsgefangenenlager Bayerns
1914 - 1918
World War I – high training activity – Grafenwoehr becomes the largest prisoner of war camp in Bavaria

Zeittafel 1900 - 1945 Chronology

1918 - 1935
Zeit des 100 000-Mann-Heeres – wenig Übungstätigkeit mit Einsatz von Panzerattrappen – junge Soldaten wie Heinz Guderian und Claus von Stauffenberg (Deutscher Widerstand im Dritten Reich) leisten unter anderem Dienst bei der Reichswehr in Grafenwöhr

1918 - 1935
Time of the 100,000-Soldier-Army – little training activity – training with tank mockups – young soldiers like Heinz Guderian and Claus von Stauffenberg (part of the German resistance during the Third Reich) are stationed with the so-called Reichswehr in Grafenwoehr

1933/1935
Machtübernahme durch Hitler/Wiedereinführung der Wehrpflicht

1933/1935
Seizure of power by Hitler – re-establishment of the military draft

1937 - 1940
Neubau des Südlagers bei Vilseck - Erweiterung des Hauptlagers Grafenwöhr – Bau des Westlagers bei Bernreuth (12000 Mann) Bau der Westwall-Testbunker (1938)

1937 - 1940
Construction of the South Camp near Vilseck - expansion of the main camp at Grafenwoehr – construction of the western camp near Bernreuth (12,000 soldiers) - construction of the West Wall test bunkers (1938)

1926
Truppenbesichtigung durch Reichspräsident Paul von Hindenburg - Bau des Bleidorn-Turms auf dem Schwarzen Berg

1926
Troop review by Reich's President Paul von Hindenburg – Construction of the Bleidorn Tower on Schwarzen Berg mountain

1936 - 1939
Erweiterung des Übungsplatzes auf 23364 Hektar - Umsiedelung von über 3500 Menschen aus 57 Dörfern, Weilern und Gehöften

1936 - 1939
Expansion of the training area to 23,364 hectare – Resettlement of more than 3,500 people from 57 villages, hamlets and farms

1939 -1945
Zweiter Weltkrieg - Aufstellung und Ausbildung von Kampftruppen sowie Auffrischung von Fronttruppen – Truppenbesuche und Aufenthalte in Grafenwöhr von Hitler, Göring, Himmler, Keitel und anderen NS-Größen

1939 -1945
World War II – deployment and training of fighting units as well as re-training of front-line troops – troop visits and stays at Grafenwoehr by Hitler, Göring, Himmler, Keitel and other NS-leaders

Zeittafel 1900 - 1945 Chronology

ab November 1943
Ausbildung der italienischen Division „San Marco" - Besuch des „Duce", Benito Mussolini (April 1944)
since November 1943
Training of the Italian division "San Marco" – Visit of the "Duce," Benito Mussolini (April 1944)

5. und 8. April 1945
Bombardierung von Grafenwöhr und Vilseck
April 5 and 8, 1945
Bombardment of Grafenwoehr and Vilseck

20. April 1945
Kommandant General Wilhelm Rupprecht übergibt den Truppenübungsplatz Grafenwöhr an die Amerikaner
April 20, 1945
Commander General Wilhelm Rupprecht turns the training area over to the Americans

Juli 1941
Zusammenstellung der spanischen „Blauen Division"
July 1941
Deployment of the Spanish "Blue Division"

1944
General Heinz Guderian richtet den „Arbeitsstab Panzer" ein
1944
General Heinz Guderian establishes the "Tank Working Group"

19. April 1945
Besetzung Grafenwöhrs durch amerikanische Truppen – „Dora" wird bei Metzenhof gesprengt
April 19, 1945
Occupation of Grafenwoehr by American troops – "Dora" is demolished near Metzenhof

Zeittafel 1945 – 2010 Chronology

November 1945
Wiederaufnahme des beschränkten Schieß- und Übungsbetriebs
November 1945
Resumption of limited shooting and training activities

1947
Neueinteilung des Übungsplatzes – Ausweisung der Impact Area – Bau von Schießbahnen, Panzerstraßen, Wiederaufbau im Lager
1947
Reclassification of the training area; designation of the impact area – construction of ranges, tank road, reconstruction of main post

1948/49
Vilseck wird Panzerübungszentrum der 7. US-Armee
1948/49
Vilseck is turned into the 7th Army's tank training center

1949
Große Truppenparaden zur Demonstration militärischer Stärke
1949
Large troop parades to demonstrate military strength

1950 - 1953
Ausbau des Lagers – Bau der Camps, Aachen, Algier und Normandie sowie der Zeltlager Tunisia, Cheb und Kasserine
1950 - 1953
Extension of main post – Construction of Camps Aachen, Algiers and Normandy and the tent camps Tunisia, Cheb and Kasserine

1945 – 1948
Bernreuth und Vilseck werden Kriegsgefangenenlager für deutsche Soldaten – Sammelstelle für jüdische und deutsche Flüchtlinge, Polen und Ukrainer
1945 – 1948
Bernreuth and Vilseck are turned into prisoner of war camps for German soldiers and a collection point for Jewish and German refugees as well as Poles and Ukrainians

1947/48
Aufnahme des Schieß- und Übungsbetriebs für Großverbände
1947/48
Resumption of shooting and training activities for large units

1948 – 1951
Aussiedelung ziviler Bewohner und Kriegsflüchtlinge
1948 – 1951
Resettlement of civilian residents and war refugees

Mai 1950
Dwight D. Eisenhower („Ike"), Oberbefehlshaber der NATO und späterer US-Präsident, besichtigt Grafenwöhr
May 1950
Dwight D. Eisenhower ("Ike"), Supreme Commander of NATO and future president of the United States visits Grafenwoehr

Zeittafel 1945 - 2010 Chronology

1955
Grafenwöhr ist größter US-Truppenübungsplatz außerhalb der USA

1955
Grafenwoehr is the largest U.S. training area outside of the United States of America

1958 und 1960
Elvis Presley ist als Manöversoldat in Grafenwöhr

1958 and 1960
Elvis Presley takes part in maneuvers in Grafenwoehr

Januar 1969
Grafenwöhr wird in das größte NATO-Manöver in Europa „REFORGER" einbezogen – Präsenz der USA im Kalten Krieg

January 1969
Grafenwoehr is part of "REFORGER" – the largest NATO maneuver in Europe – Presence of the USA during the Cold War

1. Juli 1976
Ausbildungskommando der 7. US-Armee (7th ATC) wird in Dienst gestellt

July 1, 1976
Commissioning of the 7th U.S. Army Training Command (7th ATC)

1952
Südlager Vilseck wird zur Erinnerung an US-Generalmajor Maurice Rose in „Rose Barracks" umbenannt

1952
Vilseck is renamed as "Rose Barracks" in commemoration of U.S. Major General Maurice Rose

1956/57
Standortverwaltung und Verbindungskommando der Bundeswehr werden in Grafenwöhr eingerichtet – erste Einheiten der Bundeswehr nehmen den Übungsbetrieb auf

1956/57
Garrison command and liaison command are established in Grafenwoehr – the first German Army units start their training activities

ab 1965
Zeitweise Ausbildung für Vietnam-Einsatz – Rückkehr von Vietnam-Kriegsteilnehmern

since 1965
Temporary training for deployment to Vietnam – Return of soldiers deployed to Vietnam

1970 – 1973
Bau mehrerer Wohnblocks im Hauptlager

1970 – 1973
Construction of apartment houses on main post

Zeittafel 1945 – 2010 Chronology

1982 – 1985
Umfangreiches Modernisierungsprogramm – Bau von computergesteuerten Schießbahnen für insgesamt 100 Millionen US-Dollar – Grafenwöhr wird modernster Übungsplatz in Europa

1982 – 1985
Extensive modernization – construction of computer-operated ranges for a total of 100 million U.S. dollars – Grafenwoehr becomes the most modern training area in Europe

19. März 1986
Bundeskanzler Dr. Helmut Kohl und US-Verteidigungsminister Caspar Weinberger besuchen deutsche und amerikanische Truppen

March 19, 1986
German Chancellor Dr. Helmut Kohl and U.S. Secretary of Defense Caspar Weinberger visit German and American troops

ab 1987
Verlegung der 1. Brigade der 1. US-Panzerdivision aus Mittelfranken ins Südlager Vilseck

since 1987
Re-stationing of the U.S. 1st Brigade, 1st Armored Division from Central Franconia to Vilseck South Camp

1991
Die NCO-Akademie (Unteroffiziersschule) des 7. US-Ausbildungskommandos wird von Bad Tölz nach Grafenwöhr verlegt

1991
The NCO Academy of the 7th Army's Training Command moves from Bad Tölz to Grafenwoehr

24. Mai 1985
Besuch von Bundespräsident Richard von Weizsäcker

May 24, 1985
Visit of German President Richard von Weizsäcker

1981 – 1993
Vilsecker „Rose Barracks" werden zur Garnison ausgebaut – Investitionen von einer Milliarde US-Dollar

1981 – 1993
"Rose Barracks" in Vilseck is developed into a garrison – an investment of more than one billion U.S. dollars

1987
Beschäftigung erreicht mit 3600 deutschen Arbeitnehmern den Höchststand – Personalabbau mit Ende des Kalten Krieges – 2010 sind zirka 3000 Deutsche in Vilseck und Grafenwöhr beschäftigt

1987
Employment reaches its all-time high with 3,600 German employees – reduction of employees at the end of the Cold War – In 2010 approximately 3,000 Germans are employed in Vilseck and Grafenwoehr

Zeittafel 1945 - 2010 Chronology

Oktober 1991
100. Area Support Group (Gebietsunterstützungsgruppe) wird für Standortaufgaben eingerichtet – Untergliederungen sind Base Support Battalions/Teams (Unterstützungsbataillone/Teams)

October 1991
Commissioning of the 100th Area Support Group to supervise installation management by the Base Support Battalions and Teams (BSB and BST)

1993
Neueinteilung der Schießzeiten – Einschränkung der Nacht- und Wochenendschießzeiten – Nutzungsrückgang durch allgemeinen Truppenabbau – Politischer Einsatz für den Erhalt der Bundeswehr in Grafenwöhr

1993
Restructuring of firing hours – Reduction of night-time and weekend firing hours – decrease of use due to a general reduction of troops – political campaign for the continued stationing of German troops in Grafenwoehr

1995
US-Militärsender AFN Nürnberg kommt ins Südlager Vilseck und wird in AFN Bavaria umbenannt

1995
U.S. military broadcast station AFN Nuremberg moves to Vilseck South Camp and is renamed as AFN Bavaria

ab 1993
US-Militärgemeinde Grafenwöhr gewinnt mehrmals den Wettbewerb ACOE (Army Community of Excellence) und wird als weltweit schönste und beste US-Militärgemeinde ausgezeichnet

since 1993
The U.S. Military Community Grafenwoehr wins the ACOE (Army Community of Excellence) award several times as the Army's best and most beautiful military installation world-wide

November 1994
ATLANTIC RESOLVE 94 ersetzt die jährliche REFORGER-Übung – bislang größte computerunterstützte Militärübung des 7th ATC

November 1994
ATLANTIC RESOLVE 94 replaces the annual REFORGER exercise – largest computer-supported training exercise of the 7th ATC to date

1997
Bundeswehrverbindungskommando wird in „Deutscher Militärischer Vertreter" (DMV) umbenannt und umgegliedert

1997
German Army Liaison Command is renamed and restructured as the Office of the German Military Representative (DMV)

Zeittafel 1945 - 2010 Chronology

2002
Beginn von „Efficient Basing - Grafenwoehr" (Standortoptimierung Grafenwöhr) – Gesamtinvestition für Kasernenbauten und ziviles Wohnungsbauprogramm zirka eine Milliarde Euro
2002
Start of the "Efficient Basing - Grafenwoehr" construction program with a total investment of about one billion Euro for military construction and civilian construction of housing units

Oktober 2005
100. Area Support Group wird zur „US-Armee Garnison Grafenwöhr"
October 2005
100th Area Support Group becomes the U.S. Army Garrison Grafenwoehr

April 2006
3500 Soldaten des 2. Stryker Kavallerieregiments werden von Fort Lewis im US-Bundesstaat Washington nach Vilseck verlegt
April 2006
3,500 soldiers of the 2d Stryker Cavalry Regiment are moved from Fort Lewis, Washington, to be stationed in Vilseck

seit 1996
Vorbereitung und einsatzbezogene Ausbildung für Missionen in Bosnien, Irak und Afghanistan
since 1996
Preparation and deployment-oriented training for missions in Bosnia, Iraq and Afghanistan

2005
Grafenwöhr feiert das 95. Übungsplatzjubiläum – 60 Jahre US-Armee in Grafenwöhr – 50-jähriges Bestehen der Bundeswehr
2005
Grafenwoehr celebrates the 95th anniversary of the training area, the 60th anniversary of the U.S. Army's presence in Grafenwoehr and the 50th anniversary of the German Armed Forces (Bundeswehr)

Januar 2006
7th ATC wird in „Joint Multinational Training Command" umbenannt (JMTC – Gemeinsames Multinationales Ausbildungskommando der 7. US-Armee)
January 2006
7th ATC is renamed as Joint Multinational Training Command (JMTC)

Juni 2007
JMTC eröffnet Medizinisches Ausbildungszentrum im Südlager Vilseck
June 2007
JMTC opens its medical training center at South Camp Vilseck

Zeittafel 1945 - 2010 Chronology

Oktober 2007
Südlager Vilseck wird Standort von vier „Warrior Transition Units" (Reha-Einheiten für Soldaten mit Kriegsverletzungen

October 2007
South Camp Vilseck is designated as the location for four Warrior Transition Units (rehabilitation units for soldiers with battlefield injuries

August 2008
Medizinische und zahnmedizinische Kommandos werden nach Vilseck verlegt (zuvor Auflösung des US-Hospitals Würzburg)

August 2008
Medical and Dental Commands are moved to Vilseck after the closure of the U.S. hospital in Wurzburg

Frühjahr 2008
Erste Soldaten der 172. Infantriebrigade (Blackhawk) werden von Schweinfurt nach Grafenwöhr verlegt

Spring 2008
The first soldiers of the 172d Infantry Brigade (Blackhawk) are moved from Schweinfurt to Grafenwoehr

September 2008
Übergabe der letzten Häuser des U.S. Wohngebiets Netzaberg an die Garnison

September 2008
The last houses of Netzaberg Housing Area are turned over to the garrison

November 2008
JMTC Simulation Center setzt neue Maßstäbe für digital unterstütztes Training

November 2008
JMTC Simulation Center sets new standards for digitally supported training

27. Juni – 4. Juli 2010
Festwoche und Jubiläumsfeier „100 Jahre Truppenübungsplatz Grafenwöhr"

June 27 – July, 4 2010
Fest week and 100th anniversary of the Grafenwoehr Training Area

Zeittafel Forst / Chronology of the Forest Office

1907 - 1909
Älterer Teil des heutigen Platzes wird durch die Militärverwaltung angekauft – von 9160 Hektar sind 5753 Hektar Wald

1907 - 1909
The military administration purchases the older part of today's training area – 5,753 hectare of the total of 9160 hectare are forest

1910
Bau des Forstamtsgebäudes im alpenländischen Stil direkt neben dem Wasserturm

1910
Construction completed of the Forest House in Alpine architectural style next to the Water Tower

1923
Wechsel zum Reichswehrministerium – Aufbau der Heeresforstverwaltung und Bewirtschaftung nach militärischen und ökologischen Belangen

1923
Forest office becomes part of the Reich's War Ministry – establishment of the Army Forest Administration and management in accordance with military and ecological needs

1937/38
Ankauf von 14310 Hektar Gelände für die Erweiterung – Absiedelung – Anwachsen auf 23364 Hektar – es kommen zirka 7000 Hektar Wald dazu

1937/38
Purchase of 14,310 hectare land for the expansion – resettlement – expansion to 23,364 hectare, incl. about 7,000 hectare of additional forest

1. April 1910
Prinzregent Luitpold von Bayern ernennt das königlich-bayerische Militär-Forstamt Grafenwöhr – Gründung der Reviere Tanzfleck, Weihern, Dorfgmünd, Fenkenhof und Erzhäusl

April 1, 1910
Prince Regent Luitpold of Bavaria directs the establishment of the Royal-Bavarian Military Forest Office Grafenwoehr – establishment of the forest districts Tanzfleck, Weihern, Dorfgmünd, Fenkenhof and Erzhäusl

1918
Forstamt wird dem neugebildeten Reichsschatzministerium unterstellt

1918
The forest office becomes part of the newly established Reich's Treasury Ministry

1924
Gründung der Forstinspektion II für süddeutsche Übungsplätze beim Heeresforstamt Grafenwöhr – der Leiter wird „Reichsforstmeister"

1924
Establishment of the Forestry Inspection II for training areas in southern Germany at the Army Forest Administration Grafenwoehr – the director carries the title "Reich's Forest Master"

1938
Umzug in das Gut Altneuhaus bei Sorghof – Gründung der Reviere Schwarzen Berg, Vilseck, Hannesreuth, Nitzlbuch und Luisenhof

1938
Move to Altneuhaus Manor near Sorghof – establishment of the forest districts Schwarzen Berg, Vilseck, Hannesreuth, Nitzlbuch and Luisenhof

Zeittafel Forst / *Chronology of the Forest Office*

1939 – 1945
Großer Beitrag mit hohen Hiebsätzen zur nationalen Rohholzversorgung – 149 Waldarbeiter und 72 Waldarbeiterinnen sind beschäftigt – Einsatz von Kriegsgefangenen – 500 Hektar Wasserfläche werden durch eigenen Fischereimeister bewirtschaftet

1939 – 1945
A large contribution to the national wood supply occurs due to extensive clearing – 149 male and 72 female forest workers are employed – Employment of prisoners of war – 500 hectare of lakes are managed by independent fishery masters

1935 – 1945

1945
US-Streitkräfte beschlagnahmen das Dienstgebäude – Notunterkunft im Dienstgehöft Schwarzen Berg – das Reichsvermögen wird der Militärregierung unterstellt

1945
The U.S. Forces occupy the administration building – Emergency accommodation at the Schwarzen Berg forest house – the Reich's property is put under the control of the U.S. military government

Herbst 1947
Riesige Waldbrände – wertvolle Waldbestände werden unnötig zerschossen

Fall 1947
Extensive forest fires – valuable forest area is destroyed by shooting

1949

7. März 1948
Übernahme durch die Bayerische Staatsforstverwaltung – aus dem Heeresforstamt wird das Bayerische Forstamt Altneuhaus

March 7, 1948
Consolidation by the Bavarian State Forest Administration – the Army Forestry Administration becomes the Bavarian Forestry Office Altneuhaus

1950

1949
Forstamtsdienstgebäude in Altneuhaus wird abgebrochen

1949
The forest office in Altneuhaus is demolished

1951
Bau des jetzigen Forstgebäudes in Axtheid-Berg bei Vilseck – in 10 Revieren sind 112 Waldarbeiter beschäftigt – großflächige Verwüstungen, gefährliche Erosionen und Gewässerverschmutzungen durch wilde Geländenutzung

1951
Construction completed of the current forest office in Axtheid-Berg near Vilseck – 112 forest workers are employed in ten forest districts – uncontrolled land use leads to extensive destruction, dangerous erosion and water pollution

19. Juni 1956
Übernahme durch die Bundesvermögensverwaltung – aus dem Bayerischen Forstamt wird das Forstamt Grafenwöhr

June 19, 1956
Consolidation by the Federal Assets Office – The Bavarian forest office becomes the Forest Office Grafenwoehr

1956

Zeittafel Forst / Chronology of the Forest Office

ab 1965
Stärkere Kontrolle der übenden Truppe – Sinneswandel der Nutzer zu mehr Natur- und Landschaftsschutz – Anpflanzen von Neukulturen

since 1965
Stronger oversight of troops during training – Users engage in more natural environmental protection methods – Planting of new tree cultures

1976
Intensive Waldbrandbekämpfung mit eigenen Mitteln – enge Zusammenarbeit mit der Lagerfeuerwehr

1976
Intensive efforts made fighting and preventing forest fires with forestry funds – close cooperation with the military fire department

1971
Umbenennung in Bundesforstamt Grafenwöhr

1971
Renamed as Federal Forest Office Grafenwoehr

nach 1989
Truppenreduzierungen und Veränderungen in der militärischen Nutzung

after 1989
Troop reductions and changes in the military use of the training area

1990
Erster Brutversuch der Seeadler – vermehrte Beobachtungen

1990
First Forestry Office breeding attempt of white-tailed eagles – increased observations

1967
Erstes Sanierungsprogramm – Vereinbarung mit der US-Armee für Sanierungsmaßnahmen und Umwelt-Programme

1967
Introduction of a new rehabilitation program – Agreement reached with the U.S. Army concerning rehabilitation measures and environmental programs

ab 1970
Zunahme des Wildbestandes, der durch unkontrollierten Abschuss reduziert war – der Übungsplatz entwickelt sich zur ökologischen Nische für viele bedrohte Tier- und Pflanzenarten

since 1970
Increase of wildlife stocks, which had been reduced by uncontrolled hunting – the training area develops into an ecological niche for endangered animal and plant species

1985
75. Jubiläum – 47 Waldarbeiter, 6 Angestellte und 14 Beamte sind beschäftigt – Grafenwöhr wird Ausbildungsforstamt

1985
75th anniversary of the Forest Office Grafenwoehr– a staff of 47 forest workers, six civilian employees and 14 civil servants are employed – Grafenwoehr becomes a forest office that trains apprentices

Zeittafel Forst / Chronology of the Forest Office

1997
Förderung der Laubholzbeimischungen in den Waldbeständen
1997
Funding approved for the planting of deciduous trees in the forests

2003
Zirka 85 Prozent des Übungsplatzes werden als NATURA 2000-Gebiet (FFH-Schutzgebiet) an die EU-Kommission gemeldet
2003
About 85 percent of the training area is dedicated as a NATURA 2000-area (FFH protection zone) and reported to the EU Commission

August 2005
Ergebnisvorstellung 2003 - 2005: Anhebung des Hiebsatzes auf 93000 Festmeter pro Jahr – Umbau zu Mischwald durch Naturverjüngung – Planung des Naturschutzes nach Erfordernissen der NATURA 2000
August 2005
Presentation of results 2003 - 2005: Tree cutting increased to 93,000 solid cubic meters per year – transfer to deciduous forest through rejuvenation – Planning of natural protection IAW the demands of NATURA 2000

2008
Forschungsprojekt zur Habitatnutzung des Rotwildes
2008
Research project starts to determine habitat use by red deer

2010
Bundesforst Grafenwöhr feiert sein 100-jähriges Bestehen
2010
Federal Forest Office Grafenwoehr celebrates its 100th anniversary

1991
Große Drückjagden auch außerhalb der Weihnachtsschießpause
1991
Large driven hunts occur, even outside the Christmas shooting pause

1998
Umorganisation in der Bundesforstverwaltung – das Forstrevier Neualbenreuth wird angegliedert
1998
Reorganization of the Federal Forest Administration – consolidation of the forest district in Neualbenreuth.

1. Januar 2005
Angliederung an die Bundesanstalt für Immobilienaufgaben (BImA) „Sparte Bundesforst" - die Bundesforstämter werden zu Bundesforst-Hauptstellen
January 1, 2005
Consolidation with the Federal Real Estate Management Office (BImA), Section Federal Forest - the Federal Forest Offices become Main Forest Offices

1. Juli 2007
Neu eingerichteter Fachbereich Naturschutz nimmt die Arbeit auf
July 1, 2007
Newly established natural protection section becomes operable.

1. Oktober 2009
Umgliederungen auf Bundesebene – keine Veränderungen in Grafenwöhr – 37 Waldarbeiter, 10 Bürobedienstete und 14 Forstbeamte sind beschäftigt
October 1, 2009
Federal reorganization – no changes in Grafenwoehr – A staff of 37 forest workers, 10 administration assistants and 14 civil servants are employed

Die handgeschnitzte Weihnachtskrippe auf dem Grafenwöhrer Markplatz
The hand-carved wooden Christmas manger on the Grafenwoehr marketplace

Frieden für die Welt
Peace to the World

Grafenwöhr ist Bethlehem

Eine Weihnachtsgeschichte über Grafenwöhr nach dem Krieg von Monsignore James J. Murray, New York

Der Präses der Kolpingsfamilie New York, Monsignore James J. Murray, schrieb Weihnachten 1986 für das dortige Kolpingsblatt folgenden Artikel über Weihachten 1945, das er in Grafenwöhr als Soldat verbracht hatte. Die Geschichte gelangte über Walter Pruschowitz, den Pfarrer der Dreifaltigkeitskirche von New York, nach Grafenwöhr. Kreisheimatpflegerin Leonore Böhm veröffentlichte diese „Weihnachtsbotschaft" in der Dezember-Ausgabe 1991 erstmals im Grafenwöhrer Stadtanzeiger.

Weihnachten 1945 in Grafenwöhr

Mein schönstes Weihnachtserlebnis war vor 41 Jahren die Christmette im Jahr 1945. Der Ort war Grafenwöhr in Deutschland, eine kleine ländliche Stadt im östlichen Bayern, ungefähr 30 Meilen von der tschechischen Grenze entfernt, an der sich die russischen Truppen gesammelt hatten.

Eine trostlose Weihnachtsszene

Wir waren eine kleine Gruppe amerikanischer Soldaten – ungefähr 140. Der Krieg gegen Deutschland hatte vor sieben Monaten geendet und gegen Japan vor drei Monaten. Wir lebten in ehemaligen deutschen Panzerbaracken, drei Meilen außerhalb des Ortes. Es war eine trostlose Weihnachtsszene. Die Verwüstungen des Krieges waren überall zu sehen. Bei zwei Luftangriffen waren viele Baracken zerstört worden, außer den fünf, in denen wir lebten. 82 Personen starben im Lager. Selbst im Dezember, sieben Monate nach Kriegsende, mussten wir vorsichtig sein, um nicht auf eine Landmine zu treten.

Grafenwoehr is Bethlehem

A Christmas Story about Grafenwoehr after the War by Monsignor James J. Murray, New York

Christmas 1986, the head of the Kolping family, New York Monsignor James J. Murray wrote the following article for the Kolping bulletin about Christmas 1945 which he spent as a soldier in Grafenwoehr. Walter Pruschowitz, the chaplain of Trinity Church in New York sent it to Grafenwoehr. Local historian Leonore Böhm published this "Christmas message" for the first time in the December 1991 of the Grafenwoehr City Bulletin.

Christmas 1945 in Grafenwoehr

My most beautiful Christmas experience was the Christmas mass 41 years ago in 1945. The location was Grafenwoehr in Germany, a small rural town in Eastern Bavaria, approximately 30 miles from the Czech border where Russian troops had assembled.

A desperate Christmas scenery

We were a small group of American soldiers, approximately 140. The war against Germany had ended seven months before the war against Japan three months prior. We lived in former German soldiers' barracks, three miles outside of town. It was a desperate Christmas scenery. The desolation of war could be seen everywhere. Many barracks had been destroyed during two air raids, except for the five in which we lived. Eighty-two persons died in the camp. Even in December, seven months after the end of the war, we had to be careful not to step on a land mine.

Das Lager Grafenwöhr mit Wasserturm im Raureif auf einer alten Postkarte
Camp Grafenwoehr with the Water Tower covered in white frost shown on an old post card

Es war zwar eine ländliche Gegend, aber als wir im Juni 1945 hinkamen, gab es nur sehr wenig Bauern dort. Buben und ältere Männer wurden im letzten Jahre des Krieges eingezogen, und wenn sie nicht gefallen waren, dann waren sie noch nicht aus der amerikanischen Gefangenschaft oder aus dem Lazarett entlassen worden. Was es sonst an Landarbeit gab, wurde von Frauen und Kindern verrichtet und von DPs (displaced persons). Diese waren Flüchtlinge aus den östlichen Ländern, die nach Deutschland geflüchtet waren, um, wie alle hofften, vor der russischen Armee sicher zu sein. In unserer Gegend waren es meistens polnische DPs. Sie standen unter unserem Schutz und wurden von uns mit Wohnung und Nahrung versorgt.

Neues Leben erwacht

Als der Sommer 1945 Herbst wurde und der Herbst Winter, kamen die Menschen wieder nach und nach zurück und die kleine Stadt Grafenwöhr erwachte wieder zu neuem Leben, wenn man es so bezeichnen kann. Die Straßen wurden vom Schutt befreit, die kleinen Geschäfte, deren Türen und Fenster mit Brettern vernagelt waren, wurden wieder geöffnet. Die Uhr am Turm in der Mitte des Marktplatzes wurde gerichtet und begann wieder zu schlagen, während der Fliegerangriffe hatte sie aufgehört. Das Leben im Ort wurde wieder halbwegs normal nach sechs Jahren des Krieges.

Am Sonntag vor Weihnachten gingen drei von uns die drei Meilen nach Grafenwöhr. Als wir an die eine Ecke des Marktplatzes kamen, bemerkten wir ein Schild an der Kirchentür: Die Kirche würde zu Weihnachten geöffnet sein und zum ersten Mal seit sechs Jahren wird die Christmette wieder in Frieden gefeiert.

Das durften wir nicht verpassen. Wir mussten hin zur Christmette. Wir hatten eine kleine, einstöckige Kapelle auf unserem Militärstützpunkt gebaut, die von katholischen und protestantischen Militärkaplänen benutzt wurde. Sie kamen am Sonntag von Nürnberg, ungefähr 60 Meilen entfernt. Wir hatten die Kapelle am Nachmittag des Heiligen Abends fertig gebaut und das Presbyterium mit Tannenbäumen und Girlanden dekoriert. Aber beim Abendessen in der Kantine stand für uns drei der Entschluss fest: Wir gehen zur Christmette in die Stadt. Wir gingen von Tisch zu Tisch und aus uns Dreien wurden zwanzig Soldaten.

It was a rural area but when we arrived there in June 1945, there were very few farmers. Boys and old men had been drafted during the last year of the war and if they did not die in action, they had not yet been released from American imprisonment or the field hospitals. All farm work was done by women and children and by displaced persons (DPs). Those were refugees from Eastern countries who had fled to Germany to be saved, as we all hoped, from the Russian Army. In our area, it was mostly Polish DPs. They fell under our protection and we provided them with food and shelter.

Grafenwoehr comes back to life

When the summer of 1945 turned into fall and the fall turned into winter, people came back, one after the other, and the small town of Grafenwoehr came back to new life, if that's what you want to call it. The streets were freed from debris and the small stores whose doors and windows had been barricaded with planks were reopened. The clock on the tower in the middle of the market place was fixed and started to ring again. During the air raids it had stopped. Life in town slowly began to return to normal after six years of war.

On the Sunday before Christmas, three of us went the three miles into Grafenwoehr. When we arrived at the corner of the market place, we noticed a sign on the church door: the church would be open on Christmas and for the first time in six years Christmas mass would be celebrated during peace.

That was something we could not miss. We had to go to Christmas mass. We had built a small, one story chapel at our military installation which was used by catholic and protestant military chaplains. Every Sunday, they came over from Nuremberg which was about 60 miles away. We had finished the chapel in the afternoon of Christmas Eve and decorated the presbytery with pine trees and garlands. But during dinner, the three of us had come to the conclusion that we would go to attend the Christmas mass downtown. We went from table to table and the three of us became twenty soldiers.

Christmette in der Maria Himmelfahrts-Kirche

Ich werde diese kalte Nacht nie vergessen. Es war mein schönstes Weihnachtserlebnis. Es fiel ein leichter Schnee, als wir den Lkw bestiegen. Wir erreichten die Stadt gerade, als die Kirchentür geöffnet wurde, ungefähr um 23 Uhr. Wir gingen nach vorne und setzten uns in zwei oder drei Kirchenbänke in der Mitte der linken Seite der Kirche. Da wir die ersten waren und nicht den örtlichen Brauch kannten, dass die Männer rechts sitzen und die Frauen links, setzten wir uns auf die linke Seite. Später trauten wir uns nicht mehr, unsere Plätze zu wechseln. Außerdem gab es auch keine Plätze mehr auf der rechten Seite, denn die Kirche war voller Menschen.

Die Kirche hatte eine Orgel, auch einen kleinen Kirchenchor und sogar Ministranten – wir hatten schon lange keine mehr gesehen. Aber es war nicht geheizt. Die Leute saßen da, in ihre ärmliche Kleidung eingehüllt, damit sie nicht froren.

Es wurde still in der Kirche. Pünktlich um Mitternacht begann die Orgel zu spielen, der Chor sang und die Ministranten setzten sich in Bewegung, gefolgt vom Pfarrer Dr. Adolf Schosser. Er ging aufrecht und näherte sich dem Altar, um die Messe für sein Volk aufzuopfern, das erste Mal im Frieden nach sechs langen, furchtbaren Jahren.

Maria Himmelfahrts-Kirche

Maria Himmelfahrt-Church

Christmas mass at Maria Himmelfahrt-Church

I will never forget that cold night. It was my most beautiful Christmas experience. It snowed lightly when we stepped onto the truck. We arrived in town just when the church door was opened around 11 p.m. We went to the front and sat down in two or three church benches in the center of the left side of church. Since we were the first ones there and did not know the local custom that men sit on the right and women on the left, we sat on the left. Later, we were afraid to change our seats, especially since there weren't any seats on the right anymore because the church was packed with people.

The church had an organ, a small church choir and even altar servers who we had not seen in a while. But there was no heat. People sat there, wrapped in their poor clothes so they would not be cold.

It got quiet in church and right at midnight the organ started playing, the choir started singing and the altar servers started moving, followed by Chaplain Dr. Adolf Schosser. He walked straight and approached the altar to celebrate mass for the people – for the first time during peace after six long and horrible years.

Frohe Weihnachten in alle Welt:
Alljährlich werden bei der Tree-Lighting-Ceremony die Lichter am großen Weihnachtsbaum am Paradefeld unter dem Wasserturm feierlich entzündet. Die Lichter und der Stern am Baum sollen ein Zeichen für die deutsch-amerikanische Freundschaft sein. Sie leuchten für alle Soldaten und zivilen Angestellten, die weltweit zur Sicherung von Frieden und Freiheit und getrennt von ihren Familien im Einsatz sind.

Merry Christmas to the whole world:
Every year, the lights of the tall Christmas tree next to the parade field and below the Water Tower are lit during a festive tree-lighting ceremony. The lights and the star on top of the tree are a sign of German-American friendship. They shine for all soldiers and civilian employees who are deployed world-wide and separated from their families during the holidays to secure freedom and peace.

Die Messe war noch in Lateinisch, aber die Predigt war auf Deutsch. Und obwohl die zwanzig von uns nicht viel Deutsch konnten, so folgten wir trotzdem jedem seiner Worte und verstanden sie. Man konnte an den Gesichtern seiner Pfarrkinder die Gefühle der Freude und der Trauer sehen. Seine Predigt war schlicht und ergreifend. Grafenwöhr, sagte er, ist Bethlehem. Die zwei Orte teilen dieselben Probleme: Armut, Heimatlosigkeit und Hoffnungslosigkeit. Sie litten unter dem Druck der Armeen und der Mächtigen, die die kleinen Leute umherschoben. Aber in Bethlehem kamen neues Leben und neues Licht in die Welt des Schattens und des Todes. Und mit der Geburt des Christkindes kamen Liebe, Hoffnung und Glaube. Christus kam als Retter. Er wollte mit den Menschen sein, um sie von ihren Sünden zu befreien und von der Macht Satans.

Die Botschaft des Pfarrers an seine Gemeinde war folgende:

„Grafenwöhr ist Bethlehem. Vergesst die Vergangenheit und begrabt sie! Ihr wurdet errettet und durch das Christkind heute Nacht habt Ihr eine Zukunft. Möge es eine gute Zukunft sein. Mögt Ihr Glauben haben und Hoffnung und Liebe."

Mass was still celebrated in Latin but the sermon was held in German. And although all twenty of us did not speak a lot of German, we followed each of his words and understood them. You could see the joy and the mourning in the faces of his parishioners. His sermon was simple but moving. Grafenwoehr, he said, is Bethlehem. Both towns share the same problems: poverty, homelessness and hopelessness. They suffered from the pressure of the armies and powerful which pushed the little people around. But in Bethlehem new life and new light came into a world of shadow and death. And with the birth of Jesus came love, hope and belief. Christ came to be the savior. He wanted to be among the people to free them from their sins and the power of Satan.

The chaplain's message to his parishioners was the following:

"Grafenwoehr is Bethlehem. Forget the past and bury it! You were saved and through the birth of Jesus tonight you are given a future. May it be a good one. May you have belief, hope and love."

Lichterketten schmücken zur Weihnachtszeit die hohe Tanne im Garten des Forsthauses am Wasserturm.
During Christmas time, chains of light decorate the tall pine tree in the garden of the Forest House next to the Water Tower.

Gedenksteine Memorials

Unglücksfälle auf dem Übungsplatz

Ein Übungsplatz mit einem umfangreichen Schieß- und Übungsbetrieb ist ein Bereich, der für Soldaten und zivile Mitarbeiter wie auch für die Bevölkerung besondere Gefahren birgt. Seit der Gründung des Platzes im Jahre 1910 wurden Menschen bei Unfällen, Schieß- und Explosionsunglücken verletzt und getötet. Zwei Ereignisse ragen besonders heraus.

Das „Muna-Unglück" 1940 forderte 13 Menschenleben. In der Munitionsanstalt in der Nähe des Geismannskeller wurde tschechische Beutemunition geprüft und wieder an die Truppe ausgegeben. Beim Verladen von tschechischen Eierhandgranaten auf dem Ringbahnhof am 14. September 1940 hantierte ein Arbeiter unsachgemäß mit der Munition und löste das Unglück aus. Die Sprengkraft der Beutemunition war derart stark, dass unter anderem die Achsen der Eisenbahnwaggons zerbarsten und Metallteile bis in die Stadt geschleudert wurden.

Das bisher schwerste Unglück in der Geschichte des Truppenübungsplatzes war der Schießunfall im Camp Kasserine am 2. September 1960. Ein Artilleriegeschoss, dass das Ziel um drei Kilometer verfehlte schlug dort n die Unterkunftszelte ein. Sechzehn US-Soldaten fanden dabei den Tod, annähernd 30 wurden verletzt. Gedenksteine und Erinnerungstafeln halten uns die Unfälle im Gedächtnis.

Accidents on the training area

A training area where many live-fire and exercises take place is also an area that involves dangers for soldiers, civilian employees and the local population. People have been injured or killed in work, live-fire accidents and explosions since the training area was established in 1910. Two accidents stick out: The so-called "Muna accident" in 1940 claimed 13 lives. Ammunition captured from the Czech military was tested in the ammunition facility near Geismannskeller and re-issued to the troops. On Sept. 14, 1940, a worker improperly handled Czech hand grenades while loading them at the train station, causing an explosion. The explosive force of the ammunition was so strong that it even burst apart axles of railway cars and catapulted metal parts into town. The most serious accident in the history of the training area was the live fire accident Sept. 2, 1960 in Camp Kasserine. An artillery round missed its target by three kilometers and hit one of the tents. Sixteen U.S. soldiers were killed and nearly 30 were injured. Memorials commemorate these accidents. In August 2015, a new memorial was put up at the Water Tower.

Gefallenenehrung und Übergabe des Mahnmals in der Nähe des alten Lazaretts 1927
Tribute to the fallen soldiers and dedication of the memorial near the military hospital in 1927

Angehörige, Ehrengäste und Militärs bei der Segnung des neuen Gedenksteins vor dem Wasserturm im August 2015.
Relatives, guests and soldiers at the blessing of the new memorial in front of the Water Tower in August 2015.

Neuer Gedenkstein vor dem Wasserturm

Im August 2015 wurde ein neuer Gedenkstein vor dem Wasserturm errichtet. Dem damaligen Kommandanten der Truppenübungsplatzkommandantur, Oberstleutnant Hans Joachim Gehrlein war es ein Anliegen, eine würdige Gedenkstelle einzurichten und den Schleier des Vergessens zu entfernen. Der Stein ist den Opfern des Muna-Unglücks und vier weiterer Unglücksfälle auf dem Truppenübungsplatz gewidmet. Gedacht wird auf der Tafel dem am 4. Juni 1913 verunglückten Hauptmann August Hickl, den 13 Toten des „Muna-Unglück" vom 14. September 1940, dem Zielbauarbeiter Johann Heindl, der am 25. November 1969 ums Leben kam sowie den Mitarbeitern der Firma Diehl: Herbert Sedlmayer, verstorben am 6. Mai 1976 und Schießmeister Georg Strobl, verstorben am 26. Januar 1981.

Ruhestandsgeistlicher Monsignore Karl Wohlgut segnete den Gedenkstein vor dem Wasserturm. Militärs, Ehrengäste und Angehörige der Verunglückten gedachten bei der Feier der Toten.

Garnisonskommandeur Oberst Mark A. Colbrook sah den Wasserturm als Symbol für den Übungsplatz. Dies sei eine angemessene Stelle um den Toten zu gedenken. Der Stein sei auch ein Hinweis auf gemeinsames Trainieren und Ausbilden von Soldaten in einem gefährlichen Umfeld und man solle sich stets der Sicherheitsvorkehrungen bewusst sein.

Blackhawk Memorial

Im November 2012 wurde auf dem Paradefeld ein Gedenkstein der 172. US-Infanteriebrigade errichtet. Die „Blackhawks" verabschiedeten sich von ihren gefallenen Helden. Bei den Einsätzen im Irak und in Afghanistan verloren 19 Kameraden ihr Leben. Der Gedenkstein, der von der Grafenwöhrer Firma Reiter gefertigt wurde, ist die letzte bleibende Erinnerung an die „Blackhawks". Die 172. US-Infanteriebrigade wurde im Mai 2013 in Grafenwöhr aufgelöst.

Patriots Day und Gedenkfeier für die Anschläge am 11. September
Patriots Day and 9/11 Memorial Ceremony

New Memorial in front of the Water Tower

Lt. Col. Hans Joachim Gehrlein, former commander of the German Army unit at Grafenwoehr Training Area, was committed to build a dignified memorial to ensure the victims will not be forgotten. The memorial is dedicated to the victims of the "Muna accident" and four other accidents on the training area. They include Capt. August Hickl, who was killed June 4, 1913; the 13 victims of the "Muna accident;" range maintenance worker Johann Heindl, who was killed on Nov. 25, 1969; and employees of Diehl Co., Herbert Sedlmayer, who was killed May 6, 1976 and shooter Georg Strobl, who died on Jan. 26, 1981.

Retired chaplain Karl Wohlgut blessed the memorial at the Water Tower. Soldiers, guests and relatives remembered the deceased during the ceremony. Garrison Commander Col. Mark A. Colbrook said the Water Tower is the symbol of the training area and, therefore, the appropriate place to commemorate the deceased. The stone, he said, is also a reminder of the joint exercises and training of soldiers in a dangerous environment and that all safety measures should always be followed.

In 2012, the 172nd Infantry Brigade "Blackhawks" built a memorial on the parade field to bid farewell to their fallen heroes. Nineteen soldiers lost their lives during deployments to Iraq and Afghanistan. The memorial, constructed by Reiter Co. from Grafenwoehr, is the only lasting reminder of the "Blackhawks." The 172nd Infantry Brigade was deactivated in May 2013 in Grafenwoehr.

Zum Nachdenken

Die Bilder von herrlicher Natur, unberührter Landschaft, außergewöhnlichem Artenreichtum, Waffeneinsätzen, faszinierender Technik, von Soldatenromantik und Sonnenuntergängen zeigen die „schöne" Seite des Übungsplatzes. Aber wie alles auf dieser Welt, hat sicher auch der Truppenübungsplatz die berühmte „Kehrseite der Medaille".

Seit 100 Jahren wird das Gelände als militärisches Übungsgebiet mit den verschiedensten Waffen und unterschiedlichsten Munitionssorten sehr intensiv genutzt. Militärisches Üben, technische Entwicklungen und unsere vor Jahrzehnten noch unbekümmerte Wegwerfmentalität hinterließen viel Unrat und Altlasten. Vieles konnte in den vergangenen 30 Jahren repariert werden. Ausdrücklich sollen die enormen finanziellen Aufwendungen, die Bemühungen der US-Streitkräfte und aller Verantwortlichen unserer Tage zur Wiederherstellung und zum Erhalt einer intakten Natur gewürdigt werden. Das Buch zeigt auch diese Erfolge in Texten und Bildern.

Mit der enormen wirtschaftlichen Bedeutung und dem Leben von und mit dem Platz sind auch Nachteile verbunden. Eine Belastung durch Schieß- und Fluglärm, stärkeres Verkehrsaufkommen, Emissionen und Immissionen, erhöhte Mietpreise auf dem freien Wohnungsmarkt, eine einseitige, wirtschaftliche Abhängigkeit und weiteres können kritisch angemerkt werden. Es bleibt jedem Einzelnen überlassen, die Vor- und Nachteile abzuwägen.

Something to think about

The photos of pristine nature and landscapes, an extraordinary diversity of species, weapons' deployments, fascinating technical equipment, a soldier's romance and beautiful sunsets show the "beautiful" aspect of the training area. But like with many other things in this world, there is also the infamous other side of the coin.

For 100 years, the area has been intensively used as a military training area for various military weapons and a large variety of types of ammunition. Military training, technical developments and the carefree throw-away-mentality that characterized us for many decades have left behind waste and pollution. We were able to repair much of that over the past 30 years. Here, I would like to especially recognize the enormous financial expenditures and the efforts of the U.S. Forces and others to restore and preserve an intact nature. The book also portrays those successful efforts with texts and photos.

However, there are also disadvantages concerning the economic impact of living with and from the training area. A negative impact due to firing and flight noise pollution, more traffic, emissions and immissions, higher rental prices on the public real estate market, a one-sided economic dependency and many more aspects that can be looked at critically. It is up to the individual to weigh the pros and cons.

Der Faszination des Soldatenberufes stehen Verwundungen von Körper und Geist, oft auch der Tod gegenüber. „Nichts hasst der Soldat mehr als den Krieg" – das gilt auch und vor allem wieder in unseren Tagen. Die überwiegende Mehrheit der Soldaten sieht ihren Auftrag darin, durch gute Ausbildung und ständiges Training bereit für Einsätze zu sein und in diese auch zu gehen. Über Jahrzehnte war es notwendig durch militärische Aufrüstung das Gleichgewicht zwischen den Machtblöcken zu halten. Es ist gelungen, den Frieden in Europa zu sichern und uns allen seit 1945 ein Leben in Freiheit zu ermöglichen. Frieden schaffende Missionen und Verwendungen fern unserer Heimat sind die Aufträge der Gegenwart und der Zukunft. Solange es kriegerische Auseinandersetzungen gibt, wird es notwendig sein, Soldaten eine gute Ausstattung und bestmögliche Ausbildung zu geben; dafür steht Grafenwöhr in hervorragender Weise. An Außenstehende ist der Appell gerichtet, nicht leichtfertig und unbekümmert zu glauben: „Na ja, das ist ja der Job der Soldaten." Einsätze bedeuten immer Entbehrungen und Schmerz und hinterlassen bei den Soldaten und deren Familien oft tiefe Narben.

Nicht zuletzt soll mit diesem Buch auch aller Soldaten und Zivilisten gedacht werden, die in der 100-jährigen Geschichte des Platzes den Tod fanden oder Leid und Verwundung ertragen mussten – 1910 bei der Gründung, in den Jahren der beiden Weltkriege oder bei den aktuellen Einsätzen unserer Zeit.

The fascination of a soldier's life is juxtaposed by injuries of the body and the soul, and often death. "A soldier hates nothing more than war," – that is true and especially true these days. The vast majority of soldiers view their mission as being prepared for deployment through excellent and continuous training to go on deployments. For decades, it was necessary to keep the balance between the blocks of power through a military build-up of arms. As a result, peace in Europe was successfully secured and we were given the chance to live a free life since 1945. Peacekeeping missions and deployments far away from our homeland are the tasks of the present and the future. It will be necessary to provide soldiers with good equipment and the best possible training as long as there are warlike conflicts; Grafenwoehr provides both in an outstanding manner. An appeal goes to outsiders to not lightheartedly and unconcernedly say that "oh well, this is the job of a soldier." Deployments always include deprivation and pain and often leave behind deep scars on the soldiers and their families.

Last but not least, this book is intended to commemorate all soldiers and civilians who died, suffered or were wounded during the 100-year history of the training area – during the establishment in 1910, during the years of both World Wars, or during the current deployments of our times.

Dank

Abschließend will ich allen danken, die mir die Erstellung dieses Buches ermöglicht und mich dabei unterstützt haben. Mein besonderer Dank gilt den Dienststellen und Einheiten von Bundeswehr und US-Armee für ihre Beiträge und ihre Kooperation.

Hervorragende Unterstützung erfuhr ich vom Büro für Öffentlichkeitsarbeit der US-Armee Garnison Bavaria mit Ray Johnson, Susanne Bartsch, Franz Zeilmann, und Andreas Kreuzer sowie vom Public Affairs Office des JMTC unter der Leitung von OTL Brian Carlin.

US-Armee, Bundeswehr, die Umweltabteilung der Garnison, Bauverwaltung, der Bundesforst mit seinen Revierförstern, Heimatverein, die Fotofreunde und viele mehr lieferten ein interessantes und tolles Bildmaterial. Die Fotografen ob bekannt (siehe Bildnachweis) oder unbekannt haben sehr zum Gelingen des Buches beigetragen.

Ein Dankeschön für die Beiträge und Zitate zum Buch, für das Landrat Andreas Meier die Patenschaft übernommen hat. Die Herstellung der weiteren Ausgabe lag in den Händen der Druckerei Hutzler. Laura Volkmer und vor allem Christian Krink kümmerten sich mit viel Einfühlungsvermögen und Kreativität um Satz und Gestaltung. Hannes, Bernd und Tanja Hutzler waren sehr engagiert und arbeiteten mit ihrem Team zuverlässig und termingerecht.

Einen großen Anteil am Gelingen des Werks hatte Susanne Bartsch. Sie übersetzte die Texte ins Englische und wirkte an der Gestaltung sowie Feinabstimmung des Buches mit.

Viel Unterstützung und Verständnis erfuhr ich von meiner Familie und meinen Freunden. Zu Schluss danke ich allen Lesern und Interessenten die durch ihre Nachfrage die erneute Auflage von „Truppenübungsplatz Grafenwöhr, Gestern - Heute" möglich machen, ich freue mich auf eine positive Resonanz.

Thanks

Lastly, I would like to thank all those who have assisted and supported me in putting this book together. A special thank you goes to the German and U.S. Army offices and units for their contributions and cooperation.

I received excellent support from the Public Affairs Office of the U.S .Army Garrison Bavaria with Ray Johnson, Susanne Bartsch, Franz Zeilmann and Andreas Kreuzer, and the JMTC Public Affairs Office headed by Lt. Col. Brian Carlin.

U.S. Army, German Army, the garrison environmental office, construction administration, the Federal Forest Office and its district forest rangers, the historical society, Photo Friends club and many more, whether known (see photo credits) or unknown have all made large contributions to make this book possible.

A thank you goes to all who provided input and remarks for the book, for which County Commissioner Andreas Meier was kind enough to accept the patronage. This new edition of the book was produced by Hutzler Print Shop. Laura Volkmer and primarily Christian Krink took care of the layout with a lot of creativity and empathy. Hannes, Bernd and Tanja Hutzler and their team were very dedicated, providing reliable and timely work.

Susanne Bartsch made a large contribution to the success of the project. She translated the texts into English and contributed to the layout and fine tuning of the book.

I received a lot of support and understanding from my family and friends. Finally, I would like to thank my readers whose interest and demand made this new edition of "Grafenwoehr Training Area, Yesterday – Today," possible.

Gerald Morgenstern